GOVERNOR OF THE CORDILLERA

A VOLUME IN THE

NIU SOUTHEAST ASIAN SERIES

Edited by Kenton Clymer

For a list of books in the series, visit our website at cornellpress.cornell.edu.

GOVERNOR OF THE CORDILLERA

JOHN C. EARLY AMONG THE PHILIPPINE HIGHLANDERS

SHELTON WOODS

NORTHERN ILLINOIS UNIVERSITY PRESS
AN IMPRINT OF CORNELL UNIVERSITY PRESS
Ithaca and London

First published 2023 by Cornell University Press

Library of Congress Cataloging-in-Publication Data

Names: Woods, L. Shelton, author.
Title: Governor of the Cordillera : John C. Early among the Philippine highlanders / Shelton Woods.
Description: Ithaca : Northern Illinois University Press an imprint of Cornell University Press, 2023. | Series: NIU series in Southeast Asian Studies | Includes bibliographical references and index.
Identifiers: LCCN 2022044163 (print) | LCCN 2022044164 (ebook) | ISBN 9781501769955 (hardcover) | ISBN 9781501769962 (paperback) | ISBN 9781501769979 (epub) | ISBN 9781501769986 (pdf)
Subjects: LCSH: Early, John C., 1878–1932. | Igorot (Philippine people)—Colonization—Philippines. | Philippines—Colonization—History—20th century. | Philippines—History—1898-1946.
Classification: LCC DS685 .W78 2023 (print) | LCC DS685 (ebook) | DDC 959.9/03—dc23/eng/20220928
LC record available at https://lccn.loc.gov/2022044163
LC ebook record available at https://lccn.loc.gov/2022044164

For Karen and Damon

And

Daytoy ket para kadagijay kakabsat ken gagayem
ko iday Cordillera ngà dimakkelak.
Agyamanak launay kadakayo.

I have a dream that my four little children will one day live in a nation where they will not be judged by the color of their skin but by the content of their character.
　—Martin Luther King Jr.

Contents

PREFACE

"Shelton, can you hear me?" I barely caught my father's question as I drifted in and out of consciousness. After hours of expelling food and water from my body, I didn't have the strength to respond. We were in Dacalan, a village in Kalinga province in the Cordillera Mountains of the Philippines' main island of Luzon.

We had entered the village three days earlier after an arduous two-day hike. During the journey, the seasonal monsoon rains descended on us, muddying the narrow steep trails and bringing out the leeches. When we made it to the village, I took off my jeans and counted twenty-seven bites on my legs, some with the predatory worms still drinking my blood.

We were in Dacalan to inspect a mountainside landing strip for my father's Cessna 180. He had flown over it several times, but he never landed his planes on village grounds until he inspected them on foot. Such landing areas—he called them postage stamps—served to provide emergency medical relief as well as food supplies to places inaccessible by four-wheel vehicles. Ham radio communication alerted my father to emergencies throughout Kalinga's barrios.

On this inspection trip, however, he forgot to bring emergency medical supplies, and I became deathly ill with cholera. It was 4:00 a.m., and the Dacalan elders appointed twenty-two of their strongest men to carry me down the mountains on a makeshift stretcher with bamboo poles and a blanket, safely transporting me to where my father had parked his red Chevrolet truck. My mother did not recognize me when we arrived home three days later. The Dacalan men saved my life, and I returned to thank them years later.

My parents were both in the medical section of the US Army during the Korean War and met at an Army hospital near Boston following a surgery. In 1958 they moved to the Philippines to work among the Igorots (a generic term for the indigenous people living in Luzon's Cordillera range). Two years later, their third child was born, and they named him Shelton.

I spent my first eighteen years in the city of Baguio, learning the English language at home but speaking Ilocano with my closest friends and learning the national language of Tagalog in school. My deepest friendships were with people of the mountains—theirs was my culture, and they shaped my *ugali* (character).

During the summer of 1978, I moved to Los Angeles for university training and to play collegiate basketball. The southern California Filipino-American community made my difficult cultural transition easier. In 1993, I earned a PhD in Southeast Asian history at UCLA and promptly began teaching there. The following year my wife, Karen, our five-year-old son, Damon, and I moved to Boise, Idaho, where I established my career as a professor and administrator. In time, I authored scores of articles and half a dozen books, but the following pages are what I have longed for people to read. It is about my home, my people.

This book's genesis came on a late afternoon at the University of Michigan's Bentley Historical Library. After days of archival research for my first book, I approached the archivist to say goodbye and thank her. She noticed my Idaho identification and asked, "So you're from Idaho?" I replied I'd recently moved to the state, but my roots were in the mountains of the Philippine Cordillera. She stared at me for an uncomfortable thirty seconds, then asked the question I'll never forget: "Have you heard of John Early?" When I shook my head no, she then continued, "He left Idaho and became governor of the entire Cordillera and died in 1932 in a city called Baguio."

Remaining composed on the outside, I asked, "Are his papers here? Are they extensive? Has someone written his biography?" She said that Bentley did hold his papers, but his story remained largely unknown. Fascinated, I extended my stay in Ann Arbor, and for the next three days I was the library's first and last patron as I pored over Early's files. This started a journey that sent me to a dozen archives and several countries.

Various issues made writing this book difficult. Early had no children, and his wife, a high school dropout, stopped communicating with John's colleagues several years after his death. I was told that she died in a New York City hotel room in 1971, with her husband's papers stashed under her bed. These were eventually donated to the University of Michigan. Early also distorted the facts about his parents and childhood in both his writings and the stories he told his closest friends. Consequently, untangling his family history took a great deal of research.

The more I learned about Early, the greater a Dickensian narrative emerged. His mother died when he was seven; three years later his eldest sister died as did his closest brother. His tragic childhood was followed by a professional life that resembled a train wreck: he was bankrupted at twenty-five, dropped out of three colleges, unsuccessfully pursued a get-rich scheme for gold in the Klondike, quit or was dismissed from his first post-collegiate teaching jobs, failed at both farming and journalism endeavors. Then, after rising from a position of school teacher to become lieutenant governor in America's Southeast Asian colony, he was ignominiously dismissed for supporting the indigenous peoples against American officials and entrepreneurs who exploited and slaughtered them. But Early persevered. After being fired for protecting the Igorots, he was exiled to teach in the Philippines' central islands where he faithfully labored despite sneers from American colonial racists and the challenges of a difficult marriage.

But then, almost as from a Victorian novel, sweet vindication. He rose again—not as the lieutenant governor of a subprovince—but as governor of arguably the most notable province of the Philippines. After reviewing his work, Henry Stimson, America's secretary of state, made a public announcement that "John Early is the best governor in the Philippine Islands." The Igorots also repeatedly wrote that they worshiped Early. And just as he was on the precipice of becoming the Philippines' vice governor, his body betrayed him, and his story was lost to the archives. But no longer.

What is presented in the following pages is not a defense or condemnation of colonialism; there are many books on both sides of that issue. Neither is this a book of uncritical praise for one man. Early had his flaws as the reader will learn. This volume is also not strictly a biography; rather, it is a larger story, like multiple streams that coalesce into a river. But the thread that ties the following history together—the river in which all the streams join—is John Chrysostom Early and his extraordinary life.

Countless people made this book possible. It is with profound gratitude and irreparable debts that I mention them below.

Kenton Clymer provided guidance from the outset. His book on early American missionaries in the Philippines and his article on David Barrows confirmed that there was a hidden story behind John Early's time among the Igorots. Amy Farranto at Cornell University Press believed in this book from our first meeting. Her encouragement and direction saw this book into publication. I greatly appreciate the editorial assistance from Arielle Lewis. Thank you to Michelle Scott, who served as the production editor.

Archivists and employees at numerous libraries and historical societies were always excited to help with this project. This includes the Manuscripts, Archives & Special Collections at Washington State University; the Rare Books and Manuscripts Section of the National Library of the Philippines; the Knox County Historical Society and Museum; the archives in St. Joseph Catholic Church in Edina, Missouri; the Bentley Historical Library at the University of Michigan; the archives in the Bancroft Library, University of California, Berkeley;

the Houghton Library archives at Harvard University; the Yale University Library archives; the Clay County Historical Society, Moorhead, Minnesota; and the consistent assistance from the librarians at Albertsons Library, Boise State University. I'm so grateful to Clara Adams, who worked on the maps for this book and other logistical aspects of this project.

At Boise State University, Les Alm and Steph Witt shared many Friday lunches with me and were eager listeners to the Early story and a source of encouragement. The Honors College staff with whom I work are the best colleagues. We are a high-functioning team that is more like a family as we put students first in our daily work. Kate Huebschmann read and commented on the entire manuscript and provided helpful suggestions.

I'm also thankful for the many years of friendship from Brad and Erin Chaney, and Dirk and Pam Carlson.

Frank Jenista is my professional inspiration. He has allowed our relationship to evolve from mentorship to friendship. I met him when I was in fifth grade in Baguio, and as an adult I read his groundbreaking book, *The White Apos*. At the time, I didn't know that John Early's picture was on the book's cover, but that was another important piece to the Early puzzle. Keith Eirenberg took time to communicate with me over the past two decades, met with me in Washington, DC, and shared material he had found at the National Archives. I look forward to reading his book. Pat Afable's work on the Igorots at the world's fairs provided a new perspective on this topic. She also took time to meet with me on both sides of the Pacific. I'm also thankful to my colleagues at the University of the Philippines Baguio, including Raymundo Rovillos, Lorelei Mendoza, Julius Mendoza, Ikin Salvador-Amores, and June Prill-Brett.

My formative years were spent in the Cordillera from the time of my birth until I permanently moved to the US when I was twenty-three. During those years I was befriended by the Peace Corps volunteers Thomas Churma and Mark Bosley. Churma and I played a lot of basketball together, and Mark introduced me to many new things, including Wisconsin bratwursts.

Deep friendships and love came through my friends at Brent School, including Renee Case, Gaye Tyner, Liz Viduya, Marjorie Domondon, Odette Nassr, Ruth Q. Dy, Ruby Ramos, Carmela Javellana, Lisa Marks, Doug McCallister, Steve and Jim Jepson, Jeff McCullough, Carter Glass, Elizabeth Salapong, Greg Clavano, Ross Van Vactor, Mark Walther, Fred Thomas, Mamerto Manois, and especially Jasminda Salapong and Steve Pate, who shared their lives and time with me. In Manila, Eddie, Greg and Cherrie Lyons provided great friendships, as did my Cebu friends, Karen and Cindy Hughes.

I was enveloped by love and acceptance from the time of birth by my Cordillera brothers and sisters who took me into their Baguio and Trinidad homes and hearts. I cannot mention all of them, but it is the time with them and their friendship that I wish to acknowledge as the foundation of this book. This includes the families of Abrera; Alario; Angway (thank you, Apo Jimmy, for all your assistance); Benito; Buaquen; Caoili; Caparas; Chan; Demandante; Garcia; Giron; Guerrero; Idio; Imong; Jocson; Oracion (thank you, Attorney Caesar, for your kindness to me and Karen during our latest visit); Perdigon (thank you, manong Amor); Purugganan; Piza (thank you, manong Adriano and manang Josie); Sacla; Sagayo; Tello; Viernes; and Zafra. There are many others, and I thank you all.

At the top of the list is my dear friend Benedict as well as his wife, my childhood friend Daisy Mae. Thank you both for an enduring relationship based on our love for each other. Dick, we were born the same year, lived half a kilometer from each other, and were inseparable growing up. I look forward to many more years together.

Many thanks to manang Diana, my auntie and dear friend. Many thanks to the Schreiners, who welcomed me into your family. Thanks to Florence Loveless, perhaps forgotten by most but often in my mind.

While completing this book, my father and sister, Michelle, were often in my thoughts. They are gone but not forgotten. Thanks to Mark Johnson, who cared for my sister through many of her physical struggles. Manong Damon took me in when I moved to the US, and his consistent gracious support shaped my life, and his kindness is also exhibited by his wife, Guia. My ading Rachel teaches me what it means to give without expecting reciprocity. Our years of growing up together remain golden in my mind. My mother sacrificed a great deal in raising four children. Having endured so much in her ninety years, she still greets each day with an infectious smile and a sharp mind.

Damon fills my life with joy. Our father-son relationship has evolved into the deepest of friendships and mutual admiration. I never knew how much I could love until you came along.

I cannot write these last lines with clear eyes. If Damon taught me how much I could love, Karen taught me how to love. While I've mentioned many names above, it is Karen who made this book possible by her selfless love and daily reminder of grace. This is for you.

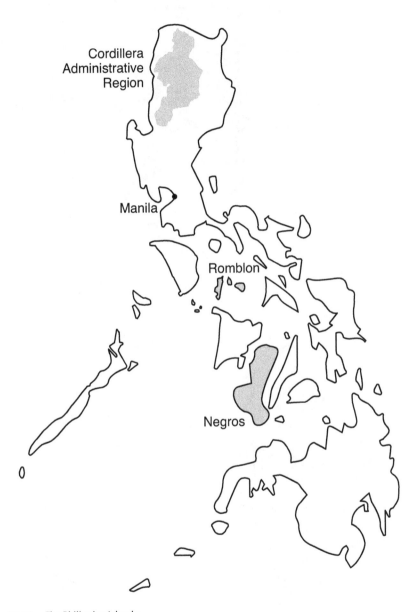

MAP 1. The Philippine Islands

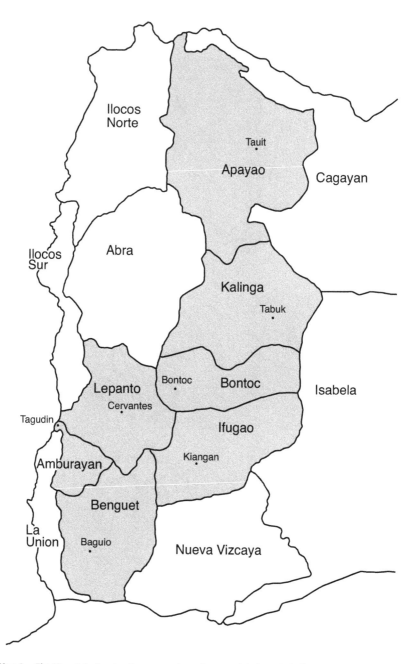

MAP 2. The Mountain Province's seven subprovinces and their capitals (1918)

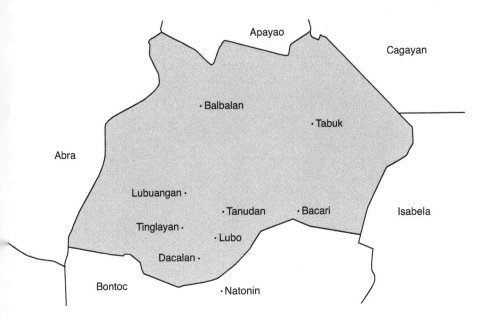

MAP 3. Kalinga subprovince (1911)

GOVERNOR OF THE CORDILLERA

Introduction

Mornings are cold in the mountain town of Bontoc. June 14, 1911, was a particularly cold morning for John C. Early, Bontoc's disgraced lieutenant governor. As he packed his belongings and saddled his horse before sunrise, his American rivals celebrated his departure while the indigenous peoples mourned his exit. He rode slowly through the town's muddy streets to begin the long descent through the winding mountains and into historical obscurity. Five days earlier he had ignominiously lost his job for trying to defend the Cordillera tribal peoples known collectively as Igorots from a slaughter planned and executed by American officials. But history has a way of vindicating promoters of justice and mercy long after its actors have departed the stage. So goes the story of John Early.

When America took control of the Philippines following the 1898 Spanish-American War, it claimed that benevolence dictated the decision. As William Howard Taft, the first American governor-general in the Philippines, stated, the Filipinos were to be America's "little brown brothers."[1] American colonial officials' worldview was rooted in social Darwinism and American exceptionalism; they insisted that America would be a kind mother, but still a mother, and so she would guide and discipline her child.[2] It would take on the "white man's burden."

Unlike Filipino lowlanders, the indigenous highlanders living in the Cordillera had not acquiesced to Spanish rule. They remained free and accepted

minimal interaction with the outside world. Known for their fierce indepen
dence, headhunting, and remarkable rice terraces, they represented exotic noble savages to the most influential Americans on both sides of the Pacific
Ocean. In the early years of American rule, entrepreneurs paraded them at
fairs and expositions across America and Europe, with a special stop at the 1904
St. Louis World's Fair.

Dean Conant Worcester, a leading American official during America's first
two decades in the Philippines, manipulated laws and policies so that he controlled the Cordillera area and its peoples. He despised Filipino lowland officials
and did everything in his power to keep the Igorots from being "contaminated"
by Filipino Christians. He bullied, intimidated, and verbally assaulted anyone
who challenged his ideological paradigm for governing the Igorots. He chose
American maverick soldiers to rule the area and expected them to use his
style of intimidation and bullying, even approving the slaughter of entire villages. This system worked for Worcester, until he appointed an obscure American teacher as a lieutenant governor for one of Cordillera's seven subprovinces.

The following chapters unveil hidden truths about Igorot-American interactions through the viewpoints of various characters. The first pages introduce John Early. His first thirty-three years (1873–1906) were marked more by
sorrows than triumphs. His mother died when he was seven, and at twenty-
two he lost everything when he was forced to declare bankruptcy. He studied
sociology in college and became convinced of the equality of all peoples. In
1906, Early escaped another financial debacle by accepting a teaching job
in the Philippines.

He volunteered to teach in the most dangerous region of the Cordillera,
and his effectiveness caught the attention of Worcester, who appointed him
lieutenant governor in 1909. Early used his influence to protect the Igorots
from colonial abuses. For this, Worcester fired him in 1911.

In the following decade, Early labored in obscurity as a teacher and then
superintendent in the Philippines' central islands. As American colonial policies shifted due to the ascendency of the Democrats, and President Woodrow
Wilson in particular, changes occurred throughout the islands, including how
the Igorots were governed.

The 1920s were volatile years for Philippine-American relations due to the
Republicans' return to the White House and the appointment of Governor-
General Leonard Wood. It was at this point that the Igorots were given a voice
as to their governance, and they requested that Early return as governor of all
the Igorots. Unfortunately, Wood's dysfunctional relationship with the Philippine Senate placed Early in the middle of a three-year battle for his appointment as permanent governor.

Wood's death in 1927 cleared the way for Early's official appointment by the Philippine Senate. Early's meaningful friendships with the Igorots took many aback. But what was even more surprising was the deep friendship he shared with Governor-General Henry L. Stimson. Early deeply cared for the highlanders and remained ever thankful for his professional vindication, though his governance was cut short due to a brave but ultimately futile battle with cancer.

It has taken a century for his story to be written. Perhaps this is because Early did not fit the ideological colonial profile of his colleagues. Still, there were repeated calls for a public examination of his life. Stimson wrote to Early's widow, "It is with a great feeling of sadness that I have heard of the passing of your noble-hearted husband, my very dear friend Governor Early. . . . His service, to which he gave his life was one of which all Americans should be proud, and I hope it will be so written up that Americans generally will have a chance to know of it."[3]

But it was not only Americans who needed to know about Early's life. A 1939 book on the Episcopal Church in the Philippines asserted, "Of Governor Early it is only necessary to record what the Igorots said of him, 'He is our father.' . . . his active concern for [Igorots] calls for a volume instead of a paragraph."[4] And in the 1980s, the distinguished historian Kenton Clymer wrote that a biography of Early might add nuance to American colonial history in the Philippines.[5]

The following pages answer these and many other requests for an assessment of Early's life among the Igorots. And like Early's professional life and passion for the Philippines, this book's focus is never far from the people of the Cordillera. Their stories are woven within the years that Early lived among them. His dying wish was that the world would come to know the greatness and dignity of the Igorots. May it be so.

Early's 1906 move to the Cordillera came thirteen years after Frederick Jackson Turner, a young professor from the University of Wisconsin, stood before a scholarly audience in Chicago and read his soon-to-be famous paper, "The Significance of the Frontier in American History." Turner's thesis was that coal-driven trains and steel mills, among other factors, had brought the US frontier days to a close. Human drive and technology had conquered the West. But Turner quickly added that America's expansion would continue. And it did. Historians have argued that one cause of American imperial expansion began with Turner. With his assertion that the frontier had ended, America's energy turned to overseas expansion.

The history of American imperial expansion, particularly in the wake of the Spanish-American War in 1898, has produced an extensive body of historical writing over several decades. Yet the acquisition of an overseas empire left Americans uneasy. They had, after all, fought a war for independence against the greatest empire in the Western world. As Daniel Immerwahr puts it in his book *How to Hide an Empire*, America played hide-and-seek with its overseas empire—more hide than seek.[6] Still, Immerwahr contends that the United States could—and should—come to terms with its imperial history and suggests that "other nations like Britain and France have acknowledged their imperial pasts and are all the better for doing so."[7] And as one reviewer notes, "Immerwahr's attempt to expose more Americans to their heritage of empire may only be the beginning of a long process [of acknowledgement], albeit an important one."[8]

As this suggests, most writing about American expansion has focused on causation and analysis of specific imperial events, such as the acquisition of Hawaii and the Philippine Islands. One early influential account was Julius W. Pratt's *Expansionists of 1898: The Acquisition of Hawaii and the Spanish Islands*, published in 1936. Very few of these historians went on to discuss how the Americans governed, much less interacted with, their new colonial subjects. About the only exception was Pratt, who published *America's Colonial Experiment: How the United States Gained, Governed, and in Part Gave Away a Colonial Empire*.[9]

With the Vietnam War in the 1960s, that began to change. First, historians rediscovered the Philippine-American War (1899–1902), formerly misleadingly known as the Philippine Insurrection. The war was America's first major Asian war, and some saw striking similarities with Vietnam. Prior to the Vietnam War, there had been only two semi-scholarly accounts of the Philippine-American conflict.[10] Now there are dozens.

A new generation of scholars writing in the 1960s, 1970s, and 1980s, such as Theodore Friend, Bonifacio S. Salamanca, Peter W. Stanley, and Glenn A. May, delved into American governance of the islands.[11] The writing has continued, with newer works going beyond traditional accounts by emphasizing different themes. Thus, for example, Paul Kramer in his well-received book *The Blood of Government* posits that race was the primary—if not the exclusive—motive for US actions and policies in its Southeast Asian colony, an assertion that some have challenged because it assumes an "unlikely uniformity in imperial outlook among Americans."[12]

A few authors have pursued innovative and creative analyses of American colonial rule and interactions with Filipinos. For example, Vicente Rafael's *White Love* describes American motives and colonial resistance by exploring the experience of American women who hired domestic workers, as well as nationalist plays, photographs, and the Philippine census records of 1905.[13] A different but equally creative approach is *Taste of Control: Food and the Filipino Colonial Mentality* by René Alexander D. Orquiza Jr.[14] Finally, Christopher Capozzola's excellent work *Bound by War* demonstrates how the US-Philippine relationship established America's Pacific Century.[15]

There are also some accounts of American missionaries and teachers in the Philippines, and a few about important colonial officials, notably Dean C. Worcester.[16] Also available are two well-known overviews of the American experience in the Philippines: Stanley Karnow's 1990 Pulitzer Prize–winning book, *In Our Image: America's Empire in the Philippines*, and H. W. Brands's *Bound to Empire: The United States and the Philippines*, published in 1992.[17]

Important as these works are, they offer limited information about the remarkable indigenous peoples and geography of Luzon's Cordillera area.[18] This is unfortunate because American intrusion and subjugation of Cordillera's indigenous population differed from the conventional social, religious, and political paradigms used by Spanish and American officials throughout the Philippine lowlands. The Cordillera became significant to the Americans because, following the patterns of the French, British, and Dutch Asian colonies, the Americans established a hill station in the mountain village of Baguio, which eventually became the colonial government's summer capital.[19]

The Igorots were illiterate prior to the establishment of American colonial rule, and the outsiders assumed that they were a people without a history. The primary volume that demythologized that idea is William Henry Scott's *The Discovery of the Igorots*.[20] Only a few other historians have written significant books about the region, notably Frank Jenista's *The White Apos: American Governors on the Cordillera Central* and Edward Dozier's *The Kalinga of Northern Luzon, Philippines*.[21] These important studies focus on individual tribes (the Ifugao and Kalinga) rather than the region as a whole. The definitive work on American-Igorot interaction between 1898 and 1936 is Howard Fry's *A History of the Mountain Province*, an impressively researched account. From its opening pages, Fry details the first heady days of Igorot-American interaction. He meticulously surveys each administrative entity in the Cordillera, making use of a well-defined chronological approach.[22] Finally, Alfred McCoy includes a chapter on American–Igorot interaction in his monumental *Policing America's Empire*.[23] A few sensational and historical fiction narratives of this period include *The Half Way Sun: Life among the Headhunters of the Philippines*, along with stories about the Igorots brought to Western fairs found in Claire Prentice's *The Lost Tribe of Coney Island*.[24] In all these books, John Early is mostly absent or at best is mentioned merely in passing.

There are hints of American-Igorot interaction sprinkled in the memoirs and biographies of colonial officials. For example, Governor-General Cameron

Forbes "had a special fascination with the non Christian tribesmen of Mountain Province."[25] The tenures of other prominent officials, such as Dean Worcester and David Prescott Barrows, were marked by their time among the indigenous peoples, and their biographers bring this out.[26]

But the broad brushstrokes by which this period and region are painted leave the reader assuming a uniformity of motives, actions, and worldviews of American officials. It is easier to focus on the prominent officials (their voluminous records are accessible) and place them in the same ideological camp. Hence it is possible to miss the outlier, the misfit, the humanitarian imperialist, and the quiet heroic figure lost to history.

The following pages unveil a story that has been either forgotten, unknown, or ignored. John Early lived, taught, and worked among the Igorots and eventually governed the entire Cordillera, yet he is scarcely mentioned in the books of the leading officials of his day, including the massive works by Worcester in which he mentions all his lieutenants, except for Early. Early is also missing from the scholarly and popular works of Karnow and Stanley. The only time Early is mentioned at length is in Joseph Ralston Hayden's book, *The Philippines: A Study in National Development*, published in 1942.[27] Hayden pays tribute to Early, placing his picture on the book's earliest pages along with a five-page biography. But Hayden's presentation of Early's life is marked by glaring inaccuracies, particularly regarding his first thirty-three years.

When Early died, his colleagues and wards never imagined that he would be forgotten. But even his grave marker cannot be found today in Baguio Municipal Cemetery. Meanwhile, the city's main thoroughfares are named after a governor-general (Francis Burton Harrison) who reportedly loathed the Igorots, a governor (William Pack) who regularly referred to the Igorots as savages, and a governor-general (Leonard Wood) who refused to meet alone with Filipino officials because of his deep-seated racism. Yet Early's name is not found on any street or town in the entire Cordillera.

The following pages attempt to set the record straight. There was an American official, in fact a governor, who publicly insisted that all races and peoples were equal. And though he was reprimanded and persecuted for his views, he persevered. In our current social climate, Early's story is needed more than ever, for amid extreme political tribalism and racial discrimination—both then and now—comes the tale of a person who was maltreated for his love of humanity but was then vindicated.

PART ONE

*John Early's Path
to the Igorots
(1521–1906)*

CHAPTER 1

The Making of a Governor

When John Chrysostom Early started writing his life's story in the spring of 1931, he knew that he had only months left to live. He began his story with a simple statement: "In 1906 I was publishing a newspaper in Southern Idaho called 'The Southern Idaho Review.'"[1] In 1906, Early was thirty-three years old, and two-thirds of his life was over. His memoir's abrupt start might have made sense had he returned to his childhood later in the manuscript; yet he wrote his entire memoir as if he magically appeared in 1906. He does not mention his parents, his nine siblings, or any aspects of his youth. In his later years, whenever he spoke of his pre-1906 life, he distorted the facts, presuming that no one would take the time to investigate his deceit. He sought to hide his deepest wounds.

Early's circuitous route to the Philippine highlands began in Tyrone County in Northern Ireland's Ulster Province. Fleeing religious persecution and economic despair, Early's granduncle Peter left Ireland for the United States in 1818 and made his way to the small village of Edina, Missouri, where, using his hands and money, he built St. Joseph Catholic Church. Peter's brother William and his family left Ireland in the 1850s and settled among Edina's Irish Catholics. William's son John, who was born in Ireland in 1836, helped the family establish a brick company in Edina.

As the US Civil War storm clouds gathered, John married the Irish-born nineteen-year-old Anastasia Kinsella on April 8, 1860, in Edina's St. Joseph

Church. Nine months after the marriage, Anastasia gave birth to Mary Ellen, the first of their ten children born over the next nineteen years. They named their eighth child, who was born on November 11, 1873, John Chrysostom Early.

In 1878, the Earlys moved to Moorhead, Minnesota. The family business thrived, and a *Moorhead Weekly* article noted that John Early Sr. employed sixteen men in a brickyard that annually produced two million bricks. But domestic tragedy overshadowed the family's professional success. In 1880 Anastasia was diagnosed with the feared disease consumption (tuberculosis). She died on April 3, 1881.

The grieving seven-year-old John found solace in his eldest sibling Mary and younger brother Alfred. But just three years after their mother's death, Mary also died of consumption. Three months later, Alfred succumbed to encephalitis. Before reaching puberty, Early had lost his three dearest family members. Perhaps this sadness explains why his college classmates would later claim: "he [John] has a face like a benediction."[2]

Early buried his grief with work and school. From a young age, he believed that education was his ticket out of brickmaking and poverty. While working long hours, he found time to complete high school, and subsequently studied for several semesters at Fargo College and the Moorhead Normal School, what is today known as Minnesota State University.

Eventually all his siblings left Minnesota, leaving Early to single-handedly run the family farm and brick business. His father deserted the fledgling business, which eventually went bankrupt, with the banks auctioning off all the land and equipment. At twenty-six, Early moved to Seattle for a fresh start. After failing to find gold in the Klondike, he moved to Pullman, Washington, where he enrolled in the nascent Washington Agricultural College (WAC), which eventually became Washington State University. He flourished during his 1900–1904 stint at WAC.

The first known photographs of Early are found in the 1902 WAC yearbook. At twenty-nine (though he listed his age as twenty-six), he sported thick black hair parted in the middle, and his muscled body filled out his suits and football uniform. He was a handsome man with well-proportioned facial features. Despite his classmates' kidding about his somber affect, in his pictures his face suggests a smile more than a frown, and gives the impression of a person in a hurry, ready to get on with life.

Early found security and a sense of belonging at WAC. His long list of extracurricular activities included being editor of both the school paper *Evergreen* and the annual yearbook *Chinook*, secretary of the Oratorical Society, manager of the baseball team, captain of the football team, and chairman of the

Discipline Committee. Known as a serious student with strong opinions, he was teased by his colleagues during his senior year for both his solemnity and his interest in a female classmate: "There was a brave Senior named Early, Whose manner last year was quite surly; 'Till he met charming Bess—The result you may guess—And now burly Early's not surly."[3]

Choosing economic science and history as his major, Early found particular inspiration in the lectures of professor Walter Greenwood Beach (1868–1948), who became a famous sociologist of his day. Influenced by the writings of Émile Durkheim and Karl Marx, Beach believed all races were equal and that exploitation accompanied colonialism and unrestrained capitalism. Early's senior thesis, "The Present Status of Child Labor in the United States," reflected Beach's theories.

Early earned his bachelor's degree in 1904, and he began teaching in nearby school districts, but resigned several positions after serving just a few months, citing what he called "the incompetence of the school board members." In 1905, he sought a superintendent position in Colfax, Washington. He asked Enoch Bryan, WAC's president, to use his influence with one of the city's prominent citizens who served on the search committee. Bryan agreed to do this, but counseled greater humility: "Replying to yours of March 8, I shall be very glad indeed to have a frank talk with Mr. Canfield in regard to your qualifications. I think perhaps you realize that even with myself I would look with some degree of anxiety upon so large an undertaking for one with so little experience as the Colfax superintendency."[4] Early didn't get the job.

With no prospects as a teacher, Early's next move was to southeast Idaho, where he accepted an eighty-four-acre homestead as part of what became known as the Minidoka Project. Along with hundreds of others, Early staked his future on the US government's promise that irrigated water would flow to this barren region, and farmers could have viable farms within three years. If the farms succeeded within that timeframe, the government would give each successful farmer their eighty-four-acre homestead free and clear.

During that time, Early also partnered with Frank Adams, a former *Chicago Daily News* reporter, and they established a local paper called *The Southern Idaho Review*. Throughout 1905 and early 1906, Early's influence and popularity among the homestead families grew. Later, in 1947, W. E. Dunham, a seasoned pioneer of the early Minidoka Project, remembered how the Irish-Catholic WAC graduate served as both a physical and emotional support for the starving families. He also recalled that Early "was a brilliant writer."[5] But writing did not pay the bills or bring water to the homestead, and Early was in trouble. The paper went bankrupt within a year, and the promised irrigated water was delayed by two years. Without irrigated water, he would not be able to prove he had a viable farm within the government's timeframe. Despite his enviable college degree, Early faced bankruptcy once again. But, as he later wrote, fortune finally came his way: "Those who could get out and still hold their land did so. I sought and found a way."[6] He learned that homesteaders could extend the time limit to improve their land if they qualified for a two-year government service stint as teachers in the Philippines. This offer meant very little to most homesteaders because their families could not accompany them to Asia, and very few farmers possessed the requisite education required for such employment. Early, however, was in luck.

He had learned about the Philippines at WAC from classmate A. C. Smith, who fought in the Philippine-American War. Professor Beach had also awakened him to the plight of America's colonized peoples. Thus, while still a senior at WAC, Early had passed an exam to teach in the Philippines as an alternate professional possibility, and this backup plan now became his only option. After thirty-three years defined by failure, he gambled his future on a place 8,000 miles from his home—there was little else he could do.

Early arrived in Seattle during the final days of April 1906, following his life's journey toward the West: Missouri, Minnesota, and now America's Pacific Coast. Borne out of dwindling prospects, the Irish-American placed his hope across the Pacific Ocean. As he reminisced on his situation, he gave no hint of either discouragement or excitement about his new adventure; he simply wrote, "In April 1906 I found myself in Seattle booked to sail on the SS 'Minnesota' for Hong Kong."[7]

On April 29, the *Minnesota* left Seattle for Yokohama, as its captain hoped to arrive in Japan ahead of the typhoon season. After a month in Japan, the *Minnesota* proceeded south and docked at Shanghai. The Shanghai of 1906 offered every pleasure under the sun—for a price. While there, Early witnessed a once-great civilization teetering on the precipice of collapse. China's last imperial dynasty, the Qing (1644–1912), was in its death throes. Led by the aging Dowager Cixi and her eunuchs, China unraveled while Japan industrialized. Between 1842 and 1906, China lost battles to the British, French, Japanese, and a multinational force that occupied Peking following the failed 1900 Boxer Rebellion.

Early's observations of Western chauvinism in Shanghai and his comments about the treatment of the Chinese represented his beliefs on racial equality and human rights—beliefs that, in a few years, would cost him his job:

> From Japan we went to Shanghai where we lay again for several days, discharging cargo, and in that time we came in contact with the first symptoms of the disagreeable in the contact between East and West. In

China more of misery was apparent, more professional beggars, more diseased people, more harshness in bargaining between strangers and natives, and every agreeable feature of places within the town of Shanghai forbidden to Chinese—signs up: "Dogs and Chinese Not Allowed . . ." This attitude of the Westerner toward the Easterner, although we did not analyze it then, was no doubt the underlying cause of the great upheaval in China during the past several years.[8]

The *Minnesota* continued south and docked at the growing British colony of Hong Kong. From there Early boarded the steamship *Rubi*, which he described as a tub compared to the massive *Minnesota*. After several pleasant days on the vessel, he spotted the lights of Manila. He was a long way from Edina, Missouri. Stretched out before him in the humid air was an uncertain future, a new life in which he could prove he was not a failure. Now, on the other side of the world, there was no one to blame but himself for his success or failure. He was not alone in hoping a new country would mean a new life; the Philippines had been a haven of Western adventurers, explorers, religious zealots, and colony collectors since the sixteenth century. But Early proved to be a different type of foreigner.

CHAPTER 2

Eight Million Souls for Twenty Million Dollars

Unlike many of his teaching colleagues, Early stepped onto Philippine soil with some understanding of the Philippines' place in history. As a graduate of the Washington Agricultural College, his social science background included world history courses, and his academic advisers included a veteran of the Philippine–American War. Tucked away in American history books, the Philippine-American War came on the heels of the 1898 Spanish-American War, which Secretary of State John Hay termed "A Splendid Little War." But the subsequent Philippine-American War was neither splendid nor little. Yet Early understood that the reasons for his arrival in the Philippines included certain precious spices that led to Spain's three-and-a-half-century colonial rule over the islands.

"The history of the Spanish in the Philippines begins and ends with the friar."[1] While there is a great deal of insight in that sentence, gold came before God in Spain's stumbling onto the Philippines. In fifteenth-century Europe, three spices were treasured: nutmeg, cloves, and mace. These spices, used in Rome in the first century CE, were valued for their medicinal, flavoring, and preserving qualities. But they were scarce with mysterious origins. Along with pepper, they made their way to Europe from India, which served as a bridge between the fabled Spice Islands and the West. Until the eighteenth century, these spices only grew on small volcanic islands in Indonesia's eastern Moluccas archipelago. Western European contact with the spices increased during the Crusades in the Middle East, and a post-Crusade trading pattern emerged in which the spices were shipped from Southeast Asia to India, then transported to the trading centers of Baghdad, Alexandria, and Constantinople. This arrangement flourished until 1453, when Constantinople fell to Ottoman forces. Muslim merchants subsequently monopolized spice distribution west of the Indian subcontinent, and Europeans bought the merchandise from Ottoman traders via Jewish middlemen in Venice and Genoa.

Constantinople's fall to the Ottomans damaged Christian Europe's prestige, economy, and diet. But Spain and Portugal determined they would end Islam's spice monopoly. Their successful *Reconquista* of the Iberian Peninsula proved that they could compete, at least militarily, with the Ottoman armies. If spices could not come to Christians, then Christians would go to the spices. Consequently, Spain and Portugal raced across oceans to find the Spice Islands, Spain sailing west and Portugal south and east. The two massive American continents and an ocean covering one-third of the planet kept the Spanish from reaching the Spice Islands before Portuguese explorers found them in 1512. Undeterred, Spain's King Charles V commissioned a five-ship fleet in 1519 to find a westward passage to the islands.

Led by Ferdinand Magellan, a Portuguese who betrayed his king and country due to perceived insults, the Spanish carracks made the epic journey across the Atlantic, down the coast of South America, and into the Pacific. It then took Magellan four months to cross the uncharted Pacific Ocean. Finally, in March 1521, Magellan and the fleet's three remaining ships discovered the seven thousand island archipelago that was later given the name *Islas Filipinas* in honor of Spain's Prince Philip. The Philippines was not part of the spice island archipelago, but it did sit just above the Moluccas islands and served as a southern doorway into China. Within fifty years, Spain established its colonial rule in the Philippines, choosing Manila as its political, religious, and economic capital.

Spain served as the Philippines' colonial master from 1565 to 1898, even though the archipelago proved an economic disappointment. Unlike the American colonies, the Philippines offered minimal natural resources, and unlike in the New World, it was the Spaniards who died due to disease, not the indigenous peoples. For centuries, traders from around Asia exposed the archipelago's inhabitants to global diseases, so they were not decimated by the germs the Spanish brought to the Philippines. For the Europeans, however, the Philippines' oppressive heat and humidity wore down their physical and mental stamina. Additionally, the twenty or more annual typhoons along with the ever-present danger of earthquakes, averaging five a day in the archipelago, left the Spaniards literally and figuratively on shaky ground. Spanish officials and soldiers sent to manage Spain's far-flung Asian colony often viewed the assignment as a punishment.

But there was one group of Spaniards who enthusiastically embraced their Asian colony. Friars from Roman Catholic religious and apostolic orders found a home in the Philippines and effectively spread their faith as they had done in Mexico and Peru. Of great importance to these men was the pope's special dispensation allowing them to serve as parish priests in the Philippines, something they could not do in Europe or the New World. As a result, the friars embedded themselves in local communities with no plans to retire or leave the islands. Over the centuries of Spanish rule, the friars emerged as the Philippines' greatest economic, social, and political influence. In short, they held the colony together and remained fanatically loyal to their orders and Spain.

But for all their power in the Philippines, the friars could not control world events such as the February 15, 1898, sinking of the USS *Maine* in Havana's harbor, which killed over 250 men. While the cause of the explosion is still debated, its political ripples are much clearer. As the nineteenth century ended, a younger generation of American men untempered by the realities of war dreamed of the heroism from tales of Civil War and Indian War battles. Americans also watched European states become global powers as they collected distant colonies. America would not be left behind, and some might have recalled the words of the country's first president in a letter he wrote to the Marquis de Lafayette: "However unimportant America may be considered at present, & however Britain may affect to despise her trade, there will assuredly come a day when this country will have some weight in the scale of Empires."[2]

While America's global influence rose in the late nineteenth century, Spain's power had reached its height during the sixteenth century. When the Spanish first arrived in the Philippines in 1521 they, like their friends back home, believed they were "God's new chosen people, destined to execute the plans of Providence."[3] But by the end of the nineteenth century, Spain's once mighty empire merely consisted of Cuba, the Philippines, and a few other inconsequential colonies. Nonetheless, Spain intended to keep its remaining outposts, especially Cuba and the Philippines—both places that were on the verge of revolution.

In Cuba, local revolutionaries sought independence, finding American sympathy, if not outright support, for their dreams of freedom. Tension on the island led American politicians to direct the USS *Maine* to Havana's harbor to protect American citizens. Its explosion or implosion on February 15, 1898, provided the opportunity for America to expand its regional influence. President William McKinley, unable to convince Spain to undertake reforms he thought were needed, reluctantly decided in April to support intervention in Cuba, and Congress then declared war.

Theodore Roosevelt, arguably the loudest and most confident voice of American exceptionalism, resigned his post as undersecretary of the US Navy to ride into battle against the Spanish in Cuba. A devout believer in Alfred Mahan's theory on the primacy of naval power, Roosevelt placed the US Pacific squadron led by Commodore George Dewey on high alert even before the war started, and he gathered US warships at Hong Kong. Dewey received word on April 22, 1898, that the US and Spain were at war. The American fleet made its way to Manila Bay to attack the Spanish ships. In the early hours of May 1, 1898, the one-sided battled commenced, and at the end of the day, every Spanish ship was either captured or sunk. Over 350 Spanish sailors perished, while Dewey reported only one fatality on the American side—an unfortunate soul who succumbed to either a heart attack or heat exhaustion. But Dewey's smashing naval victory did not weaken the Spanish Army or fortress in Manila. Fortunately, America had a significant Filipino ally.

Less than three weeks after Dewey's victory, the USS *McCulloch* carried Emilio Aguinaldo from Hong Kong to Cavite, a town along Manila Bay. Aguinaldo was in Hong Kong due to his leadership in the 1896 Philippine Revolution—an uprising that came after more than three centuries of Spanish rule. The freedom-fighting Filipino Army proved more potent than Spain anticipated, and Spanish officials believed that removing the revolution's leader would deflate the movement, so they promised Aguinaldo eight hundred thousand pesos in exchange for his departure from the Philippines. Aguinaldo accepted the money, moved to Hong Kong, and promptly planned his return to help liberate the Philippines. Spain also underestimated the extent of rebellion in Philippine society, and Aguinaldo's exile did little to stem the fervor of Philippine nationalism. Upon Aguinaldo's American-aided return, the revolution gained even more steam, and while American ships guarded Manila Bay, keeping the Spanish from escaping by sea, Philippine revolutionary forces closed in on Manila from surrounding provinces.

Since the sixteenth century, Manila-based Spaniards had lived in the 166-acre walled city of Intramuros, which contained Fort Santiago. With a moat as added protection, Intramuros was a Spanish enclave amid Malay and Chinese communities. Following Dewey's victory, the Spanish flocked into their walled city, increasing its inhabitants from ten thousand to sixty thousand. But while Aguinaldo's soldiers tightened the noose around Intramuros, more ominous developments spelled eventual disaster for the Filipino revolutionaries.

American military strategists believed the US needed to send an army to defeat the Spanish in the Philippines, just as it had in Cuba. Consequently, during the summer of 1898, an American volunteer army gathered in San Francisco for training and eventual transport across the Pacific. Thousands of young men across America volunteered to fight in the Philippines, motivated by adventure, salary, and opportunities for heroism. Between May and August of 1898, more than twenty thousand American soldiers crossed the Pacific to fight the Spaniards while Dewey patrolled Manila Bay, biding his time until their arrival. Meanwhile, the Filipino revolutionary army prepared to deliver its final victory over the exhausted and deflated Spanish in Intramuros. Yet Dewey did not support the Filipinos. Aguinaldo and his officers, particularly General Antonio Luna, correctly surmised that the US withheld aid because it did not support an independent Philippines, and, in fact, it intended to take the Philippines away from Spain for itself. Additionally, internal division marred Aguinaldo's revolutionary cause. Luna, for example, was shot and hacked to death by Aguinaldo's allies on June 5, 1899. Several elite Filipinos assured Dewey that the so-called Philippine Revolution merely mirrored a storm in a teacup and that most Filipinos welcomed American rule. Still, by the summer of 1898, Filipino revolutionary soldiers controlled large swaths of the Philippines.

In Washington, President McKinley appointed Major General Wesley Merritt, a Civil War hero and a man who fought with General Custer against the Lakota Sioux, to lead the Philippine-bound volunteers. By August 1, 1898, the American soldiers were entrenched around Manila. US military officers pressured Aguinaldo to move his forces and make room for the Americans.

Draped in wool uniforms and arriving at the height of the monsoon season, the American soldiers' initial enthusiasm gave way to heat exhaustion, dysentery, and malaria. The only thing cold in Manila's climate was Merritt and Aguinaldo's relationship. American military personnel in Manila, from Dewey to Merritt to the lowest-ranked soldier, considered the Filipino Army a nuisance, not an asset. Filipino soldiers stood in the way of America's glorious victory against the Spanish remnant trapped in Intramuros.

But Merritt faced a greater challenge than the Filipino Army and the Spanish soldiers. He still did not know what his president wanted him to do, and there was no clear objective as President McKinley continued to waffle on the nature of America's role in the Philippines. For their part, Merritt and his lieutenants wanted to let their soldiers loose across Manila and the entire archipelago with the hopes of rooting out the Spanish and perhaps establishing American rule. But McKinley was not ready to go that far, and so Merritt waited for his orders.

Tensions between the occupying American soldiers and the entrenched revolutionary Filipino Army increased as the summer wore on. Pervasive racial bias against the Filipinos characterized the American soldiers' worldview.

Though outsiders, the Americans persisted in calling their hosts "monkeys" and "n——." Americans pushed Filipino soldiers aside and built trenches around Intramuros.

Spanish officials trapped within their walled city knew theirs was a lost cause, and they hatched a plan to save face: they would surrender to the Americans after a mock battle. This killed two birds with one stone. First and foremost, they would avoid the humiliation and greater danger of surrendering to the Filipinos, a people they despised, alienated, and exploited for hundreds of years. Second, Spanish soldiers could proudly say they fought to protect Intramuros.

Spanish and American officers secretly agreed to the ruse and, following a sham battle on August 13, the Spanish opened Intramuros's gate and surrendered to the Americans. The Filipino people were the losers in all of this. After years of fighting the Spanish, they could not claim their hard-won victory, and Aguinaldo was not even allowed to attend the surrender ceremony.

Just days after Intramuros's fall, Merritt returned to the US, frustrated with McKinley's continued indecisiveness. But a few weeks after Merritt's departure, McKinley made up his mind. He would support those who advocated for America's entrance into the global colonial game. McKinley credited divine guidance for his decision: "I went down on my knees and prayed [to] Almighty God for light and guidance. . . . In one night late it came to me this way—I don't know how it was, but it came: that there was nothing left for us to do but to take them all, and to educate the Filipinos, and uplift and civilize and Christianize them, and by God's grace do the very best we could by them, as our fellow-men for whom Christ also died."[4] The American delegation sent to the Paris peace conference in September 1898 carried this directive from McKinley: get the Philippines (Filipinos were not invited to the Spanish-American negotiations). As for Cuba, the US Congress voted to recognize the island's independence.

While making these monumental decisions, McKinley ignored the fact that at a June 12, 1898, ceremony in Cavite, General Aguinaldo had declared the Philippines' independence, which was signed by ninety-seven witnesses including an American who was formerly in the US Army. Nonetheless, Filipinos were not invited to the Paris negotiations, and the country's future was in the hands of Western diplomats.

Back in the Philippines, the dramatic increase of US soldiers in Manila (there were over twenty-two thousand by September), created more opportunities for conflict between Filipino and American troops. Aguinaldo and his fellow nationalists remained patient because they knew that many Americans did not covet an Asian colony. In particular, many Democrat legislators, the

Anti-Imperialist League, and prominent citizens such as Andrew Carnegie and Mark Twain opposed McKinley's plan to seize the Philippines. Furthermore, at the Paris negotiations, Spain remained intransigent regarding its hold on the Philippines and refused to give up its Asian possession.

American negotiators, who represented the war's clear victor, offered Spain twenty million dollars in exchange for the Philippines. Spain agreed. Philippine nationalists' hopes were further dashed when the US Senate passed the treaty by one vote on February 6, 1899, thus making the Philippines and its eight million inhabitants a US colony.

After Merritt's August 30, 1898, departure from the Philippines, McKinley entrusted the Philippines to a military governor, Major General Elwell S. Otis. Otis sent friendly overtures to Aguinaldo, and the two communicated throughout the fall of 1898. But they failed to keep the peace between their soldiers. On the evening of February 4, 1899, American soldiers opened fire on Filipino men who did not properly respond to English commands. America was now involved in a much more serious war, one that would eventually cost the lives of over two hundred thousand soldiers and civilians.

CHAPTER 3

War and Colonial Policies

While the Filipino troops bravely stood their ground around Manila, superior American weaponry overwhelmed the entrenched indigenous soldiers. Aguinaldo and his army withdrew to Luzon's vast countryside and the following year adopted effective guerrilla tactics against an ever-increasing American volunteer army (by the summer of 1899, more than sixty thousand American troops occupied the Philippines). As the urban battles ceased and a general peace settled over most of the Philippines, General Otis hoped to make his soldiers' presence appear as a benevolent act rather than a hostile takeover. Soldiers used their non-combatant time to hold classes for Filipino children and adults; corpsmen cared for the local population; and Americans facilitated town and municipal elections to establish a rudimentary democracy-based local government.

Otis's embryonic hearts and minds strategy did not appease the American anti-imperialists, who daily condemned the Philippine-American War and McKinley's colonial policies. The president responded to his critics by turning to the academician Jacob Gould Schurman, a professor of philosophy and president of Cornell University. In early 1899, Schurman led an investigative team known as Schurman's Commission to the Philippines with an assignment to provide a unbiased assessment of the situation and to recommend a political paradigm for the Philippines. Schurman's team included Charles Denby, a Democratic diplomat in China, and Dean Worcester, a University of Michigan professor of anthropology. Of the three, only Worcester possessed extensive experience in the Philippines. He would also profoundly shape John Early's professional and personal life.

Arriving in Manila on March 4, 1899, the Schurman Commission called upon General Otis and Admiral Dewey, who were also slated to be part of the team, but they intimated that they were too busy to join a civilian-led fact-finding enterprise. After just one month, Schurman's group produced a document that served as an outline for America's future in the islands. It proposed that wide reforms take place in the judicial, educational, and government spheres. It also recommended that those changes, including universal education, be executed by a nationally elected governing body. Nonetheless, the real authority should be in the hands of a US presidentially appointed governor-general along with American secretaries of education, the interior, and other spheres of a colonial government.

Professor Dean Worcester enjoyed inordinate influence over the Schurman Commission's conclusions. His social Darwinian worldview emphasized the inequality of races, and he believed that Filipinos needed white men to govern them. His imperialist and racist biases confirmed American expansionist ideas. Worcester noted that with proper guidance American colonial servants would make Filipinos "more American than the Americans themselves."[1] President McKinley endorsed the commission's recommendations, and he formed a second Philippine commission to establish American rule in the Philippines and transfer authority from military personnel to civil servants. This five-man commission would chart America's new role as a colonial mother, and the success or failure of America's rule largely depended on this second commission. With such high stakes, McKinley needed an extraordinary man to serve as its leader. He found his man in William Howard Taft, a fellow Ohioan and a gifted lawyer and judge.

Born into a highly educated family, Taft studied at Yale, where he joined the college's secret Skull and Bones society, an organization founded by his father, Alphonso Taft (1810–1891), who graduated from Yale in 1833 and served as President Ulysses S. Grant's secretary of war. The younger Taft returned to his Cincinnati home following his 1878 graduation from Yale. He was keenly attracted to studying law and he enrolled at the University of Cincinnati's College of Law, graduating in 1880. In 1892 he began his tenure as a federal circuit judge with a burning ambition for an appointment to the US Supreme Court. But Taft's career trajectory took a decidedly strange turn in 1900 when he received a mid-January message from the United States president: "I would like to see you in Washington on important business within the next few days."[2] Taft's dream that the invitation meant a judicial appointment was dashed when

McKinley asked him to serve as the Philippine Commission's lead figure. He respectfully declined the opportunity, citing his anti-colonial stance and his pursuit of a law career. McKinley persuasively insisted that Taft lead this vital mission. The president argued that the Philippines had been thrust on America, and it was now its duty and responsibility to enlighten the archipelago's inhabitants. To sweeten the offer, McKinley noted that service in the Philippines provided excellent experience for a seat on the US Supreme Court. Chiming in, Secretary of War Elihu Root appealed to Taft's sense of patriotic duty. Taft reluctantly agreed to lead the commission, which became known as both the Taft Commission and Philippine Commission—a political unit that largely controlled the Philippines until 1916.

Just weeks after Taft's Washington meeting, Dean Worcester wrote home and told his family that he, too, was asked to join the Philippine Commission as the only holdover member from the Schurman Commission. He intimated that this prestigious appointment most likely meant a plum position in America's new colony, maybe even a governorship in the archipelago. Along with Taft and Worcester, the commission included Luke Wright, Tennessee's attorney general; Bernard Moses, a University of California professor of Latin American history; and the Vermont lawyer Henry Ide.

On April 17, 1900, the commission departed from San Francisco, and after stops in Japan and Hong Kong, it arrived in Manila on June 4. At the time, Aguinaldo and his army remained at large, and sporadic rural battles continued. Still under martial law, with the American general Arthur MacArthur Jr. as the supreme commander, the country continued to operate in crisis mode. McKinley appointed Taft as the Philippines' civilian governor and he immediately took charge. MacArthur was unhappy with Taft's new role, but the civilian governor changed the tone of America's presence through his affable approach to Filipino leaders and his effective administrative skills. He delegated his fellow commissioners to take charge of the islands' most pressing needs. The commission evolved into a civilian legislative body with the task of establishing democracy, peace, and education.

When Early arrived in Manila in 1906, Taft's social engineering policies were in their sixth year. For Early, as well as most American observers, Taft's education reform was of greatest importance, and during the commission's first years, people noted its steady progress even while dissension and heated philosophical and pedagogical arguments persisted. Even before Taft left for the Philippines, McKinley had wrested the Philippine education efforts away from the American volunteer soldiers and given them to civilians.

Taft, on the recommendations of Harvard president Charles W. Eliot, hired Fred Atkinson to create and nurture a Philippine public school system. A thirty-five-year-old Harvard graduate with a doctorate from Leipzig University, Atkinson seemed the ideal choice. The charismatic Atkinson was six-foot-four, and his credentials included a successful administrative stint at a Springfield, Massachusetts high school. Atkinson was very interested in the position, and he met with the Philippine Commission in Washington, DC.

Transcripts of his Washington interview reveal that he knew little about the Philippines or how he might approach educating a Southeast Asian populace. Bernard Moses, whose commission portfolio included education, was disappointed by Atkinson's answers, rightly judging that he would not contextualize his methods to fit with the indigenous cultures. Taft, however, remained impressed with the Harvard graduate and appointed him as the Philippines' first American director of education in 1900.

Atkinson promptly set out to hire one thousand American teachers, and the call for teachers brought in over eight thousand applications. About two-thirds of the candidates chosen were male, and most of the successful applicants possessed college credits and teaching experience. Their motives for going to the Philippines included thoughts of adventure, economic considerations (their monthly salaries were as high as $125, which was more than teachers in the US were paid), Protestant evangelistic zeal, and joining a relative or loved one stationed in the Philippines. To finance the new policy of universal education, the commission ordered each Philippine municipality to use its tax receipts to build and maintain school buildings. The colonial government paid for the teachers' salaries, transportation, and textbooks.

The successes of America's embryonic colonial education were mixed and largely depended on the motivations and dispositions of its teachers. Some American instructors became heroes in their assigned towns and provinces because of their compassion and commitment to educating their students. On the other hand, many of the foreign teachers despised the local culture and overtly flaunted their sense of racial superiority.

Unfortunately, Atkinson's two-year tenure as director of education was marked by his ineffective leadership and controversy. As early as May 1901, Taft realized his error in appointing Atkinson and said as much in a letter to his younger brother Horace Taft: "Confidentially, Atkinson is not what the Commission hoped for. . . . Atkinson has already begun to talk of an advance in salary above six thousand dollars, which he receives. I gently intimated to him that if I were he I would not refer such a request to the Commission until he had demonstrated his ability to control the situation by an inauguration of the system of schools. I should think that such an opportunity as he has would make him think of anything but salary. . . . He lacks, it seems to me, in force."[3]

The colonial education scheme limped through its first years and followed a curriculum that emphasized "practical education." In America, this method of schooling focused on producing a post–Civil War workforce for the nation's industrial expansion. A life worth living no longer focused on Socrates's self-examination; rather, vocational skills marked human success. Atkinson endorsed this approach and sought to implement it in the Philippines, and so vocational training dominated the colonial curriculum, preparing Filipinos to become more effective local tenant farmers while remaining subservient to foreign colonial masters. Atkinson's failure at almost every level in the Philippines culminated with Taft firing him just before 1903. Eight months later, after a more thorough vetting process, the commissioners asked Prescott Barrows to lead the beleaguered colonial Bureau of Education. The Philippines would never be the same.

Raised in California's Ventura County, David Prescott Barrows (1873–1954) typified the restless, ambitious American young men of the early twentieth century who believed they had limitless opportunities. Earning a PhD in anthropology from the University of Chicago in 1897, Barrows, like many others, saw an opportunity for quick professional advancement through service in the Philippines. In 1900 he became the superintendent of the Manila schools. One year later, in October 1901, he received a new appointment as the first head of the Bureau of Non-Christian Tribes (BNCT). He excelled in this role, catching the eye of Commissioner Bernard Moses, his former professor, whose portfolio included education.

In 1903, Barrows accepted the commission's offer to replace Atkinson and determined to turn around the floundering colonial education program. He quickly gained the confidence of teachers who had suffered through years of Atkinson's inept leadership. He also shifted the previous education paradigm, and his new approach mirrored the differences between Barrows's and Atkinson's history.

In contrast to Atkinson, Barrows spent less time with rich Filipinos, as he sought to break the power of the oligarchy and the landed elite. Taking his cue from American founder Thomas Jefferson, Barrows believed an educated agrarian class could avoid economic exploitation. At one point, Barrows claimed, "Two years of instruction in arithmetic given to every child will in a generation destroy that repellent 'peonage' or bonded indebtedness that prevails throughout this country."[4]

Barrows believed that the only way to effectively educate the Filipinos was to fundamentally change the existing system. He reduced the primary courses from four years to three, began training Filipino teachers who could replace

Americans in the classroom, and introduced more accessible and culturally relevant textbooks. Unfortunately, his belief that education would end centuries of oppression did not hold true. First, for all his idealism, three years of education could not upend the stranglehold the economic elite and the Roman Catholic friars held over the poor. But the greatest challenge was that American officials wanted the Philippines to serve as an economic boon for the US. They sought a colonial population with just enough education to effectively bring the Philippines into the US economy. In a 1908 report, one year before he resigned his position, Barrows overtly criticized the commission's educational philosophy: "To those who advocate 'practical instruction,' I reply that the most practical thing obtainable for men is a civilized community, and their most desirable acquisition is literacy."[5] Barrows left the Philippines with his educational dream for the Filipinos unfulfilled. His professional ambitions, however, were still intact, and within a decade he rose to become the president of the University of California, Berkeley.

John Early arrived in the Philippines during Barrows's tenure as director of education. When the new recruits met with Barrows for an initial orientation session, Barrows asked for a volunteer to serve in the remote mountains in northern Luzon. As the former director of the BNCT, he knew the difficulty of working among the mountain tribes. Early's hand shot up—he was the only volunteer for the assignment—and spontaneous applause broke out for his bravery. After the meeting, Barrows asked Early to remain for a private conversation. He then warned him that he was going to a dangerous region of the country and offered him a face-saving way to quietly back out of his public commitment. If Barrows thought that Early's bravado was for public adulation, he learned that this was not the case. Early remained the same man in private. As he later recalled, "What he [Barrows] told me had, however, excited my interest, and I declined to withdraw."[6]

A few days following the meeting with Barrows, Early began his journey to Luzon's highlands. The mountains and its peoples would bring Early his greatest pain and joy. It was a region rarely understood by outsiders—truly a place and people unlike any other in the world.

CHAPTER 4

The Discovery of the Igorots

From Miguel López de Legazpi's (1502–1572) perspective, his life represented a series of dismal failures. Descended from a Basque family in Spain, the middle-aged Legazpi fled Europe for the New World with hopes of better opportunities in Mexico. He proved to be good with numbers and records, but no grand fortune awaited him in Mexico. When the viceroy of Spain's American colonies called on him to lead a massive 1565 expedition to establish Spain's rule in the Philippines, Legazpi believed this would finally lead to his long-sought economic and social prestige. But after a difficult three-month voyage across the Pacific, he found even greater disappointment. The Southeast Asian archipelago was not a rich place, and the natives were hostile. He nonetheless followed orders, planted the Spanish flag on the island of Cebu, and set his five hundred soldiers to work.

Legazpi was distraught, as he wanted something better than to rule the most undesirable spot in Spain's expanding empire. Then everything changed. Just a few weeks after his mid-February 1565 arrival, he was told that gold mines existed in northern Luzon, the archipelago's largest and most populous island. Consequently, after establishing Spanish rule in Manila, Governor-General Legazpi sent his grandson, Juan de Salcedo, to lead a company of soldiers to find the gold mines with the hope that this would bring back the glory days of the conquistadors and the discovery of enormous wealth in the Americas. The fruitless exploration of northern Luzon revealed a landlocked spine of mountains running approximately 220 miles in length and 70 miles in width, which collectively became known as the Cordillera.

The disastrous results of Legazpi's get-rich plan perfectly previewed the next three hundred years of Spanish interaction with northern Luzon's mountainous tribes. He died on August 20, 1572, in abject poverty; his grandson followed him four years later at the age of twenty-seven while in northern Luzon trying to establish rule over the hill people whom the lowlanders feared. Spain would never control Luzon's northern indigenous peoples.

Scholars are divided as to the origins of Luzon's northern highlanders, who are collectively known as Igorots. The name "Igorot" evolved from Spanish documents that identified the Cordillera inhabitants as *Ygolotes*. Following the global historical pattern, Luzon's highlanders were less sophisticated than the lowlanders in terms of literacy, as oral traditions preserved their historical memory rather than written records. Archaeological investigations and a few travel accounts from outsiders who survived incursions into the dangerous mountains add to oral accounts in piecing together Igorot history.

Subsequent ethnolinguistic studies reveal six major groups/tribes among the Igorots: Bontoc, Ifugao, Kankanaey, Ibaloi, Kalinga, and Apayao. Each tribe possesses a distinctive culture, dialect, and set of folktales, dances, metaphysical ceremonies, textile patterns, and gods. Prior to the American colonial era, the Cordillera tribes did not identify as one collective group; however, similar patterns existed among all the highlanders. For example, they were profoundly religious, living in fear of unseen spirits and unappeased ancestors. Social life revolved around *cañaos* (feasts) consisting of animal sacrifices along with days of dancing, eating, and alcohol consumption. These feasts were part of celebratory events such as weddings and military victories, as well as more somber occasions such as propitiation offerings and funerals. Igorots largely subsisted on wet-rice agriculture along with their one other staple, *camote* (sweet potato). Their meat sources included pigs, fowl, dogs, cattle, and wild game. Trade with lowlanders occurred when Igorots occasionally traversed down the western and eastern slopes of the Cordillera to pick up salt and tools in exchange for the gold found in the mountains.

Igorots also practiced head-hunting, and both Spanish and early American colonial officials were astonished that the highlanders accepted perpetual head-hunting as a way of life. Harmony between villages and tribes existed through limited peace pacts, though lowlanders and colonials described the entire region as a land of existential danger. But this was the outsiders' perspective. For the Igorots, life was not nasty, brutish, or short. One heard laughter much more than weeping in the mountains, and that joy came through clan relations, deep and abiding friendships established from one's youth to the grave, and, above all, freedom. No king or foreign power impinged on the Igorot way of life.

Spanish officials, soldiers, and priests learned the hard way that Igorots would not compromise their liberty for a governor-general or a new god. Numerous sensational tales of martyred friars and doomed military expeditions in the Cordillera fill the Spanish colonial records. In the nineteenth century alone, there were seventy-five military expeditions into Luzon's highlands.[1] But when soldiers burned villages and destroyed rice paddies, the Igorots simply moved deeper into the mountains with a clear message: "You can destroy our homes, and we will rebuild them. However, you will not be able to get your heads back."

Three issues compelled the Spanish to persevere in their attempts to civilize the Igorots. First, from the very beginning of Spain's foray in Asia, Iberian-based merchants and officials complained that the Philippines represented an economic and political quagmire for Spain—a proverbial bottomless pit of misery. Even though officials in the New World administered the Philippines, the bureaucrats in Europe knew that the Philippines' annual deficit was only offset by the budget surplus of Spain's American colonies. Additionally, the Spanish crown justified Spain's economic losses in the Philippines with religious rhetoric, noting that no price was too much to save one pagan soul. Thus, the Igorot's stubborn refusal to accept Spanish rule and the Catholic faith justified Spain's continued colonial presence. Neglecting the Cordillera peoples meant forsaking Spain's very mission and imperial purpose.

Secondly, Spain's desire to control the Cordillera had a component of regional legitimacy. Igorots occasionally beheaded Christian lowlanders who lived near the mountain/lowland borders. These Christianized, tax-paying colonial subjects expected protection by European soldiers and officials who assumed racial superiority over the native peoples. If Spain projected colonial authority, then it certainly should protect its wards, but as long as Igorots continued harassing their lowland neighbors, Spanish authority appeared much more a concept than a reality.

Finally, beyond religious and safety considerations, colonial officials could not ignore the Cordillera region for financial reasons. Labeled a "fiscal nightmare," Spain's Southeast Asian colony ran an annual deficit of between 85,000 and 338,000 pesos, and during its first 250 years of rule, there were only two economic bright spots for its Manila-based government.[2] The first became known as the Manila galleon trade. Merchants in Manila loaded Acapulco-bound galleons with products from China, and the vessels returned to Manila full of silver from the New World's mines. But this promising trade became highly regulated, with extreme limits placed on it due to Iberian merchants' complaints that they suffered economically from competition from China's cheaper and superior products.

While this first economic bright spot did not affect Spanish-Igorot relations, the second did. In 1780, Governor General José Basco generated a bright but brief fiscal windfall such that for several years the colony actually produced a financial surplus. The new economic scheme implemented a government monopoly on the production and sale of tobacco. After the initial years of success, however, the program went awry as Igorots grew contraband tobacco and sold it to lowland merchants. As highland tobacco siphoned sales away from the government, Spain turned to indefatigable soldier Lieutenant Colonel Guillermo Galvey. In 1829, he began a decade-long campaign to extinguish Igorot resistance to Spanish rule. He destroyed and burned scores of villages and demolished hundreds of rice paddies along with all the Cordillera tobacco plants. To prove his mettle, he built forts and stationed Spanish soldiers in half a dozen mountain regions. Yet, after over forty raids, the highlanders remained defiant. They moved deeper into the mountains, preferring domestic inconvenience to foreign subjugation. Galvey's campaign failed to stop Igorot resistance to Spanish rule, and the tobacco monopoly ended. Galvey left the Cordillera, and the Spanish abandoned their mountain forts.

The most intense attempts to integrate the Igorots into a Christian, taxpaying colony occurred during Spain's final two decades of rule. Several socially liberal governor-generals insisted that Spain lift the highlanders into civilization. Spanish soldiers established at least five military-political centers among the Igorots by the 1890s. But it was too little, too late, and they proved unsustainable. Only three priests remained in the entire Cordillera region in 1889.[3] Following the failed 1896 Philippine Revolution and the 1898 American victory over Spain, the Spanish abandoned their handful of Cordillera forts.

In 1900, as American officials established colonial rule in the islands, the Cordillera remained autonomous, and Commissioner Worcester set out to change that. Appointed as the secretary of the interior in 1900, his portfolio included "Quarantine Service of the Marine Hospital Corps, the Weather Bureau, and the bureaus of forestry, mining, agriculture, fisheries, public lands, government laboratories, patents and copyrights, and non-Christian tribes."[4]

Worcester first heard about Luzon's Cordillera area in 1890 as he was collecting bird specimens in the Philippines' southern islands. He was told that the Cordillera contained pine forests, cool air, and a sanitarium for Spanish officials and soldiers. Then, as a member of the Schurman Commission in 1899, he interviewed José Camps, who managed a hotel in the Cordillera town of Trinidad. Camps reported that he had made more than three thousand dollars a year from this operation as he housed recuperating Spanish officials and

soldiers. Americans who had spent time in Trinidad and its neighboring village of Baguio told Worcester that the area's climate mirrored that of late
spring in New England.

Worcester resolved to see this area and asked fellow commissioner Luke
Wright to join his northern expedition on July 30, 1900. They traveled north
from Manila by boat along Luzon's west coast, disembarking at San Fernando,
La Union, near the Cordillera's base. They began climbing into the mountains
at Naguilian, which was about 25 miles from Trinidad. The narrow, slick paths
made for a precarious horseback ride, and much of the trip had to be completed on foot. Nonetheless, they eventually made it to Trinidad and its
neighboring village of Baguio. The area's beauty surpassed Worcester's expectations. More than ten years after his first glimpse of Baguio, Worcester wrote
about it in his multivolume work, *The Philippines Past and Present*:

> While experience has taught me that I cannot convey by words alone
> any adequate conception of what Baguio is like, I must nevertheless here
> make an attempt. . . . The scenery is everywhere beautiful, and in many
> sections truly magnificent. . . . Major-General J. Franklin Bell, who was
> given special attention to mountain resorts the world over, vigorously
> asserts that Baguio has no equal on the globe. Certainly the climate is
> more nearly perfect than any other of which I have personal knowledge,
> and the delighted coolness and the bracing air afford heavenly relief to
> jangling nerves and exhausted bodies, worn out by overwork and a too
> prolonged sojourn in tropical lowlands.[5]

While Baguio's beauty was close to indescribable, so too was its rain because
the area experiences rain half of the year, and it also experiences annual killer
typhoons. In 1911 a typhoon landed in Baguio, depositing 45 inches of rain in
a twenty-four-hour period. But the mountain air also provides relief from the
oppressive tropical heat, and Baguio became the summer capital for the commissioners, complete with a country club and an American military base.
American officials commissioned the notable urban planner Daniel Burnham
to design the city, and they designated an inordinate amount of money to build
the roads from the lowlands to Baguio.

During their initial stay in Baguio and Trinidad, Worcester and Wright were
entertained by Otto Scheerer, a German scientist who had lived there since 1896.
He impressed the commissioners with his garden, which included Irish potatoes, tomatoes, peas, beets, strawberries, coffee trees, and other vegetables and
citrus fruits.

The one other civilian foreigner in Baguio was Phelps Whitmarsh, a British journalist from Australia. At the time, American soldiers also crisscrossed

the region, as the search for Aguinaldo continued throughout 1900. Hard feelings existed between the army officers and the team of Scheerer and Whitmarsh, because the military men believed that the Europeans concealed important information about the insurgents, while the Europeans accused American soldiers of abusing the indigenous peoples. The Taft Commission added fuel to this diplomatic fire in December 1900 by appointing Scheerer and Whitmarsh as the area's top provincial officials. Unfortunately, the new appointees could not get organizational traction because of their repeated clashes with the locally stationed American military commanders. After seven months in office, they both resigned. But by this time, July 1901, Aguinaldo had been captured, and it was now time for Worcester to govern the entire Cordillera.

After his initial trip to Baguio, Worcester returned to Manila determined to learn all he could about the Igorots. He found more questions than answers. The two primary scholars he consulted disagreed on the number of ethnic groups among the highlanders: one placed the number at thirty-six and the other at twenty-six. Meanwhile, the Cordillera remained largely bereft of foreign control, and the American presence in the highlands was sparse. Around Baguio, however, discharged American soldiers with prospecting experience set up camp around the Igorot gold mines and established a modicum of local law and government. But in Manila, reports of increased tribal wars came to the commissioners' attention.

Considering the confusion and lack of knowledge about Igorots, the commission established the Bureau of Non-Christian Tribes (BNCT) in October 1901, which was led by David Prescott Barrows. The bureau's purpose was to regularly report on the situation among the non-Christian peoples and establish a fuller understanding of the ethnology of the Philippines.

Before embarking into the Cordillera, Barrows returned to the US and briefly reviewed his study of Native American tribes, the topic of his dissertation. Officials counseled Barrows that, as they saw it, the Indian reservations most closely paralleled the Igorot situation, and so he spent the first five months of 1902 on several Indian reservations. He did not like what he witnessed and noted that Indians were in a no-win situation. He returned to the Philippines convinced that the only proper way to present a successful governance plan was to spend time among the highlanders. So, from June to December 1902, Barrows climbed up and down the Cordillera, mapping the geographical locations of the various villages. He was accompanied by a photographer, interpreter, fellow academic, and soldier with the rank of lieutenant.

The group made substantial progress in understanding both the geographic and cultural boundaries within the Cordillera. Unfortunately, almost all their good work vanished in the Kalinga town of Ablug. As the party stopped to catch their breath, the lieutenant's gun and belt were stolen, and the soldier became so incensed that he killed a local man. This made the entire area rise up against the outsiders, and while racing back to Bontoc they passed through Lubuagan, where Kalinga warriors gathered against them with the intent of exacting revenge. Barrows recalled, "I really doubted saving our lives, but I talked severely to my companions and commanded that not a shot should be fired except by my own command. We could see the trail winding across the valley and climbing the next mountain, we went slowly ahead without a word or a shot and the crowd split and let us through."[6]

Barrows and his party made it to Bontoc, but he remained concerned about the Ablug incident, and he determined to make peace with the Kalingans. He left the lieutenant in Bontoc and returned to Lubuagan with about twenty Bontoc constabulary soldiers. The Lubuagan warriors returned the stolen property and killed a carabao as part of a lengthy cañao. Barrows recalled that "the people thereafter kept the peace and the region became a centre of American activity."[7]

Returning to Manila, Barrows presented a report to the commission stating that the Igorot communities lived in cultural areas rather than tribes. Further, he explained that there were just a few cultural groups, including the Apayao, Kalinga, Tinggian, Bontoc, Kankanaey, Ibaloi, and Ifugao. His assessment represented the most accurate ethnic, geographic, and cultural reality of the Cordillera and its peoples to date. But the ink was barely dry on his report when the commission reassigned Barrows to lead the education efforts for the entire Philippines. Nevertheless, his findings were corroborated by Worcester's subsequent exploring trips.

Barrows helped the commission understand the Cordillera's social and political situation, and in his later life he remembered two things about his time among the Igorots. First, he recalled that while he enjoyed his time among them, he remained unsure as to its overall benefit: "Nevertheless, I can look back on my work as Chief non-Christian [sic] as one of the most interesting periods of my life. I had explored most of the northern and southern fields of the non-Christian tribes, but I am not at all certain that I accomplished much for the political and economic relief of these two great regions."[8]

His second lasting impression centered on the powerful presence and personality of Dean Worcester. Barrows only spent a short time among the Igorots, but he recalled how Worcester dominated the highlands:

For two years, while I was Chief Non-Christian, my work was under Dean Worcester to whom I have referred. He was a good supervisor. We differed occasionally and he could use harsh language, but he was generous with me and a strong supporter. Worcester's character was well understood by his colleagues. Governor Wm. Howard Taft once remarked very cleverly, "Worcester's language," he said, "is a standing refutation of the common law doctrine that one cannot commit assault by word of mouth." Worcester remained at the head of his board and difficult department longer than any of his famous colleagues. His whole heart was in the Philippines and while he loved combating his opponents, he probably accomplished more than any other man. . . . I venture to say that he knew more of the Philippines than any man, white or native, who preceded or followed him.[9]

As the secretary of the interior, Worcester visited and explored the Igorot region five times between 1900 and 1906. Some of his forays into the mountains lasted for months, and he became keenly aware of the highland's political situation.

In addition to Barrows and Worcester, three other American entities entered Luzon's highlands between 1900 and 1905. The first group was the Philippine Constabulary (PC), a military police force led by American officers but largely composed of indigenous soldiers. This organization created unprecedented peace throughout the highlands due to its useful policies and persistent presence, as seen in the next chapter. The Episcopalian clergy and lay workers also entered Luzon's highlands shortly after the Taft Commission replaced the US military rule of the islands. And the third American community included several American volunteer soldiers from the Philippine-American War who chose to stay among the Igorots rather than return to the US. Since they were discharged from their units, they had no official status other than as American citizens in an American colony. John Early's description of these volunteers-turned-fortune-seekers presents an odd picture of men in search of peace far from their native homes:

> There was another group of Americans . . . who were a very useful element. . . . These were for the most part flotsam from the Western volunteer regiments who remained in the country when their regiments returned. These men were the highly intelligent floating laborers commonly found in and about Western mining camps a generation ago—laborers today and prospectors tomorrow. Here in the hills of Luzon they continued their course—always rich in prospect but always reduced in practice to elementals in food and clothing. This group got on marvelously well with the hillman whose customs it understood, whose hardships it shared and whose sisters it married.[10]

Of the three foreign groups among the Igorots, the officers of the PC were the most influential among the Igorots. In many ways, they set the stage for Early's entrance into the highlands.

CHAPTER 5

The Philippine Constabulary

America's first order of business in the Philippines was to establish law and order. Under Spanish rule, the approximately twenty-seven thousand police distributed throughout the islands maintained peace, but with Spain's defeat and the subsequent Philippine-American War, urban and rural areas experienced social upheaval and a power vacuum. One can imagine the confusion: Should the people obey the old guards? The followers of Aguinaldo? The Filipinos collaborating with the Americans?

Aware of this confusion, Taft created legitimate and effective peace and justice systems. He assigned fellow commissioner Luke E. Wright to provide a safe national environment where all Filipinos could enjoy the pursuit of life, liberty (under colonial rule), and happiness. Wright would go on to the prestigious positions of governor-general, ambassador to Japan, and President Teddy Roosevelt's secretary of war. But the first assignment Wright received in the Philippines was to create an institution that would provide security to all Filipinos. Wright was up to the challenge.

Born in Tennessee, Wright (1846–1922) grew up in Memphis and at fifteen joined the Confederate Army. He survived the war, earning a commendation for his actions at the 1864 Battle of Murfreesboro. Following the war, he studied law and served as Memphis's district attorney from 1870 to 1878. Given this background, Taft trusted that Wright's military exploits, along with his civilian administrative experience, made him the best choice among the five commissioners to craft a constructive national police force.

Initially Wright's options remained limited because the Philippines was still at war. However, as the conflict ended after Aguinaldo's March 23, 1901, capture, Wright got down to business. He had a head start because as American soldiers marched through municipalities, they worked with each town's leading citizens to establish an American-approved government. These local officials then appointed credible men to serve as police. Many of these police had been employed by the former colonial regime, so there was a large pool from which to choose. Building on this locally based administrative momentum, Wright created a three-tier security paradigm: the metropolitan, municipal, and constabulary forces.

The metropolitan police around Manila represented the smallest among the three organizations. The capital city teetered on anarchy after years of battles on its shores and streets, and despite its economic and cultural prominence, the city continued to be dangerous. At the end of 1901, Wright created a metropolitan force that within the year comprised close to nine hundred personnel including a secret service containing twenty-four detectives. Of the sixty-five patrol officers leading the metropolitan force, thirty-two were Filipino, and the indigenous patrolmen outnumbered their American colleagues by 416 to 382.

Outside of the Manila area, Wright worked with the elected or appointed municipal councils to establish a lightly armed local police presence that enforced local regulations and national laws. Of the three organizations, the municipal police caused the greatest headache for Wright and his successors. Since they were appointed by local authority (usually the mayor), resident politicians viewed these security men as their personal army. But despite their obvious partiality toward local officials, the municipal law enforcement provided a degree of peace under American rule.

Neither the municipal nor metropolitan police forces impacted the Igorots, but the Philippine Constabulary (PC) reshaped Igorot society. A primary catalyst for creating the PC was America's effective use and employment of Filipino spies, guides, and linguists during the Philippine-American War. Guerrilla warfare made these local collaborators invaluable in gaining the upper hand against the Filipino freedom fighters, and Wright sought to use some of these men to establish something between a municipal police force and a disciplined, bivouacked army platoon—a well-ordered unit that transcended local and military authority. For Taft and Wright, the PC killed two birds with one stone. First, by 1902 there were only fifteen thousand American soldiers left in the Philippines, down from seventy-five thousand in 1900. Without such a large military presence, the PC could patrol barrios and provide accountability for local law enforcement personnel. Second, though they were initially led by American officials, the plan was for Filipino constabulary soldiers to eventually replace Americans "for the realization of Governor-General Taft's goal of building a 'Philippines for the Filipinos.'"[1]

One of Wright's successful PC policies was to have troops stationed among their own ethnic and linguistic groups, in contrast to Spain's idea that it was best to station Filipino soldiers where they were viewed as outsiders or even the region's rivals. Wright's plan succeeded, especially among the Igorots, who almost instinctively distrusted anyone outside their cultural/linguistic community.

Nonetheless, the Cordillera posed a major challenge for the PC because its landscape was characterized by mountain peaks up to 9,000 feet high and valleys shaped by rushing rivers. The region proved ideal for guerrilla combat. During the first decade of America's rule, almost every official report from the Cordillera echoed the same theme: the difficulty of eliminating headhunting and ubiquitous tribal rivalries. Incessant warfare among the Igorots was often based on oral histories of past wrongs from rival villages. Igorots grew up hearing tales of these wrongs, which fueled hatred toward neighboring peoples and exacerbated the revenge head-taking incidents. Animus, however, was not always a primary motive in headhunting. American soldiers, teachers, officials, and missionaries slowly learned that the reasons for taking heads included revenge, placating ancestors, and rites of passage. Embedded in the young Igorot warriors' worldview was the belief that they remained inferior to their elders or colleagues who had beheaded another human being, and young women in the villages reportedly admired men who had taken heads. The human desire for acceptance and approval is strong, and in some highland cultures, killing a person and taking their head served as a prestigious badge for men. Skulls decorated the outside of warriors' homes as a sign of prowess.

The spiritual component of taking a head proved a bit more complex. Its metaphysical association meant that cañaos, along with their associated rituals, often followed head-taking raids. Taking a head from a rival community also served to placate ancestors who still bore ill will against a certain village for unaddressed past offenses. In short, the Igorots' practice of headhunting ran so deep that a strong police force would not change things; such transformations necessitated a cultural shift. The Igorot PC soldiers provided a bridge between the past and present because they revered their indigenous cultures while denouncing headhunting. The subprovince of Ifugao best illustrated the importance of the Cordillera PC and the character of its leading officers.

By the end of 1903, Lieutenant Levi Case, the top PC officer in Ifugao, had established a permanent military station in Kababuyan that served as a base for patrolling all Ifugao territory. In the first months of 1904, Ifugao PC soldiers built another four outposts, which represented an unprecedented military presence. But all was not well in Ifugao, as headhunting incidents were on the rise. Case's 1904 annual report abounds with headhunting episodes, including several tales of women and children losing their heads. His frustration with the local population boiled over in the report when he complained that "their [Ifugao's] chief failing, which it is so hard to get them to look at as a failing—[is] a fondness for the heads of strange tribes."[2]

From 1904 to 1906, Case marched up and down the mountains determined to establish the PC as the instrument of peace among the Ifugao. He became fluent in the local languages, recruited local warriors into the PC, and confiscated numerous guns the Ifugao had stolen or purchased over the centuries. His methods included a mixture of carrot and stick inducements. He offered protection and trail construction to villages that acquiesced to his rule, but severely punished any recalcitrant groups. A quick glance at his terse diary entries between September 1904 and May 1905 illustrate his approach:

> September 8—Came to Bili. Shot some hogs and ate dinner there. Arrived in Bagu. Burned three houses. Slept in Ataban. Shot some hogs there.
>
> September 9—Amduntug. Killed hogs. Burned houses and palay [rice].
>
> September 10—Baiyang. Passed through; I was wounded in the foot by a bamboo spear. Burned rice of Palao space and Antipolo. An Ifugao shot at me (with a rifle) in Antipolo.
>
> September 11—Burned rancheria of Bahag. Killed one Ifugao, and some others wounded.
>
> May 24—Expedition to Amgode. Burned a few houses, killed some hogs, and returned to Banaue at 6:45 P.M.
>
> May 26—Gave Namulditang people the alternative of paying for the rice stolen and fixing the roads, or be severely punished. They refused to pay for rice or fix roads. Several villages were burned and a large number of hogs killed.
>
> May 27—Burned another village and killed some more hogs. Also some men. Ifugaos sent word that they are willing to settle if we give them a truce in three days.
>
> May 28—Learned that we killed five men in the Namulditang fight.[3]

Seven months after this last diary entry, the area completely changed because of one man. The name and legend of Lieutenant Jeff D. Gallman still reverberates in twenty-first-century Ifugao.

Jefferson Davis Gallman was the nephew of Jefferson Davis, the Confederate States of America's president. Born in 1877, two years before his uncle died,

Gallman grew up in Holland, Texas. He enlisted in the US Army on April 28, 1898—three days after the US had declared war on Spain. He was a member of the 23rd Infantry and fought in the Muslim-dominated portion of the southern Philippines until June 1899 when he returned to Texas. He lasted only one year as a bored civilian and reenlisted on July 11, 1900. He was assigned to Company M of the 9th Infantry. For the next four years, he participated in major military campaigns in China (the Boxer Rebellion) and the most brutal fighting of the Philippine–American War in Leyte and Samar. Following an honorable discharge in 1905, he accepted a position as a commissioned officer in the PC. He was reportedly singled out as an excellent candidate to work among the Igorots, and at the end of 1905, he entered Ifugao to work under Lieutenant Case.

Gallman arrived at a crucial time in Ifugao's history. Case had mastered the language and taught it to Gallman, who was already fluent in at least two other languages (English and Spanish). Gallman's Ifugao arrival coincided with that of H. Otley Beyer, an American schoolteacher assigned to Banaue. Beyer, who

FIGURE 1. These Igorot Philippine Constabulary soldiers wear modern jackets and hats but continue to use the loincloth. The constabulary forces tried to temper Worcester's dictatorial rule over the Igorots. Howard Haines Brinton and Anna Shipley Cox Brinton Papers (HC.MC.1189), Quaker and Special Collections, Haverford College, Haverford, PA.

later founded the University of the Philippines' Anthropology Department, authored the most detailed study to date of the Ifugao people. Gallman spent his first six months in Ifugao soaking in knowledge from Beyer and Case while also immersing himself in the local culture. This prepared him to take over the Ifugao PC following Case's departure in June 1906 due to a physical and mental breakdown.

Understanding the Ifugao culture, Gallman replaced all non-Ifugao PC soldiers in the area with indigenous men, and he created a uniform of a khaki shirt, a specially embroidered loincloth, and several other pieces of distinctive equipment. Though Gallman was the second American PC commander to police Ifugao, his charisma made him overshadow Case. He admired his Ifugao soldiers, and they deeply cared for him, giving him the nickname "Kawitan" (fighting cock) due to his fearlessness in battle. He stressed discipline among his troops and insisted that they provide an example for the entire Igorot people. His warriors were by far the best marksman among all PC units. Though it went against their deeply ingrained culture and practice, Gallman's Ifugao soldiers refrained from taking the heads of their enemies killed in battle. This is not to say that Gallman followed American laws. He was both feared and loved due to his willingness to show unmitigated authority over his charges. He gave himself the title "Apo [father] of the Ifugaos" and publicly challenged anyone who wanted a fight. He also insisted that any Ifugao who desired revenge due to a murder and subsequent decapitation had to let the PC exact vengeance, with the promise that "I will go to fight those who attack you and will get your revenge so you have no need to be ashamed before the ancestors."[4]

A story orally passed down and chronicled in later written sources illustrates the type of man and administrator Gallman proved to be during his 1905–1912 tenure as the Apo of the Ifugaos. Trouble between the Banaue and Cambulo Ifugaos persisted throughout Gallman's early years in the area. In 1907 three Cambulo warriors clandestinely entered Banaue territory, beheading a man named Ngatan. The Cambulo men took the head back home, where they were celebrated for their strength, bravery, and human trophy. Following Gallman's instructions, Ngatan's relatives did not take revenge but brought the news to the PC station. Frustrated by the Cambulo's continued headhunting, he ordered his men to arms and marched on Cambulo. As they reached a bridge directly across the Cambulo hamlets, the village was eerily silent as its residents took their animals and hid in the thick surrounding forests. As the PC soldiers began to make their way down the shallow valley and up to the village, a young warrior named Hangcha broke the stillness as he climbed onto a rock in the middle of Cambulo and directed challenges and curses at Gallman. Surprisingly, Hangcha was not one of the three men the PC were after. Cambulo residents later insisted that Hangcha was motivated by the desire to be admired, particularly among the single young women. In essence, he was jealous of the attention given to the town's headhunters. Gallman silently watched the young man jump and shout. Perhaps the gesticulating young Ifugao warrior assumed he would run into the forest and join the others once Gallman started up the hill, but he never got a chance to run and hide. "As everyone watched this display of bravado Gallman leveled his rifle across the canyon and shot the dancing Hangcha in the forehead, killing him instantly."[5] Silence again descended on the village. Gallman then shouted instructions to those hiding in the forest. He wanted Ngatan's head returned to Banaue, and Hangcha's death provided the needed payment for Ngatan's death. Cambulo's residents returned Ngatan's head to Banaue, bringing peace between the villages.

Gallman's actions were illegal—he killed an unarmed young man guilty only of verbal insults. Yet the Ifugao's respect for him grew as he maneuvered his policies to fit somewhere between the colonial law and Igorot practice. As the PC authority and then the lieutenant governor of the Ifugao people, Gallman seemed oblivious to the physical and political risks he took in marching from village to village challenging any individual or group who dared oppose the new legal paradigm he had created and administered through his remarkable indigenous military unit. He was reckless at times, taking on hundreds of armed warriors with just a handful of PC soldiers, and was wounded several times, yet he always prevailed in the end. He seemed indestructible, and he administered justice as he saw fit, just as he had learned from his mentor, Lieutenant Levi Case. Within three years of Gallman's tenure, the area enjoyed an unprecedented peace. His soldiers exhibited strict discipline, and that, perhaps, was the greatest success of the PC.

PART TWO

The Creation of
Mountain Province
(1906–1908)

CHAPTER 6

John Early in the Cordillera

John Early lay in his bed staring at the ceiling while beige lizards scurried from corner to corner. The oppressive heat and tropical humidity made it impossible to sleep. He did not turn on the light because he knew it would reveal what he heard—large golden-brown cockroaches exploring the floor and lizards scampering across the ceiling. Caught between reptiles and insects, he waited for the morning, when they would flee with the sun's appearance. His room at the Hotel La Francia was little more than a closet, and the hotel's bathroom was an "afterthought."[1] His first days in Manila were much better than the evenings as he awaited his teaching assignment. Meandering through the streets, he set out to revise his wardrobe, and in Manila's Chinatown he exchanged the wool clothes that kept him warm in Idaho for tailor-made khaki and light-colored clothing.

Manila was coming into its own during the summer of 1906. Five years of American civilian rule made the capital city safer than it had been for decades, if not centuries, as colonial officials and Filipinos seeking service-oriented jobs changed the city's human landscape. For Early, this growing capital city could hardly have been farther or more different from where his life began. After thirty-three years and a journey of 8,090 miles, Manila represented an opportunity for this Missouri-born Irish American to reinvent himself.

What Early could not know during his walks along Manila Bay and his time in the Chinese tailor shops was that his life's journey had just begun. Though

Kalinga was just 200 miles from Manila, it represented a far greater journey than crossing half a continent and the Pacific. While Manila and Edina seemed like they were at least on the same planet, Luzon's Cordillera region and its remote peoples resembled another world altogether.

After volunteering for the Kalinga teaching assignment, Early booked passage on the SS *Bustamante*, a small steamer that ferried people and goods along Luzon's west coast. He noted that his transportation amenities since he left Seattle gradually deteriorated in style and convenience. He likened the *Bustamante* to Columbus's ships, adding a sardonic comment that the decks were overcrowded due to numerous pigs, chickens, and goats. But he expected that "it is likely some old arks will be navigating the Philippine waters in 2030 with its meat ration still on the hoof."[2]

Early hoped the Spanish skipper would take him to the major coastal city of Vigan, but as they approached the area, a seasonal typhoon began, and the captain ordered him to disembark at Pandan, an "open roadstead, which served as an emergency port for the town of Vigan."[3] When a boat propelled by a crew of about twenty men met the steamer, Early—along with his luggage— was unceremoniously dumped into the longboat while the *Bustamante* steamed out of sight. The paddled boat was the final vessel in his long journey, and it proved to be the most humiliating and dangerous. He sat next to the young men and used hand gestures to communicate. As the waves increased, he observed that most of the paddlers were drunk and guessed that the men needed alcohol to summon up the courage to venture into the typhoon-tossed ocean. As they drew closer to land, Early longed for *terra firma* and believed he had finally made it across oceans and seas safe and sound. But it was not to be. The closer they came to the sands of Pandan, the louder an argument became between the old steersman and a young drunken oarsman who insisted that they follow a different path to the beach. The dispute grew so intense that the young man whacked the steersman on the head, plunging him into the water. The ensuing chaos capsized the boat, but Early's excellent swimming skills saved him while his suitcases followed him later, guided to shore by the boisterous waves.

Early waited until morning to walk the three miles to Vigan, where he presented his assignment papers to the American school superintendent. From Vigan, he was ordered to make his way through the Ilocos plain to Cervantes, the town that straddled the two worlds of the lowlanders and the Cordillera's Igorots.

Early's trek from Vigan to Cervantes began with a horseback ride to Candon, an Ilocos town 40 miles south of Vigan. Candon marked the end of Early's five-month ocean affair because from the time he had stepped onto the *Minnesota* in Seattle, he had remained in viewing distance of water; now, he turned inland, as Cervantes was 45 miles east of Candon.

Though the heat and humidity wore on him, Early admired the lowland rice fields that stretched as far as the eye could see. Both rain and irrigated water filled the paddies, making it difficult to navigate the trenches and slender walking paths between the muddy pools of water. With great amusement and relief, he accepted an offer to rent a water buffalo so he could ride on its back across the fields. So it had come to this—from the world's greatest steamship, to a boat paddled by drunken men, to a horse, and now to a water buffalo. But Early relished the prospect of crossing the muddy terrain without ruining his new clothes. Everything seemed fine as the farmer rode in the lead on his own animal, slowly guiding Early's mount by a rope. Toward the end of the journey, however, the second animal became spooked by what Early termed a strange "Caucasian scent" and bolted toward the end of the rice field, where it threw its passenger into a bush of *kawayan* (razor-sharp bamboo leaves). Early noted the event ended with "not much clothing and very little skin left on me." The farmer raced to the accident and apologized in Ilocano, a language Early was just starting to grasp. He might have considered that the boat capsizing and then his falling into piercing bamboo were messages to stay clear of the Igorots. Yet he took quite the opposite view. He happily paid the farmer for the use of the water buffalo, "bade him good-bye, and kidded myself into good humor by assuring myself that there was one China-made suit of khaki I would never have to wear out."[4]

Turning east and toward the mountains, Early was now on foot. His traveling mishaps up to this point were trivial compared to the danger of crossing swollen monsoon-fed streams and rivers. After his nineteenth river-crossing, he finally reached the hamlet of Concepcion at the base of the Cordillera Mountains. Exhausted, he found a place to stay where an aged Ilocano resident used coconut oil to massage Early's soaked, bruised, and cut-up body. Accepting this kind hospitality, he cleaned up and devoured a dinner of chicken and rice. The grilled chicken on a spit tasted so good that he made sure to leave some for breakfast.

The cool breezes from the mountains along with the exhaustion from his journey made that night's sleep one of the soundest he had enjoyed in months. Excited to finally begin climbing into the mountains, Early woke up before the sun could light his path. While waiting for enough light to pick up the trail, he found the chicken and rice he had set aside for breakfast but received a shock after taking his first bite. It seemed the chicken had come to life during the night. Early's tongue received multiple sharp stings that felt like kawayan grass. He called for a light and found that an army of ants had taken residence in his evening's dinner. He skipped breakfast and prepared to climb toward Cervantes.

The switchback trails along the lower mountains made the initial climb quite enjoyable. Early passed a Philippine-American War monument commemorating where General del Pilar made a heroic and fatal stand against American soldiers, which allowed Aguinaldo to escape into the Cordillera. Shortly after passing this marker, he turned a corner and met his first Igorot. They surprised each other, and the armed Bontoc man raised his spear. Unarmed, Early simply stood still until the Igorot lowered his arm and extended a hand of friendship. Though he could not communicate in the Bontoc dialect, Early tried to convey his thanks and travel plans to Cervantes. The Bontoc man, soon joined by a few companions, seemed to wish Early well on his journey. Early's initial impression of the Igorot people stayed with him and served him well for the rest of his life: "I felt I had nothing to fear—they were intensely human, and one who is intensely human kills no one, unless he deserves it."[5]

Early tried to make it to Cervantes in one day but fell short and scrambled among the trailside bushes looking for a place to sleep as darkness fell. Dirty and hungry, he waited for the dawn and followed the narrow path leading to Cervantes. His hunger drove him to walk as fast as he could, and within two hours he reached the Abra River, which protected Cervantes and the Cordillera from the outside world. Unwilling to find an accessible ford or bridge across the river, he plunged into the water and swam across, finding himself just outside Cervantes. A quick learner, Early had picked up enough Ilocano to inquire where the American PC officer might be found. He was directed to the house occupied by Lieutenant John S. Manning.

Manning was still asleep, and so a boy employed by the PC helped Early find Manning's bathroom, where he could clean up with a shower unlike any other he had experienced. The young boy brought soap, a Standard Oil can full of water, and half a coconut shell floating on the water. The washing procedure was to lather and scrub the body, and then use the coconut shell to scoop water from the can for a good rinse. As he finished his shower, he noticed an eye peering through the crack in the door. A bit frightened, he loudly said, "This is Early. Who are you?" A friendly but very assured voice replied, "Manning. I happen to have some reason for looking about because this is my house."[6] This began a friendship that lasted for many years, and Early's introduction to the type of Americans in the PC.

Manning hosted Early for six weeks as the wide-eyed foreign teacher tried to take in the surrounding culture. He was impressed by the prevailing peace that the PC had established, and he also closely watched civilian Americans who had taken up residence in Cervantes. He likened them to the population of America's northwest mining camps that moved from place to place looking for gold. In Cervantes, these gold hunters were discharged volunteer soldiers who had remained in the Philippines. Many had married local women and created trails and roads connecting the Igorots with the outside world. While the American civilians rarely mixed with the American officials, they did socialize on the baseball field, where Early's considerable athletic prowess was just a few years removed from his time as WAC's football captain.

Early did not appear anxious to get to his assigned station in Kalinga, and it may be that his time with Manning included a welcome respite from the previous months of harrowing travel. He also awaited a safe passage. In 1906, the only officer in the entire Kalinga area was Lieutenant W. D. Harris, who was assigned to escort Early.[7] As each day passed, Early heard amazing tales about Harris's exploits so that the Kalinga-based officer "had begun to assume the proportions and attributes of a mythical man of the mountains." Everyone Early met bragged about knowing Harris, the only man who would fearlessly walk alone throughout Kalinga and "talk a wild man tame." When Harris finally arrived to accompany him into Kalinga, Early was shocked to find that the mythical man was short and painfully shy. It was a pleasant surprise as Harris's meek demeanor made Early rightfully conclude: "I can get on with such a man."[8]

Harris's and Early's journey from Cervantes to Kalinga wound through the Bontoc Igorot territory, which by the fall of 1906 included a few American missionaries. Lieutenant Harris intimated that he was anxious to get back to his Bontoc soldiers in the Kalinga town of Lubuagan to make sure they were still alive. Though only 15 miles separated Bontoc from Lubuagan, it was normally a grueling two-day journey along the Chico River and then west up and down steep mountain trails. Every few miles the hired Igorots who carried equipment handed their loads to a fresh group, who brought the material to the next set of men.

On their journey's first day, Early and Harris made it past Sadanga, "the most notable town in the high ranges and one of the fiercest aggregations of headhunters ever gotten together in any country." Just a mile outside of Sadanga their party camped for the night in a grass hut on a "little tongue of land" between two small streams.[9] Around midnight, a powerful, unseasonable typhoon landed, and the wind's first gust carried their rudimentary shelter into the rapidly swelling streams. By the time morning light appeared, the rain-soaked men saw that the streams were now raging torrents that threatened to submerge their little island. Two days of nonstop monsoon rain made it impossible for them to leave their quickly dwindling space of refuge. It was Early's first experience with Cordillera rain.

The sun emerged on the morning of the third day, and the Chico tributaries settled enough for the group to get back on the Lubuagan trail. Before nightfall, Early had finally reached his post. It had taken seven months from his April 6 Seattle departure, but he was now in his new home.

After his first week in Lubuagan, an emergency required Harris's return to Bontoc, and he left Early as the lone American in Kalinga. A Filipino lowlander, Santiago Robles, took command of the Kalinga constabulary station. Surprisingly, Early decided to leave Lubuagan and visit more remote Kalinga villages to introduce himself and invite parents to send their children to his new school. Robles reluctantly agreed to accompany him, and as they journeyed into Kalinga's interior, Early became fascinated by the physical endurance and physiques of Kalinga warriors along with the simplicity of their lives. They appeared absolutely content to enjoy their days hunting or working the rice fields, while evenings were filled with long conversations and smoking pipes around fires. Concomitantly, the Kalingans were impressed by Early's hiking abilities and willingness to venture where few, if any, lowland or American officials had entered. The only person who did not enjoy the monthlong hinterland exploration was Robles, who Early noted loved food but hated physical exercise. Just a few days outside of Lubuagan, Robles grew so exhausted that six Igorots took turns carrying him on a makeshift stretcher. Early's observation of Robles's weakness stayed with him for the rest of his life: "I judged by the looks of the disgust on the faces of the cargadores [porters] and the villagers who came to visit with us along the trail, that a man who could not travel on his own feet was not well thought of in Kalinga, and although often tempted to try a blanket, that first picture kept me from it. In all my travels in Mountain Province I went under my own power."[10]

When Early returned to Lubuagan he learned that Harris had been temporarily relieved of duty. The cryptic notation of "duty relief" often meant that the official teetered on the verge of a mental breakdown or could not stop self-medicating with alcohol. Harris's replacement, an untested "city-bred" American, seemed petrified, paranoid, and absolutely convinced that the Kalingans wanted to kill him. He was especially afraid at night, when the inebriated warriors congregated around fires and joked about past foibles. Early tried to convince the American military official that this was just the way Kalingans communicated, and nighttime was set aside for joyous camaraderie with tobacco and alcohol as social lubricants. These reassurances only convinced Harris's replacement that Early himself was part of a "conspiracy to kill him."[11]

As the weeks in Lubuagan passed, Early found a house where he could set up his books and a classroom. He began teaching the Kalingan children during the day, then used the evenings to hold classes for the Bontoc constabulary soldiers. Not much else could be done during the typhoon season, and he did not waste the opportunity for indoor schooling while storms raged outside. As November turned to December, he received a pleasant surprise when forty-seven-year-old Albert W. Hora and a Mr. Wendahl dropped in at his school and new home.

Hora previously served as the superintendent of manual training in Cervantes and then interim secretary of Lepanto-Bontoc in 1905. He did not like working for the colonial government, so he resigned, married an Igorot woman, learned the local dialect, and began a career building trails and roads throughout the Cordillera. He became the go-to person for the construction of crucial pathways that opened the way between the lowlands and highlands. He and his wife Maggy had five children, and he helped to teach Igorots not only road construction, but furniture-making as well. He eventually retired from road work and settled into a life of farming coffee in Mankayan, a Kankanaey town. Hora never returned to the United States, and when in 1918 his sister in Chicago wrote the US government to see if her brother was still alive, officials went out of their way to find Hora in Mankayan. The Bontoc provincial commander noted that "Mr. Albert W. Hora read the letter of his sister, but he declined to write for unknown reasons."[12]

Hora's December 1906 visit to Lubuagan provided Early with much-needed relief. His reputation as the "best camp cook in the Mountains" meant Early enjoyed a respite from his monotonous diet. Bridge games went late into the evenings, and on Christmas Eve, Hora played the mouth organ while Early and Wendahl "waltzed and two-stepped until midnight."[13]

Hora also tried to put Harris's sulking replacement in a better frame of mind. The wily cook and trail-builder clandestinely went through the officer's personal items and found a well-read and marked-up medical guidebook. Hora burned the book, and according to Early the depressed soldier began to "improve at once." Early remained close friends with Hora until the trailblazer died of stomach cancer in 1926, leaving Maggy the coffee farm and a twenty-year-old gold Waltham watch, forty-five cows, and 6,000 pesos to distribute to their five children. He never wrote back to his sister, and she received this cryptic notice of her brother's death: "It is with deep regret that I have to advise you of the receipt of a communication . . . informing of the death of your brother, Albert W. Hora."[14]

But in 1906, Hora and Wendahl had their hands full with building projects, and they had to move on from Lubuagan. For his part, Early continued teaching, though his diary entries are full of numerous stories of exploring Kalinga. He could not sit still. Despite warnings about traveling alone, he climbed up Kalinga's highest peaks and descended into its lowest valleys, and, at times, he carelessly plunged into rivers hoping his strength would match that of the currents so that he might visit remote villages.

CHAPTER 7

Dean Worcester and the Making of Mountain Province

Dean Conant Worcester was "the most influential man in the Philippines from 1901 to 1912" due to his "knowledge, length of tenure, organizational ability, strength of conviction and tenacity of purpose."[1] Governor-General Taft appointed Worcester as the Philippines secretary of the interior, a position whose portfolio included the Bureau of Non-Christian Tribes, among other responsibilities. He served as a commissioner until 1913, twice as long as any other member of the Philippine Commission. Worcester's inordinate influence was matched by the Filipino politicians' disdain for this blatant racist. He once made this public comment to a reporter: "honesty among Filipinos is a theme for a humorist."[2] There were, however, two Filipino groups that Worcester enjoyed spending time with. The first included the wealthy elite, who had supported Spanish colonial rule, but then welcomed their new Western overlords. They correctly assumed that their privileges and wealth would remain intact based on America's capitalist economic system. The second group was the highlanders, a community that he did not consider Filipinos. He described the highlanders in terms of the noble savage untainted by the lowlanders' dishonesty. By manipulating colonial policy, he set himself up as the semi-dictator of the Cordillera region until his 1913 resignation.

The youngest of nine children, Dean Worcester entered the world on October 1, 1866. He was from a line of prominent ministers dating back to the seventeenth century. His father, Ezra Worcester, was the only one of four sons who did not enter the ministry, as he chose to study medicine and was known throughout Thetford, Vermont, as a compassionate and professionally astute physician. The Worcesters' oldest child, William, was twenty-one years old when Dean was born. Following his father's lead, William studied at Dartmouth and in Europe, becoming a prominent figure in the diagnosis and treatment of the mentally ill.

Dean Worcester attended high school in Newton, Massachusetts, and even before finishing school he found himself drawn to the study of birds. He collected nests, eggs, and eventually birds, with a keen interest in taxidermy.

For financial reasons, Worcester attended the University of Michigan rather than one of the more expensive Ivy League schools. He entered the university in 1884 with financial assistance from William and another sibling—an arrangement that reinforced his familial loyalty. During his first college years he came under the influence of Professor Joseph Steere, the head of the Zoology Department. Steere traveled the world collecting specimens in the 1870s, including an 1874 stint in the Philippines. Once back in Ann Arbor, he decided to return to the Philippines, and Worcester volunteered to accompany his mentor. Borrowing money for the expedition, Worcester was transformed by his 1887–1888 work in the Philippines. Though this expedition landed on Luzon, its Manila stay was brief because the focus of collection activities occurred in the southern islands. It was during a visit to the island of Mindoro that Worcester ventured into the interior and stumbled across the people known as the Mangyans, whom he characterized as barely civilized savages and "harmless as children."[3] Remote tribal peoples remained a lifelong interest for Worcester.

He returned to Ann Arbor and graduated in 1889, and even before finishing his coursework the university offered him an assistant staff position in the Department of Botany, which he accepted, though the Philippines remained in the forefront of his mind. Through various connections, he contacted the Minneapolis real estate tycoon Louis F. Menage and proposed an expedition to the Philippines that would bring unparalleled scientific information and discoveries. Menage provided Worcester with a ten-thousand-dollar advance and a promise of additional monies upon the return of the two-year mission. For his part, Worcester agreed to donate all collected specimens to the Minnesota Academy of Natural Sciences. Worcester traveled to Minneapolis in July 1890 and finalized the expedition's contract.

Worcester arrived in the Philippines for his second visit on September 5, 1890. He again traveled south and spent two-and-a-half adventured-filled years collecting rare birds and learning more about the Philippines. He admired and wrote about the European entrepreneurs who had established successful sugar plantations in the southern islands. During that trip, Worcester almost died due to various tropical fevers that ravaged his body. He also ran afoul of Spanish officials, which reinforced his growing disdain for bureaucracy and petty policies that contrasted with his idea of how things should run. His observations of incompetent colonial officials laid the foundation for his future distrust of bureaucracies and their vetoes and prohibitions.

Barely clinging to life due to typhoid fever, Worcester made his way to Manila in February 1893. The doctors said he would not survive, but he did recover and arrived in San Francisco in April 1893. That same month he married Nanon Fay Leas.

Worcester expected to remain an employee of Menage, but the 1893 economic downturn exposed Menage's shaky financial dealings, and he fled to South America to avoid creditors. Consequently, Worcester's limited employment opportunities drove him back to Ann Arbor, where in 1895 he was rehired and appointed an assistant professor of zoology and curator of the university's zoological museum.

In the classroom, Worcester taught his students the latest anthropological theories, describing his firsthand observation of human evolution. He explained his belief that the Filipinos in general, and the remote tribes of Visayas in particular, were inferior physically, emotionally, and intellectually to white Americans. In his lectures he noted: "The resemblance of savages whose development has been retarded to children has been noted from the beginning. It has been my fortune to spend some time among such peoples, and I can not impress upon you too strongly the fact that in arriving at a correct estimate of the mental differences between man and the brutes you should not compare the gorilla and the orang-utan [sic] with the gentleman, but with the lowest of living men."[4] These observations referred to the Mangyans, who reportedly communicated by vocal squawks rather than words.

Worcester wrote papers about his Philippine experiences, and his articles received increasing academic attention. During this time, his personal life stabilized. At age thirty, the Worcesters owned a home in Ann Arbor and celebrated the birth of their first child, Alice. But as he settled into the routines of professorial life, the winds of revolution swept across the Philippines, and Worcester still felt pulled toward the islands.

In October 1897, as the American press vilified Spain's treatment of the Cubans, Worcester wrote an article in which he claimed that the Spanish also mistreated Filipinos, and that America should take a greater interest in the archipelago. He published six more articles on the Philippines between April and October of 1898. Following Dewey's May 1, 1898, destruction of the Spanish fleet, Worcester found himself in great demand for public speeches on the

Philippines. Not only did he have experience in the Philippines, he also possessed an ace up his sleeve. Frank Bourns, his 1890–1893 expedition companion, was in the Philippines in 1898 and sent Worcester secret, updated eyewitness accounts of the events unfolding in Manila. Because of Bourns's previous experience in the Philippines, General Otis had hired him as an intelligence officer, gathering information on the volatile situation that the army faced during their first months in Manila. Worcester had the ultimate inside scoop.

Worcester took a leave of absence from his university job and in less than two months put together a book on the Philippines based on his expeditions, Bourns's letters, and previous notes. Published in early October 1898, *The Philippine Islands and Their People* went through three reprints in its first months of publication. Worcester was a star and a hot commodity; he had more than three years' experience in the Philippines, a legitimate academic background, up-to-date information on the Americans in the Philippines, and a best-selling book.

Bourns's lengthy August 23, 1898, letter to Worcester included a detailed description of the fake battle for Intramuros and the increasing tension between Filipino and American soldiers. He told Worcester that while the American forces focused on Manila, Aguinaldo's insurgents controlled the rest of the Philippines, and he predicted that unless something quickly changed, American troops would find themselves in a bloody war for control of the entire archipelago. Alarmed by Bourns's letter, Worcester sought an audience with President McKinley. He traveled to Washington where, assisted by political connections of the University of Michigan's president, he met with Secretary of State John Hay on December 28. Hay then arranged a meeting between Worcester and McKinley. During the long interview, President McKinley showed Worcester a document that indicated that if the United States Senate should pass the treaty with Spain, America's policy toward the Philippines would be that of benevolent assimilation. In short, America would take the Philippines as a colony. Not to be outdone, Worcester showed Bourns's letter to the president, who asked if he could keep it. The president then surprised Worcester by requesting that he serve as one of three civilians in the Schurman Commission to the Philippines. Worcester accepted the offer, which came with an annual salary of five thousand dollars plus personal and travel expenses, doubling his University of Michigan compensation.

So it was that in late January 1899, Worcester once again made his way to the Philippines. While on a stopover at Yokohama, the commission learned that war between the Philippine insurrectionists and the American volunteer troops had broken out on February 4. They also learned that the Treaty of Paris, which ceded the Philippines to the US, had passed the US Senate by one vote. Both news items shaped their work once they arrived in Manila.

On March 4, Worcester spotted the now familiar outline of Manila Bay and arrived as a prestigious official rather than a zoologist hoping to get through the Spanish bureaucracy. As he suspected, conditions were not good in the Philippines. Daily bloody battles led both sides to engage in horrendous brutality. In short order, Worcester took charge, and though Schurman was the commission's president, Worcester's past connections placed him at the forefront of diplomacy between the commission and the Philippines' foreign, social, and economic leaders. When Schurman sent a preliminary report to John Hay claiming that the Filipinos were capable of self-government, Worcester sent his own report explaining that the rest of the commission believed that the only hope for Filipinos was for America to rule over the islands. John Hay's response to Schurman vaguely scolded the Cornell president for not including the majority opinion in his report. Worcester's fluency in Spanish, his contacts with Manila's social elite and foreign businessmen, his previous experience in the Philippines, and his domineering personality gave him inordinate influence on the Schurman Commission, whose final report included portions of forty-four interviews. Most of the interviewees were with wealthy Filipinos who stood to profit by collaborating with a new colonial power, and almost all stated that Filipinos were not ready for self-government.

During two interviews, the commission heard about Luzon's Cordillera, which began in Benguet Province. The witnesses spoke of the cool mountain air but also warned that tribal headhunters populated the region and that the Spanish failed to control the highlanders even though they had established a sanitarium in a village called Trinidad toward the end of their rule. Worcester hoped to visit the mountains, but his limited time and the danger outside of Manila made that impossible. Still, the information about the remote peoples stayed in his mind.

After seven months in the Philippines, the commission returned to America and presented their report. Even before communicating their recommendations, Worcester made public speeches proclaiming that the only hope for Filipinos was America's benevolent rule.[5] The final report, reluctantly signed by Schurman and heavily edited by Worcester, recommended that the Philippines be governed by an American governor-general with absolute power over a US-appointed Philippine judiciary and a popularly elected legislature, which Worcester assumed would be filled with pro-American Filipinos. After reading the recommendations, McKinley assembled the Taft Commission, which included Worcester.

Taft appointed Worcester the secretary of the interior. During his first year in that role, he made two brief trips into the Cordillera. His third trip into the mountains was extensive and he brought four American companions with him:

FIGURE 2. Worcester with his lieutenant governors and staff on June 9, 1909. This photograph was taken in front of Early's newly completed brick schoolhouse. Seated (*left to right*): Walter Hale; Dean Worcester; William Pack; Elmer Eckman; John Evans. Standing (*left to right*): John Early; Dr. W. E. Moss; Jeff Gallman; Samuel Kane; PC Lt. B. Nicolas; Charles Olson; PC Lt. F. J. Montgomery; William Miller; PC Capt. W. D. Harris. Owen Tomlinson Papers, Bentley Historical Library, University of Michigan.

William Dinwiddie, the governor of Lepanto-Bontoc; Dr. Albert Jenks, an anthropologist who had traveled throughout the region a year earlier; Captain C. E. Nathorst of the PC; and Samuel Kane, a former American volunteer soldier who served as an interpreter. Among their experiences on that journey the group saw the remarkable Banaue rice terraces, and a celebration of a successful headhunting war party.

Worcester had seen enough to know that he wanted to control the entire Igorot region. For the remainder of his life he romanticized the Igorots as honest, straightforward people untainted by Filipino politicians' predilections of self-interest, cunning, and deception. In 1905, two years before Taft's Commission was to share power with an elected national assembly, Worcester pushed through a bill that gave the secretary of the interior "direct executive control over the government of the wild people of the islands, excepting the Moro Province [in the archipelago's southern section]." He authored the Special Provincial Government Act (1905), which gave him unparalleled authority over all Igorots.[6] His self-proclaimed identity among the highlanders became that of the "Great White Father." Americans in the region believed this was the closest they would ever come to living under a king. He appointed the governors and lieutenant governors throughout the Cordillera, and they served at his pleasure. Two years into his rule, he created one realm for the entire Cordillera region and named it Mountain Province. It included seven subprovinces, each led by an appointed lieutenant governor, many of whom were American officers in the PC. Paradoxically, the PC became the one entity that restrained Worcester's free hand among the Igorots. The only other hindrance to Worcester's complete dictatorship was one of his lieutenant governors, who sided with the PC against him. That lone, brave soul was the most unlikely of all Worcester's lieutenant governors—a former American teacher named John Early.

CHAPTER 8

Early's Move to Bontoc
Teaching, Bricks, and Olympics

Early's work in Kalinga, and Lubuagan in particular, astonished the skeptics who thought that it was foolish to have American teachers in the province. He began constructing a school building, and during the spring of 1907, he established a routine of teaching in the morning and working on the schoolhouse in the afternoon. His second six months in Lubuagan were much more peaceful than the first, and the rains abated while the rice paddies were dry until the coming June rains triggered a new planting season. But Early would not be in Kalinga to welcome the wet season. Though full of energy and plans for his school, he was struck by trachoma in April 1907. This infectious bacterial disease made his inner eyelids rough like sandpaper, causing him great pain and a possible loss of eyesight.

He spent the month of May at the army hospital in Manila undergoing "scraping and burning at the lids and other such tortures which only doctors can invent."[1] Receiving a clean bill of health, Early returned to the Cordilleras in June but was assigned to Bontoc rather than Lubuagan, as the Bontoc teacher had been transferred out of the area, and the Department of Education deemed Kalinga too dangerous for an American schoolteacher. The constabulary in Lubuagan consisting of Bontoc soldiers struggled to keep peace among the numerous remote Kalinga villages, which were safeguarded by rivers, narrow trails, and human-constructed death traps.

Bontoc, on the other hand, was relatively peaceful and it became the capital of Mountain Province. During Spanish rule, the friars had established a parish in Bontoc, and Spanish soldiers lived in barracks, while a governor lived in a house made of hand-hued boards from Bontoc's ubiquitous pine trees. Bontoc abutted the Chico River, and before 1898 the Spanish lived on the ridge overlooking the river and rice fields. Lowland Filipinos, who served as middlemen traders and had married Bontoc women, lived in the area between the Spaniards and the Igorots who lived in the valley.

Like Kalinga, Bontoc's villages were shrouded in clouds many days of the year. Unlike Kalinga, its land was all spoken for, and most of it was owned by a few families whose wealth stretched back for generations. With a much larger, concentrated population, Bontoc's land was largely farmed by tenant farmers. Unable or unwilling to try and make a go of it in more distant areas, most families seemed content to work for their landowning neighbors. Tied to the area for ancestral burial reasons as well as physical protection, the Bontoc families multiplied until they represented the apex of the Cordillera's social and political life.

As Early moved into a Bontoc house in June 1907, he enjoyed the company of six other Americans in the town. These included the three Episcopalian missionaries: Father Clapp, Edith Oakes, and Margaret Waterman. Oakes, who was from England and had earlier served as a missionary nurse in Shanghai, would later marry Clapp. Together these missionaries established Bontoc's All Saints Church, providing education and medical services heretofore unknown to the area. Lieutenant Harris, who first brought Early to Kalinga, also lived in the town, and the two men shared a mutual admiration as they both seemed to live for work and adventure. Lieutenant Governor Elmer Eckman and his wife Daisy completed the American contingent. Early and Daisy teamed up to continue the work of the region's previous American teacher. Early supervised Daisy as she established a school for Bontoc girls, while he focused on providing a basic education for motivated students before sending them out to teach beyond Bontoc's population center. In short, he taught his students both an elementary curriculum as well as pedagogical skills. These student teachers instructed younger children in surrounding barrios during the morning and then attended Early's school in the afternoon. Before the end of 1907, Dr. Barrows visited Bontoc and gave Early's system a hearty endorsement.

Early finally settled into a routine after years of restless wandering and disappointments. At the end of the school day, the Americans played tennis, and evenings were spent together, each group taking turns hosting the small contingent. Bridge followed dinner, and then lamps were blown out and sleep came quickly as warm blankets made the cold Cordillera evenings conducive to rest.

Teaching, tennis, bridge games, an ecclesiastical commitment to Bontoc's All Saints Episcopal Church, and deepening friendships marked Early's simple Bontoc life. But three things plucked him out of his inconspicuous existence: bricks, games, and a new job. The bricks and games came about due to his past experiences, and he mentions both items in his memoir, though he omits some of the truth about his knowledge of brickmaking.

Early did not reveal his Irish Catholic heritage to his new friends, perhaps to fit in with the predominantly Protestant crowd he now worked with. He also concealed his background as a brickmaker and the son of a bankrupt brickmaker. Nonetheless, he rightly surmised that brick building could help the Igorots, and he told several officials that he believed he could make bricks because "I had taken a short course in clay working in college."[2] His extensive college transcripts show no such thing. In fact, he had spent twenty years making bricks in his father's business, identified himself as a brickmaker in the 1895 Minnesota State census, and tried to run away from this profession in college. But Early had the Igorots in mind when he offered to help make bricks, because Bontoc's annual typhoon season damaged or destroyed virtually every human-constructed dwelling. Thatched roofs were blown away by hurricane-force winds, while the houses' rudimentary walls of mud and sticks collapsed. Early overheard Samuel Kane, one of the three officers of Mountain Province, complain about Bontoc's rotten structures, and he stepped forward and asked, "Why don't you make the buildings out of brick?" Kane replied, "That would be fine. All we need is bricks, lime, masons, for a start. Any other pipe dreams?" Undeterred, Early responded, "I'm not dreaming. There is plenty of good brick clay near the river . . . I'll teach them [Igorots] how to make bricks."[3] Using his spare time, Early set out to construct solid, weather-resistant bricks, and found suitable clay near the Bontoc River. Together with Mr. Hora, he found a swath of limestone about 10 miles outside of town and began hauling it to the provincial capital.

In his memoir, Early carefully detailed the multiple experiments his team of Igorots attempted until they found the perfect formula for mixing the clay, placing it in wooden molds, and then removing the soft molds. At first, they placed the damp bricks in the sun, but the sun dried them too quickly, so Early suggested that they work at night. This worked, but the Igorots preferred to have evenings to themselves. The solution was to make the molds in the daytime, and then cover them with dried grass so that the sun would not dry them too quickly. After the bricks dried, they placed them in a constructed kiln. "We spent three days with light fires drying the brick in the kiln, and then increased the fire until the brick became incandescent. We then held the incandesce long enough for it to permeate the whole kiln, and then sealed up the kiln and permitted it to cool off slowly."⁴ The process of firing the bricks took three days, but it was worth the wait. Upon opening the kiln, they found that the one hundred thousand bricks were of excellent quality for building construction. This initial brick experiment led to an industry in which Igorots formed five thousand bricks every day until one hundred thousand were ready for the next firing.

Early's initial Bontoc brickmaking success coincided with a visit from Worcester. This 1908 inspection trip brought together an impressive contingent of Igorots from every major group for a weeklong Bontoc-centered festival. Such a massive gathering came with great risks. A seven-day cañao included substantial alcohol consumption among groups prone to fighting each other. Early's star, already on the rise in Worcester's mind due to the bricks, heightened yet again when Early suggested that the cañao should resemble an Igorot Olympic competition, and as a recent prominent collegiate athlete, he volunteered to organize the events. Worcester feared that competition between the rival Igorot groups would exacerbate their animus and rivalry. But by 1908, Early had spent two years immersed in Igorot culture and languages, and he insisted that highlanders were "gentlemen by instinct and tradition" and they would act respectfully demonstrating sportsmanship during the competition.⁵ Though Worcester doubted the games would work,

FIGURE 3. Early introduced brickmaking to the Igorots so their houses could withstand the annual typhoon winds. These rows of bricks in Bontoc are being dried by the sun. John C. Early Papers, Bentley Historical Library, University of Michigan.

he admired the brickmaker's pluck and acquiesced to the sports field day. Sprints, long-distance races, and relays were followed by events such as climbing a greased pole, with each winner receiving tools or a new woven loincloth. Of all the events, the tug-of-war garnered the most attention and enthusiasm from participants and spectators alike. Early's plan worked to perfection, and he noted with satisfaction that the Igorots "showed themselves real sportsmen—modest winners and good-natured losers."[6]

As noted previously, when Worcester gained control over the Cordillera via the 1905 Special Provincial Government Act, he began the process of creating one "super" Cordillera entity aptly named Mountain Province that included seven subprovinces: Benguet, Amburayan, Lepanto, Ifugao, Bontoc, Kalinga, and Apayao. The town of Bontoc, in the Bontoc subprovince, was designated the provincial capital. A governor, treasurer, and supervisor were the province's three primary officials; they all lived in Bontoc. Worcester appointed these three officials as well as the subprovinces' lieutenant governors. They all served at his pleasure, with no vetting process for their appointment or dismissal. Like pieces on a chessboard, officials were moved from one position to another, and Worcester chose men with whom he had traveled up and down the Cordillera trails. He poached PC officers he admired and appointed them to the more prestigious civilian political post of lieutenant governor. He wanted men cut from the same cloth who could control a challenging human and geographical landscape by force of bravery and personality.

Worcester's challenge was that he did not have enough trusted men to take on this monumental task. The first six months of the province's existence witnessed multiple appointments and resignations. The first governor of Mountain Province had lasted only half a year, and Worcester continued to juggle personnel, moving Early's good friends the Eckmans from Bontoc to Benguet, where Eckman served as the subprovince's lieutenant governor. By April of 1909, almost eight months after the creation of Mountain Province, Worcester still sought men he trusted to help govern his domain. The final piece of the political puzzle fell into place on April 3, when he appointed Bontoc's obscure American teacher to the lieutenant governorship of Amburayan. The professional break for which Early had waited a lifetime finally arrived. He packed his things and began a solitary journey to Tagudin, Amburayan's social and economic center. Early certainly had mixed feelings as he rode past Bontoc's brick buildings and his beloved students. He wrote that despite this promotion he found it difficult to leave Bontoc, because "[In Bontoc] I was quite contented and [now] set before me [was] a new problem—the reconciling of a Christianized Ilocano community to its new status as a part of a special [Igorot] province."[7]

CHAPTER 9

Lieutenant Governor of Amburayan

The problem in Amburayan centered on how Western colonial officials often took it upon themselves to redraw geographical borders to control a population economically and politically. Playing geopolitical dictator with a pencil, eraser, and ruler often led to catastrophic consequences for the colonized peoples. The Paris 1919 Peace Conference ranks as one of history's most egregious miscarriages of geopolitical justice. But just ten years earlier, Worcester provided a preview to Paris with the creation of Mountain Province, and Early would bear the brunt of the peoples' animus.

Worcester's plan to control the Igorots made him draw boundaries extremely favorable for the highlanders to flourish. He correctly surmised that the landlocked province needed access to a lowland port, but unfortunately for Worcester, the Igorots lived in the mountains, not by the sea. Undeterred, he sliced off the lowland town of Tagudin and attached it to Amburayan, an Igorot subprovince. Tagudin's Ilocano population of around five thousand had fallen on hard times. In 1908 a series of typhoons had destroyed its rice fields, and the Amburayan River, as it had for centuries, overran its banks and flooded the town. That same year almost fifty of its residents perished from cholera. But one major point of local pride remained intact, and that was that they were not politically or ethnically connected with the illiterate, uncouth Igorot communities on the western Ilocos Sur border. Worcester changed that with the stroke of a pen, and Tagudin became part of Igorot country.

It took Early two weeks to wrap up his work as a teacher in Bontoc and transition into his new administrative position. Even before he arrived in Tagudin, the local officials and residents received word that their new American lieutenant governor had spent his entire Philippine career among the Igorots and that the highlanders spoke highly of him. It was an 80-mile journey from Bontoc to Tagudin, and he entered the town on Saturday, April 17, 1909. He rode into a ghost town. Streets were abandoned, and despite the oppressive humidity, "every window was shut."[1] Two days later he learned that only his clerks would greet him; the mayor and other officials offered no welcome. Early represented a policy lumping their town with Igorots, and they did not want him. Even the legendary heat of the Ilocos coast did nothing to melt the frigid political morass he found himself in.

His first days as an administrator were a baptism by fire, and all the while Worcester sat back and waited for news from Tagudin. Most of Worcester's men would have responded to this situation with a heavy hand, demanding that the local officials either acquiesce to the colonial policies or immediately resign their positions. But Early was different. While not lacking in the self-confidence the other lieutenants shared, he did not believe that demanding respect and obedience garnered the best results. Rather, he spent his first days in office seeking advice from the local teachers on how he could best reach out to the community. They unanimously answered with one word: dances. Using his own resources, Early organized three *bailes* for the local Ilocano communities. People flocked to these events where Early, fluent in Ilocano, made it clear that he would use his position to address the region's economic challenges.

He spent his first weeks in his office reviewing the town's recent history, and it was a sad story. In the previous three years, the Ilocanos around Tagudin had suffered famine due to typhoons, flooding, and, paradoxically, drought. Some communities ate only one meal a day and slept most of the day so as not to expend calories. As he studied the latest annual report, the former lieutenant governor had ignored these issues and simply wrote about the place, "This town is the only seaport of the Mountain Province and the beginning of the avenue of reception and transportation of supplies to the capital, Bontoc."[2] Early recognized Tagudin's logistical importance and persistently requested provincial funds to construct a 4,500-foot-long wall where the Amburayan River normally overran its banks and spilled into the town. He also initiated an elaborate irrigation system to bring water into newly developed rice paddies. Whether due to his persuasive appeal or out of pity for his difficult first assignment, Charles W. Olson, the provincial treasurer, provided Early the resources he needed to construct the wall and the irrigation projects.

The following year the annual typhoon season did not destroy Tagudin, and the rice harvest proved more than enough for the town's citizens. Within just a few months of his time in the Ilocano coastal town, the municipal council members repaired the lieutenant governor's office, and he recalled, "This gave me a very dignified office as well as the coolest rooms to be had in the town."[3] He attributed the people's transformation from angry and suspicious to amiable to the fact that "I had no intention of interfering with their rights as a municipality and no intention to dictate to them as local lawmakers."[4]

Tagudin was an Ilocano town, but the Amburayan subprovince was mostly located in the highlands and populated by Kankanaey Igorots. Unlike the Ifugao, Bontoc, or Kalinga peoples, the Kankanaey were peaceful. Their farms produced potatoes, corn, berries, cabbage, and coffee. They also raised cows, which significantly boosted their economic situation. Early enjoyed the affability of the Kankanaey and their sophisticated metaphysical beliefs of a preeminent creator and lesser gods, along with ancestor spirits. These spirits' ubiquitous presence made the difference between this world and the afterlife thinner than a mango leaf.

In his notes, Early admired the Kankanaey more highly than other Igorot groups. But in Amburayan, he learned that they faced two primary dangers: their Ilocano neighbors and the more aggressive Igorot tribes. According to his reports, the Ilocano traders often swindled Kankanaeys and made enormous profits at the highlanders' expense. Ilocanos used the excuse of a shifting global economy to pay less for the rice, potatoes, and other goods from the mountains than what had previously been agreed upon. While this angered him, he was particularly vexed when educated Ilocanos tried to use the law to take property away from Kankanaeys who had worked the land for generations. In one instance he wrote, "A young Ilocano who had dabbled a little in the study of the law" presented a document to an old Kankanaey man proving that Igorots had squatted on fertile land and therefore had to move. The learned Ilocano man came to Early's office seeking support for his claim. As an administrator, Early's policy with regard to Igorot land favored those who had tilled the land for the past three generations—they didn't need proof of ownership, and most Igorots knew which families had worked the land for the past century. He bluntly stated, "[I] protected the rights of squatters." He brought the old Kankanaey man into his office to face the young Ilocano man. At the end of the day, the sophisticated lowlander conceded that if Early would not support him, he had no right to take the land away.[5]

Early's worldview, solidified by his undergraduate sociology studies, included a passionate desire to see disenfranchised people receive justice. As a lieutenant governor this served as his moral compass and would lead to both his downfall and later vindication. It also manifested itself among the Kankanaey, not just in protecting them from the lowlanders but also demanding that the more aggressive Igorots refrain from exploiting the Kankanaey.

A distinctive aspect of Early's leadership as both a teacher and official, which is mentioned often in Igorot stories about him, was his regular and extensive tours of all the villages in his jurisdiction. On one of his first outings in Amburayan he came upon a Kankanaey village where Bontoc warriors sat eating the villagers' food, including chickens and pigs they had slaughtered while "generally having an excellent time at the expense of the Kankanaeys." Having spent the past two years in Bontoc, he knew the men and their language. He demanded that they pay for their meal and the slaughtered animals, apologize to the Kankanaeys, and then leave. They complied not because he carried a gun, but because his moral suasion was based on fairness.[6]

He continued to make progress as a lieutenant governor, and while it was one thing for the American teacher to catch the eye of the secretary of the interior, it was quite another when he gained the attention of the governor-general and the US secretary of war. A combination of events placed him at the center of these officials' attention.

In 1910, several members of the Philippine National Assembly accused American officials, particularly Worcester, of buying substantial tracts of prime farmland that had belonged to friar estates. President Taft needed to send one of his cabinet members to investigate the situation. Since the Bureau of Insular Affairs was a division of the US War Department, it was appropriate that he asked his secretary of war, Jacob Dickinson, to clear up the problem.

On the east side of the Pacific in 1910, Philippine Governor-General Cameron Forbes was given little warning that his boss had scheduled an extensive trip to America's Asian colony. Forbes arranged Dickinson's six-week itinerary, which began with a visit to the remote capital of Mountain Province. A major obstacle to this plan was that the aged secretary could not make the steep climb from Tagudin to Bontoc, so a first-class 80-mile horse trail had to be carved out of the mountainsides in just six weeks so that he could reach Bontoc. Forbes and Worcester ordered Early to supervise the construction of the trail but provided no tools or dynamite for the project. Early sent an appeal to Colonel Wallace Cadet Taylor, the commander of the northern Luzon PC. He provided a few soldiers to help, but Early knew that the only way to compensate for the lack of equipment was enormous manpower. He rarely requested help from the Igorots, but he made this one appeal for volunteers, and the overwhelmingly positive response made it so that numerous villages sent "every available man they could spare." Working day and night, the army of Igorot workers and Early completed the trail within six weeks.

FIGURE 4. Early called on the Igorots for help just once, and this was to help him build the trail from Tagudin to Cervantes. John C. Early Papers, Bentley Historical Library, University of Michigan.

On July 30, 1910, just five days after Dickinson arrived in the Philippines, a military transport carried the secretary and Forbes to Tagudin. The following day they proceeded to Cervantes along the newly constructed grade-A horse trail. Beyond exhausted, it took Early and the Igorot workers weeks to recover from the project, many finding comfort in long naps brought on by strong drink.

Their remarkable accomplishment was not lost on Dickinson and Forbes. In his report to President Taft, Dickinson mentioned the Tagudin-Cervantes trail, noting that "Many miles of mountain trails of easy grade have been constructed. I passed over the one from a point 5 miles from Tagudin to Bontoc, that portion from Cervantes to Bontoc being entirely new and just opened. . . . The initial cost was comparatively small owing to the cheapness of the labor, all of which was performed by the wild men of the Mountain Province . . . and to the skill developed by those directing the work."[7]

Forbes was especially pleased with the new trail. From the time he started as the Philippine governor-general in 1909, he insisted that roads should connect all parts of the Philippines. His assistants took to calling him "William Caminero Forbes."[8] In 1912, the former governor-general of British Ceylon, Sir West Ridgeway, visited the Philippines and praised Forbes as the person who "would go down in the history of the islands as the 'road building' governor."[9] So it was no surprise that as the Dickinson party returned to Tagudin and boarded a steamship, Forbes took time to loudly praise and thank Early for his supervision of the Tagudin-Bontoc trail. As the son of the Irish brickmaker heard the praise from the governor-general and a presidential cabinet member, he pointed to the Igorot workers as the primary catalysts for the trail. Still, he basked in this public recognition. But his time of rest and reflection on a job well-done did not last long. Worcester had new plans for this trailblazer and friend of the Igorots.

CHAPTER 10

Lieutenant Governor of Bontoc

According to the May 7, 1905, feature article of *Munsey's Magazine*, Edward Y. Miller was living every American boy's dream. Born in Pennsylvania, E. Y. Miller enlisted in the 5th Illinois Volunteer Army at the outset of the Spanish-American War, and his initial assignment in Puerto Rico led to a quick transfer to the Philippines. His distinguished service earned him an appointment as an officer in the regular army. Photogenic, affable, and an inspiring leader, Miller's reputation for pacifying politically troubled hotspots caught the attention of high-ranking American colonial officials. In 1905 he was appointed governor of Palawan Province, a portion of the southern Philippines that reportedly included seventy-nine islands. Like Mountain Province, Palawan was mostly populated by non-Christians: Muslims and indigenous animists. The area mirrored the Mountain Province in its reputation for lawlessness and tribal warfare.

Miller accepted Palawan's governorship, sent for his fiancée in Illinois, and set up his headquarters at Palawan Island's Puerto Princesa. With just two other foreigners and an effective PC unit, Miller established peace throughout the region either through diplomacy or military victories. The American press gave him multiple monikers, including "Man-God," "Governor-King," and "Soldier-King." The *Munsey's Magazine* article identified him as the "King of Palawan," and claimed that most American boys dreamed "that it would be a pretty glorious thing to be a king, with or without a capital K."[1] Miller planned to establish schools throughout his domain, create a solid export economy, and integrate the indigenous interior ethnic group, the Tagbanua, into Palawan's broader society. As such, his daily inspections of school buildings and economic projects took him upriver from Puerto Princesa. On the evening of May 27, 1910, as the annual rains raised the river, Miller was returning home in his boat after an inspection. During the journey, he failed to see a thick low-hanging branch, which crushed his skull and knocked him into the river. His body was found twenty-four hours later. Soon after, the *San Francisco Call* newspaper's sensational headline proclaimed "Wanted: A New King for Palawan."[2]

In the Philippine archipelago, Palawan was about as far west and south as one could get from Tagudin, but Miller's accidental death directly impacted the rest of Early's professional and personal life. Palawan was within the domain of Worcester's non-Christian hegemonic rule, and he now had to find the King of Palawan's replacement. There was very little time for a reflective decision as Palawan's fragile peace began to unravel immediately after Miller's accident. Worcester noted that "Governor Miller's place cannot be really filled until some other man has acquired knowledge which is attainable only through long years of experience."[3] Another official wrote that Miller could not "be replaced by a company, probably not a battalion, and possibly not by a regiment of troops."[4] With such big shoes to fill and a local uprising brewing in the southern Philippines, Worcester turned to John H. Evans, the lieutenant governor of Bontoc. Tall and thin, with a long face and sharp nose, the bearded Evans would, at the very least, present a physically dominant human specimen who would serve as Miller's interim replacement to stem the piracy and theft breaking out in Palawan.

With Evans's move south, Worcester had to find a lieutenant governor for Bontoc, arguably Mountain Province's most important subprovince. Its status as the capital had transformed the town of Bontoc into a rapidly expanding city with numerous officials and merchants moving into newly built homes. Worcester chose Early. As Bontoc's previous teacher, Early knew the place and garnered praise from its inhabitants. He had built its brick buildings and established an education system that reached Bontoc's most remote areas. The governor-general had publicly lauded Early's work in Amburayan, and even President Taft had heard of the trail Early engineered.

For his part, Early was conflicted about the transfer. His fourteen months in Tagudin included successful irrigation projects, the construction of a wall that prevented annual flooding, and an increased food supply. Most importantly, the Ilocanos and Kankanaeys peacefully coexisted and were more soundly protected, and he had plans for Amburayan's future economic projects.

At the same time, Bontoc represented a promotion as it was the center of Mountain Province. He also had friends in the city, including Reverend Clapp and Lieutenant Harris, and he was a member of Bontoc's All Saints Episcopal Church. In the end, his feelings mattered little as Worcester did not ask Early about the transfer; he demanded it.

Toward the end of April 1910, Early once again packed his gear, mounted his horse, and began to ride out of Tagudin. His exit radically differed from his entrance. The initial cool reception was replaced by a warm-hearted send-off, as Tagudin's leading citizens accompanied him for the first 15 miles of his journey. He thanked them for their kindness and support and continued his leisurely three-day journey to Bontoc.

Early's initial impression of his new station was captured in one sentence: "The Bontoc to which I had returned after fourteen months' absence was not the Bontoc I left."[5] The town was now a city filled with new faces, both foreign and domestic. It also housed the province's three officers. This logistical arrangement meant that Early had to carefully navigate his subprovincial authority with that of the provincial governor, treasurer, and supervisor. Early reported to these officials, and each one had a story behind their rise to provincial officialdom.

Many were surprised that Worcester (a die-hard Republican) chose the staunch Democrat William F. Pack to be governor of Mountain Province. But they had much more in common than people realized. Like Worcester, Pack came to the Philippines from Michigan. Extremely thin, six-foot-seven, and sporting a mustache, Pack possessed superior military tactics and innate leadership qualities. Raised in Michigan's Saint Joseph County, he was thirty-eight years old when the Spanish-American War commenced.

After General Aguinaldo's March 23, 1901, capture, General Arthur MacArthur spotted Pack during a military parade at Manila's Luneta Park. Leading a company of only eighteen men, MacArthur asked why Pack had so few soldiers. He responded, "The rest of the company are dead or in the hospital."[6] MacArthur reportedly offered Pack a position in the Cordillera town of Baguio, where he found his way into the position of Benguet's governor and proceeded to tirelessly advocate that Baguio be developed for Americans. In an official report he claimed that Baguio "is a white man's climate and here may be raised products with which he is familiar. Here he may engage in stock-raising or agriculture."[7] Under Pack's leadership the influential Benguet Consolidated Mining Company was created.

Worcester appointed Pack as Mountain Province's governor in 1908 because they shared the same vision of keeping the Igorots separated from lowlanders, and they were also overt racists. A cursory glance at Pack's annual provincial reports from 1909 until his resignation in 1912 reveals that he usually re-

ferred to the Igorots as savages, barbarians, and wild people. He rarely requested additional resources for the indigenous peoples, but he regularly complained about the low wages provided to his lieutenant governors. At one
point he argued that his American officials' lack of pensions would result in
their returning to the US and ending up in the "county house" despite their
sacrificial "work among the barbarians."[8]

Tall, lanky, addicted to alcohol, and overtly dismissive of the Igorots, Pack
carved out a comfortable existence in Bontoc. The secretary of war noted in
1939 that Pack had been "one of the most valued officials of the Philippine
government."[9] Worcester praised him as an American hero: "Think of Pack,
weakened by illness which twice brought him within a hair's breadth of death,
wearing himself out riding over the Mountain Province trails, many of which
he himself had laboriously built, in order to keep the little handful of men
who control its 400,000 non-Christian inhabitants up to the high-water mark
of efficiency, when he could have gone home any day and spent his remaining years in leisurely comfort."[10] This high praise did not align with how Pack's
lieutenant governors viewed their boss. Kalinga's lieutenant governor Walter F.
Hale noted in his October 31, 1909, diary: "Talked with Gov. Evans. Gov. Pack
came to [the] phone, but said he could not hear—too old."[11] In another document, Early wrote that Pack had spent most of the summer of 1910 drunk on
whiskey, leaving the provincial supervisor, the third member of the board, to
govern the province. His name was Samuel Kane.

On a rainy New York City morning in 1895, Samuel Kane (1880–1933) secretly entered his parents' empty bedroom. His mother was in the kitchen
while his father shaved in the bathroom. He spied his father's pants on a chair
and rifled through the pockets until he found a wallet. He had never stolen
from his father before, but he justified this larceny as a short-term loan that
would lead to a massive monetary return. In the wallet he found a ten-dollar
bill, grabbed it, and returned the wallet to his father's pants pocket. Afraid he
would be caught before executing his get-rich-quick-plan, Kane breezed
through the kitchen, telling his mother that he would eat on the run. But the
get-rich scheme ended in an embarrassing debacle, and he wondered what his
father might say or do about the missing money. Kane decided he would not
stick around to find out. The fifteen-year-old New Yorker said goodbye to the
city and moved on to his next plan—to become a Texas cowboy. He never saw
his parents again. Texas also proved a disappointment to the young man as he
worked at low-paying jobs and his companions spoke only Spanish. Within
two years, the runaway was bilingual.

With limited prospects in Texas, Kane moved on to a new adventure—a
trip across the Pacific to kill Filipinos who were fighting for independence. He

joined one of the most influential and admired volunteer units of the entire Philippine-American War. Young men from Texas, Arkansas, and Oklahoma filled the ranks of the 33rd Infantry Volunteers, and they all reported to Fort Sam Houston, where they became known as the Texas Regiment.

Following a few months of intense training, they travelled to San Francisco and promptly made a mess of things by spending their wages on alcohol and prostitutes. Still, they garnered fear and respect, with one reporter noting that these "sun-browned, raw-boned, danger-tried rangers" would distinguish themselves in the Philippine War.[12] They boarded the army transport ship *Sheridan* on September 30, 1899, endured a terrifying voyage across an unusually harsh Pacific, and landed in the Philippines on October 29. One author noted that "The regiment that disembarked in the Philippines on October 29 had been mobilized, trained, and sent overseas in less than four months."[13]

The 33rd Infantry men immediately made a name for themselves in Manila so that "between November 4, 1899, and January 9, 1900, the 33rd Infantry emerged as one of the crack units in the US Army."[14] They cornered Aguinaldo while winning the battles of Magnatarem, Tirad Pass, Vigan, and Tagudin Pass. They also successfully rescued a group of American POWs in one of the most daring maneuvers of the war.[15]

Kane was part of this distinguished group, though he was barely twenty years old. The 33rd endured a high casualty rate, with over 40 percent debilitated by tropical disease. At the beginning of 1901, they gathered in Manila and Candon on the northwest coast of Luzon for their return trip to America. On March 2, 1901, the transport ship *Logan* pushed off from the Philippine shore with the 33rd Infantry. Their homecoming radically differed in tone from their departure less than two years earlier. One member of the 33rd who had returned earlier than his colleagues observed, "I was there close to shore where I could see them march to the Presidio. You could tell they were from the Tropics, tanned to near a leather color, they looked very healthy although lank and lean. . . . But, Oh! How thin their ranks were, only 469 left to come marching home, while when we left nearly two years ago we were 1,300 strong. There was no lively band music, no waving flags nor blaring trumpets, like when we were on our way to war."[16]

Samuel Kane was not one of the 469 men who disembarked at San Francisco. He had nothing waiting for him in the United States, and his time in the Cordillera had ignited an interest in the Igorots and especially their language. Having spied the decorative gold that the Igorots wore and learned that the mountains contained this precious metal, he could not shake his boyhood dream of riches. The Cordillera was a goldmine. Furthermore, he wrote about sleeping with various young Igorot women, describing their

breasts as "straight and firm, resembling two ripe pears."[17] When he announced that he planned on staying in the Philippines, his friends asked,
"Boy-boy why do you want to stay over in this God-forsaken country?"[18] But
Kane remained resolute in his decision and used his two-hundred-dollar army
pay to purchase mining equipment in Manila.

Returning to the Cordillera, Kane settled in Sabangan near the Bontoc-
Ifugao border, but panning for gold turned up only gravel. During this time,
he took up with a young Igorot woman and picked up several languages to
the point of impressive fluency. Despite his lack of formal education, Kane
possessed an innate gift for learning languages. Due to Sabangan's remoteness
and Kane's linguistic abilities, the Igorots assumed that he represented America's rule, and his was the authoritative voice of law and arbitration in and
around their villages. Kane, a twenty-one-year-old high school dropout, embraced the role of judge and arbiter, but he also learned that he could not
prevent the incessant head-taking followed by bloody battles of revenge.
Consequently, in early July 1901 he decided to travel to Manila and request
that soldiers be stationed in Sabangan to protect the weaker villages from their
aggressive neighbors. At the outset of his journey, he learned that members
of the Philippine Commission were in Cervantes. He could not believe his
luck, as the highest American officials were at his doorstep. Borrowing a horse,
he rode to Cervantes, where he found an overweight American sitting outside a tent. Kane politely introduced himself, and in response, the oversized
official broke out in loud laughter. Kane, being considerably smaller and much
younger than the roaring man, did not pick a fight but walked away in disgust, saying, "I was told that American Commissioners had arrived from Manila to investigate the possibility of organizing the mountain tribes into some
kind of government—but I must have walked into a bunch of laughing jack-
asses."[19] The laughing American called him back and introduced himself as
Dean Worcester, secretary of the interior. He said that Kane's appearance—
his oversized beard and disheveled, long-red hair—made him quite a sight that
suggested the biblical character Samson.

After this awkward initial meeting, they sat down, and Kane provided a detailed introduction to the social and economic situation of the Bontoc and
Ifugao Igorots. Over the next few days, Kane served as Worcester's interpreter,
and the commissioner was impressed that so many chiefs knew and trusted
Kane. Worcester accepted Kane's invitation to visit Bontoc, but on their way
into the mountains, he received a message to immediately return to Manila
for the July 4, 1901, inauguration of Governor-General Taft. Worcester promised to send several military companies to Cervantes and to return the following year to visit the remote Igorot towns and villages Kane had described.

Ten days later the soldiers arrived with a mandate to protect Kane's villagers. It had only been four months since Aguinaldo's capture, and the entire Cordillera remained in chaos. The Worcester-sent troops sought to bring a semblance of order, but they also needed food, and so Kane's golden egg finally landed in his lap. When the ranking military major disclosed that his men needed meat, Kane offered to supply around 300 pounds of dressed beef a day for between fifteen and twenty cents a pound. The agreement led to Kane's economic windfall. Acting as a middleman between the American military and the Igorots who raised cattle on the Cordillera hills, Kane earned $7,600 during the next year. With the money, he purchased a coffee plantation from a former Spanish official turned businessman, Don José Mills.

After just months on his coffee farm, Kane again played the role of judge and arbiter. In May 1902, the colonial government created the Lepanto-Bontoc province, which encompassed numerous Igorot groups. Cervantes served as the provincial capital and had three American officials: governor, treasurer, and supervisor.

Six months later, Taft and Worcester appointed Kane the provincial supervisor, with an annual salary of three thousand pesos. Only in the backwaters of America's first colony could a high school dropout with no administrative experience become a provincial board official. The turn of events shocked Kane himself: "The supervisorship also carried with it the power of justice of the peace, ex-officio, for the whole province, and meant that I could settle all the little difficulties of the Igorots, during my trips, in a legal manner. It was an honor I had never thought of possessing."[20]

Kane remained Lepanto-Bontoc's supervisor until 1908, when Worcester created the all-encompassing Mountain Province, and he was then appointed the provincial supervisor and worked alongside Governor Pack and the provincial treasurer, Charles Olson. Then in 1910, Early joined them as Bontoc's newly appointed lieutenant governor. It did not go well.

PART THREE

Conflict (1910–1911)

CHAPTER 11

Alcohol, Labor, and Land

Early hardly recognized Bontoc as his horse slowly climbed the final hill that led to the town's outskirts. In a place where things remained the same for hundreds of years, Bontoc appeared to have changed overnight. His former simpler days in Bontoc were forever gone. Instead, Early found that Eckman now lived in Baguio as Benguet's lieutenant governor, and Father Clapp was busy with domestic changes, having married Edith Oakes just months earlier. But these changes were mere trifles compared to the tectonic political shifts that had fundamentally changed Bontoc's society.

When Worcester created the Cordillera-encompassing Mountain Province, Baguio, and not Bontoc, seemed the logical choice for the provincial capital, since enormous resources had made Baguio accessible by vehicle, and it was the summer capital of the colonial government. Daniel Burnham drew the plans for Baguio's future development, and the Ibaloi and Kankanaey Igorots who populated Baguio and its surrounding area were the most affable and peaceful of all the Cordillera peoples. Charles Brent, the Philippines' Episcopal bishop, made Baguio the center of education for American and Igorot children, creating two outstanding schools: one for American boys and the other for Igorot children. The town was now a bourgeoning, beautiful city. If Mountain Province's capital was supposed to become the center of economic and political growth, then Baguio seemed the only city prepared for such

FIGURE 5.   In 1926 the town of Bontoc included multiple brick buildings built by Early and the Igorots when he served as Mountain Province's governor. John C. Early Papers, Bentley Historical Library, University of Michigan.

changes. But Worcester chose the much smaller, rural and inaccessible town of Bontoc as the capital because it was at the heart of the Cordillera while Baguio was at the southwest tip of Mountain Province—just 33 miles from the South China Sea. His choice of Bontoc set off a flurry of activity that the provincial supervisor Samuel Kane recalled in his autobiography: "That task that confronted me [making Bontoc the provincial capital] was a colossal one. . . . There were no stores, sawmills or any sources of supply where material could be bought, borrowed, or stolen, for the matter."[1]

Porters carried enormous amounts of material into Bontoc, and thousands of Igorot men and women were pressed into service. The town slowly took on the feel of a consumer center, with numerous indigenous people leaving their remote villages for the capital's service-oriented jobs. The most profound change, however, was not the bustling streets, increased population, new consumerist economy, or ubiquitous building projects; rather, it was the behind-the-scenes political shift that few Igorots understood.

For his provincial officers, Worcester sought like-minded men who would only defer to one authority—himself. In its first years, the Mountain Province's administrative paradigm worked. There was, however, one fundamental logistical flaw in his scheme—Bontoc. The three provincial board members resided in the town of Bontoc, but so too did the subprovince's lieutenant governor. Consequently, potential conflict was ever-present because Early was the subprovince's primary source of authority, and he had taken an oath to protect all its inhabitants. Difficulty arose when the provincial board implemented policies detrimental to Bontoc's inhabitants, and Early defended the rights of Igorots in opposition to the board. Furthermore, if he ruled against an individual in a dispute, that person could directly appeal to the provincial board and have the judgment overturned. Simple solutions to these potential conflicts included collegial communication and transparency between the offices. Unfortunately for all involved, this did not happen. The consequences of this proved disastrous for Early because there were numerous disputes noted in the historical records—the final one leading to his ignominious dismissal.

The initial conflict between Early and the provincial officials centered on the use of *cargadores*. As mentioned earlier, the trails connecting Igorot villages and towns were treacherous, narrow, and purposefully steep so as to protect communities from invasions and natural disasters. In many cases horses could not climb the trails, and so humans carried goods in and out of Bontoc. As most outsiders used all of their physical strength just to climb the mountains, they required Igorots to carry all their food, blankets, clothes, tents, pots and pans, utensils, tools, etc. Thus, an industry grew around hiring Igorots to serve as porters.

Early knew that this new business opened the door for potential exploitation because the first experiences between Americans and Igorot cargadores were horrific and widely known in Bontoc. For example, during the Philippine-American War, an American military officer shot and killed two Igorot carriers when they refused to get up after falling down from exhaustion.[2]

Once settled in his Bontoc office, Early learned that Pack and Kane had pressured so many Igorots into serving as carriers that rice paddies lay fallow, and some villagers suffered starvation as a result. Consequently, one of Early's first acts was to organize the cargadores into teams and institute a policy that these teams would only work on certain days so that they did not neglect their agricultural duties. Pack and Kane were furious when they learned that Early had curtailed their new thriving business, and matters came to a head when they ordered Early to supply hundreds of cargadores to carry lumber to a storage shed 12 miles outside of the capital for a new sawmill business. Compounding this already excessive request, Bontoc was in the midst of harvesting season. For the first, but not last, time, Early refused to obey the governor's order because this would compel him to break his oath to protect the Bontoc people. Neither side specifically recorded their compromise in the matter; Early simply wrote, "The matter seemed to have adjusted itself after a time, and we settled down to work together."[3]

FIGURE 6. Igorots were used as porters, or cargadores, to carry things in and out of the Cordillera. These four porters are taking a much-needed break. The headband straps on their heads are attached to additional straps on the loads on their backs, so that they can carry the loads up steep inclines with their arms free. Howard Haines Brinton and Anna Shipley Cox Brinton Papers (HC.MC.1189), Quaker and Special Collections, Haverford College, Haverford, PA.

Within just a few months of the cargadores conflict, however, Kane and Early almost came to blows over the importation of alcohol into Bontoc. As Early told it, in the waning weeks of 1910 a legal case came across his desk related to a Chinese merchant caught bootlegging gin and whiskey into Bontoc. This incident particularly troubled Charles Olson, the provincial treasurer. He had repeatedly insisted that this contraband broke the spirit and letter of provincial law, and he recorded his complaint in a letter to the secretary of the interior's office: "Regarding the purchase of supplies direct from Manila by others than the Provincial Treasurer, I think I have made myself clear in other letters, but I do not think I can put myself too strongly on record as being opposed to this practice."[4] It is not clear whether Olson knew who was behind the larger bootlegging operation, but he sent the merchant to Early, who then sentenced the man to serve time in jail. Early noticed that the Chinese merchant was shocked he would have to join over one hundred men in the provincial jail. The man's surprise was based on his assurance by his employer that if he were caught, he would only be fined—and he would not even have to pay that! Following the sentencing, the merchant's employer barged into

Early's office and ordered him to change his decision from jail time to a monetary payment. It turned out that Kane was the merchant's boss and had greatly profited from this business. Early stood his ground and noted that "the irate Board Member left muttering threats against me for declining to do a friend a favor. I thought little of the threats at the time, but the time was to come when I remembered them well."[5]

Relations between Kane and Early deteriorated over the next six months. While never mentioning him by name, Early wrote that Kane spent most of the rainy season sitting beside Governor Pack, consistently filling his superior's glass with whiskey. In pointed language, Early contrasted Olson and Kane's professionalism: "The Treasurer was a gentleman of university training who paid strict attention to his own business and cast his vote on the board wholly unmoved by ulterior aims, but the Third Member, as I have noted, was a man who rose from the status of laborer—a man of natural shrewdness and sharpness who had married in the country—and was in a great many ways an advantage to the Board. But from his antecedents and training lacking the inhibitions which restrain a gentleman, and so, if he became an antagonist, he was a dangerous one."[6]

The last proverbial straw that reportedly ended Early's administrative career in Bontoc was an issue very dear to Worcester: land. As secretary of the interior, Worcester's portfolio included the Philippines' resources, particularly public lands. In 1900, the Philippine Commission estimated that private individuals held about five million acres of land, leaving sixty-eight million acres in the public domain.

In 1904, the commission's Public Land Act limited the purchase of land to 40 acres for individuals and 2,500 acres for corporations. Restrictions were also placed on how much land individuals and businesses could lease. Worcester complained that this law was too restrictive because he believed that the future of the Philippines lay in American investment and ownership of Philippine land. He often remarked that Filipinos would never break out of their subsistence-based rural economy until they learned firsthand how Americans used land for large business enterprises such as coconut farms, sugar plantations, and raising cattle.

Worcester skirted the land laws by selling a sixty thousand acre former friars' estate on Mindanao Island to an American, who then sold it to other investors. He justified the sale by claiming that the friars' lands had been purchased by the Philippine government and so were not subject to the restrictions placed on public lands. He also leased land in northern Luzon to his brother and nephew. This, combined with Worcester's purchase of ten acres in Baguio (the land value of which he reportedly assessed himself as secretary of the interior), led to an investigation of his office. Colorado Congressman John A. Martin initiated the investigation. On June 13, 1910, Martin made a speech on the floor of the House of Representatives in which he uncovered Worcester's colonial land deals, noting, "These transactions [were] so criminally corrupt and immoral as to constitute malfeasance in office on the part of all the officials of the Philippine Government concerned."[7]

Worcester was recalled to the US and faced a three-month investigation (December 1910 to February 1911) led by the Committee on Insular Affairs, which waded through 8 tons of records from Manila's Bureau of Lands. Never one to back down from a fight, Worcester castigated Martin by accusing him of serving as a puppet of Colorado's sugar barons who did not wish to compete with America's colony. Toward the end of the hearings, Worcester addressed the congressional committee, claiming that Martin had "charged me with immoral, corrupt, and criminal conduct, and with malfeasance in office," but that Worcester could do nothing about these false charges because the congressman hid behind his constitutional legislative privilege. He wrote to his friend and supervisor Governor-General Forbes, "It is axiomatic that the harm accomplished by such an attack as that which representative Martin has made can never be wholly undone."[8] Worcester was correct. Even though he was "completely vindicated" by the investigation and resumed his responsibilities in the Philippines, he ever after remained connected to the friars' land scandal.[9]

He returned to the Philippines more bellicose and short-tempered than usual. This was not a time for any of his subordinates to make waves, which was unfortunate for Early, because while Worcester was in the US, a land dispute arose in Bontoc. Pack and Kane ordered Early to confiscate some land from the Bontoc Igorot families that the Board deemed public land, since no one could produce a title or deed. But Early claimed, like others who knew Bontoc culture, that for the Igorots "land was of divine origin, it was sacred . . . not subject to . . . sale, purchase, or lease. Among indigenous peoples in the Philippines, there was a widespread belief that land was held usufruct; it could not be removed from the community's use."[10] The land that Pack and Kane wanted had been part of Bontoc families' property for generations, and he refused to give it up to the colonial government. When pressed on the issue, Early took the matter to a provincial judge, who ruled in favor of the Igorots.[11]

On Monday, May 29, 1911, a tired and agitated Worcester entered Bontoc and immediately met with Pack and Kane, who presented their side of the land case. He may have had a sense of déjà vu from his recent time in Washington, but this time he would be the judge. He disagreed with Early's protection of

Bontoc land for the Igorots, and Olson noted about the situation in his June 8 diary entry, "Lt. Gov. J. C. Early is in trouble with Worcester who is on the warpath." The next day Olson wrote that Early was leaving for the US in the next seven days, and "will not return to position here."[12] Kane gloated over Early's firing, noting that Worcester claimed that "he [Worcester] had spoilt a good teacher to make a poor governor."[13]

Early gathered his belongings, and on the morning of June 14, 1911, rode past the Bontoc buildings he helped to build and began his ignominious departure from the highlands. Recalling the event later, he claimed that he "tendered [his resignation] without regret quite satisfied that the two members of the Board would overlook no trick to trip me up should I stay; and as I noted before, a man with the inhibitions of a gentleman is at a disadvantage in a rough and tumble contest with a man with no inhibitions. I was glad to go." In his view, he had kept his vow to protect the Bontoc people, and they were "sorry to see me go."[14] But was he really glad to go? Was land the real issue? A closer look at history demonstrates that Early used the land argument to hide the real reasons for his dismissal, which centered on his refusal to be silent in the face of the exploitation and massacre of the Igorots.

CHAPTER 12

The Problem of Kalinga and the Hale Solution

During the first decade of their colonial rule, American officials and soldiers described Kalinga as "the meanest country the devil ever created."[1] If Kalinga was designated the heart of Mountain Province by many observers, it was reportedly a dark heart. Like other Igorot tribes, Kalingans loved to laugh and embrace life's simple pleasures, but their sadistic cruelty and incessant warfare made theirs the Philippines' most dangerous territory. Even the PC soldiers dreaded a posting there, and neighboring Igorot groups steered clear of the borderlands. The first official American visits to Kalinga, those of David Barrows (1902) and Daniel Folkmar (1904), had led to bloodshed and their hasty retreat out of the territory.

The first anthropological studies on Kalinga included the incessant head-hunting among its inhabitants. The description of this practice explained that head-taking began when several men would form a hunting party. Their villages were placed on notice that the group had departed with two primary goals: to take at least one head and then to return safely. Often, the victim was anonymous. Targeting a specific person was the exception more than the rule. The raiding party relied on stealth as it was in enemy territory, and, if spotted, they would be attacked by a much larger number of warriors who were familiar with the terrain and possible escape routes. In a hide-and-seek game with life-and-death consequences, the invading party tried to find an individual who was alone; usually the victim was an old man, a child, or a woman.

Normally, the warriors chose their prey based on how quickly they could commit the deed and escape with a head. The targeted individual was usually working in a rice paddy or by the river washing clothes or bathing. Upon the successful head removal, the perpetrators raced back to their domains; friendly lookouts at the borders signaled if the men returned safely with their trophy. Women also alerted the community of the successful raid with distinctive shouts that circulated from village to village.

Once safely back in their village, the head was placed in a special basket, and villagers prepared for a celebratory cañao. The feast lasted a day or longer, depending on the available food and alcohol. At some point during the revelry, a detailed narrative of the hunt, stealth, decapitation, and safe return was told with rhythmic gongs as background music. During the speech, the head might be rolled across the ground and placed on a stake. Following the cañao, boiling water removed the head's flesh, and the skull's jawbone was removed. It might serve as a handle for a gong or as a badge of honor on a hut's outside wall. And while the individual who murdered and decapitated the victim would be admired, particularly by single women of marriageable age, all members of the successful raiding party received distinctive tattoos marking them as headhunting warriors.

Head-taking was dangerous, as communities often set booby traps such as concealed pits or strategically placed sharp bamboo stakes (*sugas*), whose whereabouts were only known to local villagers. Unlike other Igorot groups whose primary motives for head-taking included revenge killings or propitiation for recently deceased relatives, the primary reason for taking heads in Kalinga was to garner honor and prestige. One American soldier who spent time in Kalinga during America's first years of colonial rule noted that "Kalinga is neither a race or tribe name, but a word meaning 'enemy' or 'outlaw,' as though the hand of the people that bear it had been against everybody's [sic] else. These people have been great head-hunters, and have not yet entirely abandoned the practice. . . . They will not marry outside of their own blood, and their women, so we were told, would not look at a white man."[2]

In a time and place where colonial officials exhibited eclectic, if not bizarre, personalities, no one matched the unconventional Walter Franklin Hale. At just over five-foot-six, he was shorter than his colleagues, but no one stood taller in governing the Igorots. Described by both men and women as strikingly handsome, with a chiseled face that included a square jaw and perfectly proportioned eyes and nose, he resembled Rudolph Valentino and was nicknamed "Don Juan." His absolutely dictatorial style of governing was rooted in a sadistic enjoyment of battles and an overblown confidence, along with his dismissal of written laws and policies. Since Kalinga was the most difficult subprovince to govern, Worcester appointed Hale as its lieutenant governor. A provincial official approved of this, noting that "Hale, though educated and raised in a civilized country, was more of a primitive wild man than the wildest of his seventy-odd thousand wild head-hunting Kalingas. He was built along the lines of a large stocky gorilla and could outhike and outfight the bravest and strongest warriors of his province."[3] Worcester also reserved his highest praise for Hale, writing this after Hale's first year of governing Kalinga: "Lieutenant-Governor Hale has made remarkable progress in improving public order and in bettering sanitary conditions in this subprovince. He must be credited with being the first man to bring about the complete cleaning and sanitation of Igorot towns. He has gone practically alone to towns which threatened to take his head if he attempted to visit them, with the result that they promptly changed their minds and decided to be friendly."[4] At the same time, Hale caused Worcester many headaches, so that at one point the secretary scolded him in a letter: "You either do not know what co-operation means or are unwilling to co-operate . . . you want to run your own show, and are unwilling to make use of agencies provided by the government."[5]

Hale's relatively long tenure in Kalinga lasted from 1908 to 1913, and praises continued to be heaped on him by high officials in Manila: "Lieutenant-Governor Hale has now [1913] been in the special government longer than any other man who remains in it, and has an admirable record for quiet efficiency . . . he is a man with chilled-steel nerve."[6]

While Hale played a central role in shaping early colonial rule in Kalinga, he was also a key player in John Early's downfall. His multifaceted career and remarkable life are certainly a story in itself, and the paradoxes of his background and leadership seem unending.

Born on July 27, 1874, close to Plattsmouth, Nebraska, Walter Hale was the eldest of five children born to Samuel and Anna Belle Hale. Raised on a cattle ranch, where he mastered both horsemanship and a six-shooter, he completed an undergraduate degree and one year of graduate studies at Cotner College, a Disciples of Christ institution in Lincoln, Nebraska. In 1898 he joined the 1st Nebraska Regiment, a volunteer unit sent to the Philippines, where they disembarked in Manila on July 17, 1898; a month later the Spanish surrendered. The regiment remained in the Philippines, and from February to June 1899 it was at the forefront of the Philippine-American War and suffered a high casualty rate of sixty-four deaths and hundreds wounded, including Hale, who suffered a severe leg wound.

Less than a year after arriving in the Philippines, the Nebraska volunteers boarded the transport ship *Hancock* on July 1, arriving back in San Francisco on July 29. The soldiers were mustered out of service on August 23, 1899, but

Hale did not return with his colleagues, as he chose to leave the volunteer army and remain in the Philippines. Like Kane, he decided to try his luck finding gold in the Cordillera just north of Baguio. He met with limited success, finding just enough gold to create two small *carabao* statues, which he gave to Lepanto-Bontoc Governor William Dinwiddie.

Unlike most of the American prospectors in the area, Hale was a college graduate, and his intelligence went beyond the classroom. His gifts to the provincial governor translated into a networking bonanza as Dinwiddie introduced Hale to Worcester, which led to Hale's appointment in the new colonial government. He was not a lonely bachelor trying his hand at government. In a 1902 diary entry he noted, "I think Willie is going to be the girl I want and need. She is good and kind and above all, I believe her to be honest."[7] Her name was Guillerma Linda-Lorenzana, and when they married on January 1, 1903, she was sixteen years old. Her family was from a town just south of Tagudin, and their forty-nine-year marriage produced nine children.

Like the other Cordillera-based colonial officials, Hale's situation changed in 1908 when the entire region folded into Mountain Province. Hale was given the volatile subprovince of Kalinga, which meant that he had to leave the comfort of the lowlands and his in-laws to take on a loathsome task. The new challenge brought out sharper edges of Hale's personality, for good and ill. Along with his wife, children, and some advisers, Hale eventually made the Kalinga town Lubuagan his subprovince's capital, as there was also a PC station there.

Kalinga became Hale's fiefdom. Reading through his diaries and reviewing his life up until his Kalinga appointment, one wonders if Hale's autocratic leadership was dormant and only emerged once he found a dictatorial opportunity, or if a metamorphosis occurred once he found himself in the Philippines' most dangerous region. Whatever the case, he spent the next seven years as Kalinga's king. A characteristic example of his rule is a recorded conversation he had with a lowland visitor in Lubuagan. Hale asked the Ilocano guest, "Who is God down there [in the lowlands]?" The visitor answered, "Dyos" (the Ilocano word for the Christian God). Hale responded, "Up here I am god. You obey me."[8] He was not joking.

Neither the Spanish nor the PC could control Kalinga's perennial warfare and headhunting, but Hale accomplished what no one else could with a different governing approach. First, he created a new type of indigenous local authority. Most villages were ruled by a group of elders—often those with the most resources. He hiked throughout Kalinga and found the prominent families in each hamlet, town, and village. After numerous interviews, he appointed an individual acceptable to the residents as the local headman. This individual had to attend regularly scheduled assemblies at Lubuagan and was honored with tokens of authority such as an army jacket and new loincloths that included badges. They also garnered an annual stipend, which enhanced both their economic and social status. Serious responsibilities accompanied these privileges. For example, if an individual broke one of Hale's laws, the criminal's headman had to bring that individual to Lubuagan within twenty-four hours of the crime. If he did not do this, the entire village would be punished for the offense. William E. Dosser, the lieutenant governor of Ifugao and later governor of Mountain Province, was astounded at Hale's success in Kalinga: "Gov. Hale had a system that always worked, never to my knowledge [was there] a single failure. Any crime within the Sub-Province, be it the theft of an egg or a murder, he had the culprit behind bars within forty-eight hours. He did not have to send out police or soldiers to make an arrest. His headmen brought the culprit in promptly, frequently before the governor even knew that a crime had been committed. Governor Hale was a great character and a wonderful person."[9]

The regular gatherings of headmen (*presidentes*) in Lubuagan kept them from fighting, as these leaders faced each other in Hale's presence. If disputes between two presidentes flared at the conferences, their colleagues served as arbitrators. This consistent interaction enhanced communication between villages. If tension between leaders was so acute that one of them skipped the required gatherings, Hale marched to a village and escorted the headman to Lubuagan. If he refused to accompany Hale, he lost his position, and a new headman was appointed on the spot.

Hale was also widely known for disregarding colonial policies and provincial laws. He ignored these rules because he believed the Kalinga justice system was much easier to work with and more credible among the mountain people. In particular, he declared that peace pacts between villages served as the authoritative means for peace rather than colonial government regulations.[10] Thus, Hale accepted the killing of an individual if it restored a peace pact between villages. In one instance he demanded that a village hiding fugitives immediately hand them over or he would encourage other Kalinga towns to march on them, as his January 12, 1910, diary entry recorded: "Advised Lubuagan to break Peace-pact or cut out criminals from Lubuagan with Sumadil, Bangad, Balatok or any other town where criminals were likely to go with safety. The Headmen of Lubuagan's *Baknangs* (wealthy) agreed to do so and would leave in the morning for that purpose."[11]

Hale's colleagues and superiors knew of his arbitrary disregard for colonial law and allowed him to burn villages that refused to acknowledge his authority. One of his nicknames, "Sapao," was the name of a village whose headman refused to acquiesce to his rule. He marched on the hamlet and challenged the leader of Sapao to a fight, and the elder headman agreed to follow Hale's leadership. In his December 10, 1909, diary entry, he wrote that the use of his name brought other villages to heel: "Told them I heard they had eight guns. Advised them to turn them in. Advised them of the fact that I was *Sapao* the *Apo* of the Kalingas; wanted them to be friends with their neighbors; do what is right, work their part of [the] trail, etc. Advised them to come to Lubuagan in five or six days and visit me. In case of failure, I would send for them. Advised them to tell me their trouble. In case they thought they were fighting people, to tell me so I would see what I could do to accommodate them."[12] Hale's draconian rule was such that over a dozen villages pleaded to be placed under the jurisdiction of bordering subprovinces.

Hale's capricious interpretation or compliance with colonial policies irked other American officials. In particular, he disregarded the colonial rule on the thorny issue of taxation. The Spanish never governed the Cordillera because they demanded that Igorots, like the lowlanders, pay an annual tax. For the highlanders this meant bondage, and they would rather fight than accept outside demands. In Mountain Province, an annual tax of two pesos was placed on all able-bodied men between the ages of eighteen and fifty-five. However, they were offered the alternative option of working ten days during the year building trails. Most Igorots chose the work over the cash tax. In Kalinga, Hale arbitrarily "doubled the number of days and frequently had as many as five hundred Kalinga working on a single stretch or road."[13] Many of these construction projects were extremely dangerous, and on one site boulders fell on two workers, killing one man instantly while his companion suffered broken arms and legs. The man clung to life for close to half an hour before he also died. Hale noted about this tragedy, "The Provincial Board is morally to blame for not furnishing suitable tools and an American foreman to do and oversee difficult work."[14] The accident occurred close to the end of the workday, but Hale dismissed the possibility that it occurred because his men may have been tired and overworked.

When an American PC officer learned that Hale had doubled the workday tax, he boldly confronted him. Unrepentant, Hale wrote in his diary, "Capt. Hunt was visiting all morning. [He is] Opposed to road tax & road labor—against the provincial gov't. He is long on P.C. manual, rules and regulations. Seems to be laboring under the impression that the P.C. is about the whole thing, or a separate governing body. Separate, independent with a separate law especially created to do or not to do—unto themselves."[15]

This interaction revealed that Hale's biggest challenge in governing Kalinga was not its inhabitants; rather, it was the other colonial authority in the area, the PC. In a telling diary entry, Hale wrote, "Slowly but surely—Lt. Governors must win or else the P.C. If the P.C. are to win, it is possible that they will change and the change will cost money and lives."[16] Hale was overtly contemptuous of the PC and expressed his disdain for its officers and soldiers to Kalinga leaders. Consequently, unlike in other subprovinces, the PC found it impossible to recruit soldiers from within the subprovince it patrolled. PC soldiers dreaded their Kalinga assignment because they were viewed as outsiders and were not respected by Kalingans. Hale told the headmen that should there be a domestic or outside crisis, they should report directly to him, not the PC, as he was the sole authority and would take immediate action. He believed he was in competition with the PC for the soul of Kalinga, and he wasn't about to lose the successful social engineering project he had built. As years passed, the colonial government grew in sophistication, and Hale lost the protection of Worcester, who was eventually replaced. He was commanded to change his dictatorial rule into something resembling a democratic system. The new secretary of the interior reported on his conversation with the God of Kalinga:

> I have had a very frank talk with Governor Hale. I told him that I realized the courage and power which he has shown in Kalinga, but that I was afraid he would not be suitable to the work which remains to be done there. He understands perfectly well that he is a one-man government, and always has been and has never succeeded in cooperating with anyone else. He has no deputies or lieutenants whom he can leave in charge when he is absent. . . . The Secretary of Commerce and Police has notified me finally that if Governor Hale is retained he will positively withdraw Constabulary from Kalinga, owing to the inability of the Governor to get on harmoniously with any of the Constabulary officers who have been detailed there.[17]

But at the height of his power, Hale did not need to get along with anyone else. In addition to his forceful personality and authoritarian rule, he also garnered inordinate economic power because he monopolized the sale of rice in Kalinga. He claimed that outsiders used different scales and measurements when selling rice, so it was best to have just one source for rice distribution. Lubuagan therefore became Kalinga's economic heartbeat, where rice was collected and sold. Hale's wife and her relatives built stores, and they enjoyed his protection from other competing businesses. He used profits from these businesses for the annual stipend payment to the village presidentes, who in turn gave him their undivided loyalty.

Thus, the initial deal Worcester and the provincial board made with Hale was that they would allow a dictator to control Kalinga in exchange for unprecedented peace and the diminution of head-taking in one of the most difficult regions in the colony. John Early attempted to challenge this arrangement in January 1911; it would cost him his job.

CHAPTER 13

The Bacarri Problem

When Hale accepted his lieutenant governor position in 1908, he first moved his family to the Kalinga town of Tabuk, and one of the first matters he had to settle was a recent beheading. Three weeks prior to his February 12 arrival, seven men from the Kalinga area called Bacarri beheaded Demitrio Cauilan, a lowlander from Enrile, Cagayan, a town at the eastern edge of the Kalinga mountain territory.[1] He could not take care of the case immediately but noted that he would track down the killers.

Less than two months later, Hale was told that PC forces were bringing him much-needed supplies from the lowland town of Santa Maria. Carried by a long line of pack horses, the supplies never reached Tabuk, as heavily armed Bacarri warriors stopped the soldiers and horses three hours outside of Tabuk. The lowland-based PC soldiers were no match for the Kalinga fighters, and they retreated having failed at their resupply mission.

While supremely frustrated by the resupply debacle, Hale was occupied with more pressing matters. Having almost died of malaria in early 1903 while prospecting for gold, he feared that the mosquito-infested Tabuk was unsuitable as a home base. He and Willie were particularly concerned for the health of their three-year-old Anna Belle and one-year-old Samuel James. In July, they moved Kalinga's administrative capital 30 miles southwest to the subprovince's central town of Lubuagan. From this town, Hale established his political, military, social, and economic fiefdom. In rapid succession, scores of Kalinga villages submitted to his rule and his appointed headmen. But the Bacarri district stubbornly refused to follow his orders even though he brought transformational medical, economic, educational, infrastructural, and agricultural improvements. Ever vigilant, his energy astounded the Kalinga warriors, and rumors spread throughout the region that he possessed an *anting-anting* (protective amulet) that made him immune from harm. Remarkably, after scores of recorded battles in Kalinga, he was never seriously injured.

A January 2, 1910, incident further deteriorated relations between Hale and Bacarri. A man from Lubo named Lissuag was attacked and beheaded by three Bacarri men.[2] Lubo had come under Hale's authority, and Hale intended to demonstrate that he would protect all under his rule. Thus, just weeks after Lissuag's murder, Hale gathered loyal Kalinga warriors and marched southeast for 30 miles to Bacarri. They were attacked as they closed in on the town. Dodging spears and bullets, Hale entered the town, only to find it abandoned. He and his ragtag army managed to catch two elderly Bacarri men, and he reportedly "returned Bacarri spears thrown at us, and advised them to have a talk with their people about throwing spears and shooting at people, assuring them that such conduct would surely get their District into trouble."[3] Moving on from Bacarri, Hale stumbled into a hamlet of two dozen houses. It was abandoned save for an old woman lying on the ground with five spears pinning her down and her head gone. Hale ordered that the spears be removed and the headless corpse be buried, correctly surmising that the Bacarri peoples sent the woman's head to Lubo as a peace offering for Lissuag's decapitation a month earlier.

Two months later, the Lubuagan-based PC led by Captain Harris marched on Bacarri to arrest Lissuag's three murderers, but they too encountered a cold reception and returned to Lubuagan empty-handed. Through the summer and fall of 1910, Hale repeatedly requested that Bacarri send a representative to Lubuagan and join the other village presidentes in the peace pact paradigm.

By the fall, Hale knew the names of the men who beheaded Lissuag: Salibad, Banasan, and Uyong. He was also informed that Bacarri warriors owned more than sixty rifles and were proficient marksmen. In November, he received notice that Bacarri had indeed sent an old woman's head to Lubo as a peace offer for Lissuag's murder; Lubo rejected the offer because they trusted that Sapao would exact their desired revenge.

For Hale, the last straw came while he was in Lubuagan on January 2, 1911. On that bright and sunny Monday morning, he met with Kalinga's headmen, who told him the alarming news that Bacarri had joined an alliance with eight other hamlets to attack villages under American control. The belligerents included 870 warriors with up to 200 guns. The presidentes who informed Hale of this were particularly concerned because they had turned in all their guns to him, a demand he placed on all villages who surrendered to his rule.

Three days later, Hale typed a letter to Governor Pack explaining the situation. The letter contained a history of Bacarri's "depredations" along with the names of all the "ugly towns and rancherios" in the anti-American alliance. He proposed a multi-force attack on Bacarri. Pack supported the plan, and wanted the strike force to be adequately supplied.

Pack sent a telegram to Colonel Wallace Taylor, the PC's Mountain Province district director. The message was more of an order than a request: "I will probably want detachments Harris and Penningroth to meet in Guinabal district with Hale and Early. Please arrange."[4] Taylor simply replied: "Harris and Penningroth will meet such place as you arrange if you take up matter with them."[5] Despite these cordial exchanges, tension remained high between Worcester and the PC, and this carried over to the highest civilian and military officials in the Cordillera. However, the animus had not trickled down to lower-level officials such as Harris, Penningroth, Early, and Hale, who all got along well with each other—until the unfolding of the Bacarri campaign.

Though Pack did not anticipate much trouble from this military operation, it was significant enough that he informed Governor-General Forbes of it. Forbes responded with a two-sentence dispatch: "Your letter of January 9th received. The action taken by you is approved."[6] Having sent his letter to Forbes on January 9, Pack turned his attention to the four men leading the attack: Hale, Early, Harris, and Penningroth.

Unlike his three colleagues, Charles Penningroth's time in the Philippines represented only a brief period in his long and remarkable professional career. Just twenty-four years old at the start of the Bacarri campaign, he was the youngest American on the mission. Born in Red Oak Township in Iowa's Cedar County, he grew up on a farm, speaking only German until he entered elementary school. The oldest of ten children, he matured and embraced the discipline needed to transform a 320-acre wooded area into an enviable farm with crops, roaming livestock, and impressive structures to house people and farm animals.[7]

In 1905, he graduated at the top of his high school class with all his final grades above 95 percent. He enrolled at the University of Iowa and was part of its military training program, receiving the Governor's Award as the university's top cadet. Penningroth wanted to study at Harvard Law School but lacked the finances to do so. His academic mentor suggested he could earn money by doing a brief stint in the PC, and his parents agreed that this would be an excellent opportunity to both travel and earn tuition money. He joined the PC as a third lieutenant, arriving in Manila on April 3, 1909. From there he promptly moved on to Baguio, where he spent four months in the PC training academy. In August he was assigned to the 3rd Company, stationed in Bontoc. He served in the newly established Mountain Province for the next two years, most of it at Natonin, where he supervised the construction of a PC station.

Prior to the Bacarri mission, Penningroth was acquainted with Hale, and enjoyed a deep friendship with Early. His first interaction with Hale occurred when he entered Kalinga to capture four men accused of theft. Stopping in Lubuagan on his way to the suspects' village, he called on Hale, who told him not to return without the men. Hale proceeded to have a private conversation with the Igorot PC personnel accompanying Penningroth and instructed them to burn the accused men's village. When they arrived at the village, Penningroth stopped his soldiers from carrying out Hale's clandestine orders, saying that this was not part of the instructions he had received from Governor Pack. When he returned to Lubuagan without the prisoners, Hale rebuked him for following the governor's directions: "Don't pay any attention to orders. Now you will probably be blamed by your superiors for not having had better control of your men. Now if you do as I say there will be work here for you for two months but if you don't do the way I say then you will not get it done short of six months or probably not at all."[8] He also told Penningroth to keep their conversation private, especially from Pack.

In contrast to his prickly relationship with Hale, Penningroth's closest friend among American officials turned out to be Early. Writing in 1966 at eighty-one years old, Penningroth recalled, "Since the American occupation brick public buildings have been erected. The first one was erected by Jack Early a man who then had charge of the schools. He came from the western part of the United States and had great ambition. . . . Though much time was taken [to make the finished bricks] the structure is a credit to the Mountain province and a monument to the man."[9]

While stationed in Natonin, Penningroth regularly received letters from Early. They were full of warmth and often concluded with words like those expressed in this October 1, 1910, note: "When you come in [to Bontoc] my house is wide open and I shall feel aggrieved if you don't spend some time with me. Best wishes, Early."[10]

The PC officers Harris and Penningroth were ordered to provide soldiers for the Bacarri mission, while Hale and Early represented civilian leadership and legal legitimacy. Dated January 7, 1911, Pack's three-page, single-spaced letter to Early contained detailed instructions. He was to proceed to Natonin, where he and Penningroth, along with PC soldiers, were to set out on January 12 for Kalinga. They were ordered to rendezvous outside of Bacarri with Hale and Harris on the afternoon of January 14. Once the two groups linked up, Early was directed to defer to Hale: "Upon joining Governor Hale and Captain Harris, they will really be the senior officers of the expedition and you will accompany them, you, subject to the direction of Governor Hale who will assume the responsibility for the civil part of the expedition."[11]

Hale's plan of attack was the classic pincer movement. Early and Penningroth would enter Bacarri from the southeast while Hale and Harris would approach from the northwest. Their coordinated attack was scheduled for January 14 at noon. But what developed between January 11 and the end of the campaign turned into a debacle.

Once Early received Pack's instructions, he set out to meet Penningroth on January 10. As he approached the PC's Natonin fort, he could barely make out its structure on the hill as the fog hid the barracks, which resembled a long train with grass that served as a roof. Once there, they set out on the afternoon of January 11 along with twenty-two PC escorts and marched toward Kalinga territory for what turned out to be an eleven-day military campaign. The first three days were mostly spent climbing up and down Kalinga's mountains, and the nights were described as miserable due to mosquitoes. Early was used to the primitive aspects of the Cordillera, but he was taken aback by what he found as his party entered a part of Kalinga he had never seen before. As they made their way toward Bacarri he commented that they were now in "no man's land."[12] The very nature of indigenous economic survival in the Bacarri region was not the normal agricultural-based society of the highlanders; rather, it appeared that they were living as nomadic hunter-gatherers, and their houses were up in the trees for protection.

When word spread that the American-led party from Natonin was on its way to subdue the Bacarri people, many men gathered their weapons to join Early's group. In particular, the Balangao tribe—a group numbering just under twenty thousand, but with their own language and religion—were anxious to exact revenge for all the Bacarri-led depredations they had endured. While the PC officers appreciated this additional support, Early insisted that the Balangao stay put. Nonetheless, they continued to shadow the PC, so Early ordered the PC officers to stop and ask the Balangao warriors to come out. Believing this was a good sign, they gathered around Early. In a bold maneuver, Early ordered several soldiers to guard the Balangao men and make sure they did not follow him. This reduced Early's accompanying soldiers to about a dozen men, but he did not want the expedition to turn into a slaughter of the Bacarri alliance because, as he later wrote, "A school of thought had arisen in the Philippines which based its creed upon the postulate that you must first use force to the uttermost, then when the opponent is crushed extend him gradual leniency. Here we found people coming in contact with government for the first time, eager and willing to conform because personal safety and ordered government appealed to them. This dissipated all arguments of the advocates of flattening punishment as a matter of policy."[13] Early's conviction did not align with Hale's ideas. The Apo of Kalinga was on the move from Lubuagan, and nothing and no one was going to stop him from destroying Bacarri. A showdown between the two lieutenant governors was now just two days away.

CHAPTER 14

The Bacarri Massacre

On the morning of January 14, Early and Penningroth mustered their soldiers with the intention of making it to the Bacarri village by the appointed hour. After breakfast, they set out at 7:30, and as the dew burned off the thick foliage and sweat soaked through the mens' clothes, they may have wished that they were in the local loincloth uniform. Suddenly, their mountainous climb through the Kalinga jungle was interrupted by a gruesome change in scenery. The tall, verdant green grass changed color as streaks of red from freshly spilled blood stained the plants and slowly oxidized to brown. Penningroth consulted with Early, and "several hypotheses were framed to explain the cause."[1] As they drew closer to Bacarri, the blood began to be mixed with intestines, and as they turned a sharp corner they found the source of the blood and entrails. Scattered along the trail were the remains of Bacarri's pigs, dogs, and chickens. At that same moment, shouts from the surrounding hills were directed toward Early and his company. Straining to hear the words, they made out "Lubuagan" and "Sapao." The shouters were Kalinga warriors who had accompanied Hale for the impending Bacarri battle. According to witnesses, Early lost his temper when this group came down to meet the Natonin soldiers. If they expected praise and admiration for their recent vandalism, they were rudely surprised. He severely scolded the civilian warriors, and he warned the Lubuagan PC soldiers that the "dereliction on their part would be met with drastic actions."[2] This event caused Early and

Penningroth to arrive two hours late for their scheduled rendezvous with Hale and Harris.

As they approached the meeting point, a small stream and valley separated the two groups. Early observed that there were numerous abandoned and recently burned villages in the valley, and as they lifted their gaze to the rising mountain, they hardly knew what to say. Hale and Harris were not only accompanied by the two dozen PC personnel, but they also came to Bacarri with over six hundred Kalinga warriors, who were loudly celebrating their successful devastation of the Bacarri villages and peoples. Hale ordered Early and Penningroth to join his contingent and promised to care for their soldiers in newly constructed shelters. The Natonin men were anxious to join the much larger contingent and prepared to march across the valley, but Early told them to stand fast. They were not going to join Hale's men. Incredulous, Hale sent a courier with a message demanding Early bring his group over because the six hundred Kalinga men came from over two dozen villages (he listed each by name), and this would "probably be a good opportunity for the head-men to get acquainted."[3] Despite the numerous entreaties, Early refused to join Hale, and the following morning the two groups went their separate ways, though they would meet again after an action-filled five days.

Sunday, January 15 was relatively quiet, as Hale and Harris stayed in camp, giving the soldiers and volunteers time to recuperate from the previous day's activities. Early and Penningroth also rested and constructed a plan to confiscate the guns in the surrounding villages. They were frustrated that the Bacarri inhabitants disappeared into the thick jungle every time they approached a village, and they sought to communicate that they came to bring peace and not war. Early told the PC officers to contact the more remote Bacarri villages and reassure their inhabitants that he and Penningroth came in peace. These overtures proved effective. Early triumphantly wrote, "The people were disposed to be friendly to us after we came into contact with them and expressed themselves as wishing the protection of the Provincial Government as a refuge from the state of anarchy which had been theirs since they first sought refuge in the hills."[4]

That Sunday of rest and peace gave way to a Monday full of blood and destruction. As Early and Penningroth marched east, they saw more evidence of Hale's work, with entire villages burned to the ground. For his part, Hale reported that, like Early, he asked the Bacarri villages to make peace with Sapao, but they refused. Harris's field notes, however, told a different tale: "Today everything that could be destroyed was burned, more so with the rice houses."[5] This destruction of rice sentenced the villagers to starvation or forced them to buy rice from Sapao's stores.

On Tuesday, Harris and Hale moved from village to village destroying everything in their path. At 4:20 p.m. a message from the Bacarri warriors reached Hale inviting him to send some of his volunteers for a fair fight; this was Hale's type of battle, and he sent his best headmen and a few volunteer fighters. He believed the challenge was a bluff, until about an hour later a runner reached him. Between breaths, he told Hale that the Bacarri men not only showed up for the fight, but Hale's men "were getting killed."[6] Grabbing his gun, Hale led several hundred warriors to the fight. But the sun goes down early in the mountains, so by the time Hale reached the battle scene it was too dark to engage the Bacarri men. Revenge for daring to take on Sapao would have to wait until the next morning.

As the sun peaked over the mountains on January 18, Hale and Harris's warriors returned to the previous day's battlefield, where they found dead combatants and buried them. Over the next ten hours, Hale's men killed men, women, and children. All the while, Early and Penningroth entered numerous villages, collecting guns along the way. They came into Mabaca, a small village near the Balbalan region. With daylight fading, they camped there for the evening. The Mabaca elders informed them that Sapao's camp was close by, and they pleaded for Early to remain in the village "as long as 'Sapao' should be in the vicinity."[7] But despite his desire to protect Mabaca's inhabitants, Early and Penningroth had more villages to visit, and they left the following morning at 7:00.

That Thursday was uneventful for both Early and Hale as the mission drew to a close. While Early collected more guns, Hale burned the entire Lattang area, but he spared the barrios of Kalao because he needed their rice and pigs to feed his men. In his subsequent report, he congratulated himself for taking things from the Bacarri people so that his warriors were taken care of.

On the following day, Friday, January 20, Early opened his eyes not knowing that the day would forever change his life. Both he and Penningroth believed they had successfully fulfilled their eight-day mission, and after a brief visit to a few villages, they planned to return to Natonin. They set out at 9:00 a.m. Ninety minutes later the problems began when they met Hale and his contingent. Hale sent a runner to Harris, who was 1 mile back, notifying him that the two groups had finally connected. Harris sent the runner back, ordering Penningroth to wait for him, but when Penningroth received the message, he asked Early what he should do. This infuriated Hale because the instructions from Pack were very clear—Hale and Harris were the commanding officers in the Bacarri campaign. Sapao was even more flummoxed when Early told Penningroth that they were not going to stay with Hale, and Hale scolded the two men, reminding them that he was not requesting but ordering them to join his group. For ten minutes Early followed Sapao but then could not stomach what he saw. Hundreds of Hale's men were carrying stolen items from the burned villages, and this was too much for Early. He told Penningroth that they should quietly break away from Hale's men.

Once Hale and Harris learned that their subordinates had slipped away, they sent scouts to find them and deliver a stern message to immediately rejoin the group. Despite repeated commands, Early refused to return, as the Kalinga fighters prepared to destroy even more villages the following day. Hale's frustration with the situation spilled over in his post-expedition report: "After lunch, Captain Harris sent 4 P. C. with note and guides again asking Lieutenant Penningroth to come into camp. . . . The actions and conduct of Lieutenant-Governor Early as well as that of Lieutenant Penningroth under the circumstances would seem to resemble that of two very small boys, rather than two full grown men holding responsible positions in the Mountain Province."[8]

Early's party continued east toward Natonin, and as they passed through the village of Abugao, its elders begged them to write a letter that they could show to Hale's men indicating that they were under Early's protection. That exhausting day came to an end when they finally reached Butigui—the last stop before the final hike to Natonin. They rose early the next morning, Saturday, January 21, and by late afternoon they reached Natonin, reporting that no member of their party had suffered injury and that they encountered no resistance or *sugas* (hidden bamboo stakes) during the ten-day expedition. On that same day, however, Hale and Harris faced a new crisis. Rumors had spread throughout Kalinga that Sapao was in trouble, so three hundred men from Lubo, Dacalan, and Falangao rallied to support him with a message to Bacarri that if Sapao was hurt "they would tear them to pieces."[9] Hale's volunteer army now numbered close to one thousand men, all itching for a fight. Even with all his unquestioned authority, he was losing control of the situation, and he demanded that all the volunteers return to their villages. Now with only a few PC soldiers, Hale and Harris returned to Lubuagan, satisfied that they had imposed their rule over the Bacarri population, or what was left of it.

During the ensuing days, the four Americans who participated in the campaign typed up their interpretation of what happened; they all agreed it was a great success. It seemed like a routine exercise, and it would have passed as a forgotten episode in the lives of its participants had it not been for one short paragraph from Penningroth's report. Those few lines poured gasoline on the fire between Worcester and the PC. They would also create an unbreachable chasm between Early and the secretary of the interior.

CHAPTER 15

The Report

After ten days of fighting the Bacarri alliance, Hale and Harris, along with twenty-two Kalinga-based PC officers, walked into Lubuagan at 2:30 p.m. on Monday, January 23, 1911. They had not captured the three men they sought but still believed the expedition represented a brilliant success: they crushed the backbone of Kalinga's only remaining anti-colonial region, confiscated fifty-four guns, and within several weeks the three murderers of Lissuag surrendered themselves to the Apo of Kalinga. Hale had destroyed his enemies, and the subprovince was his and his alone.

On that same day in Natonin, just 20 miles south of Lubuagan, Lieutenant Penningroth typed up his report on the campaign for William Moore, the administrative assistant to Colonel Taylor. The three-page, single-spaced report changed history. In his narrative, Penningroth noted that Hale enlisted six hundred Kalinga warriors who looted, burned, and butchered as they moved from village to village. He concluded the report by claiming that "Throughout the trip not one suga was seen by nor was any hostility shown to Lt.-Gov. Early and his escort."[1] He also reported that numerous village headmen begged Early to protect them from Hale and his army.

Penningroth's report was the smoking gun the PC needed to put Worcester in his place, because since the 1908 creation of Mountain Province, Worcester had engaged in a bitter political fight with Brigadier General

Harry Hill Bandholtz, who led the PC. They battled over who should control the Cordillera, for it was the PC, not Worcester, who had finally brought law and order to the mountains, and the region largely remained a police state. In 1908, Worcester wrested control and authority away from the PC by choosing some of its officers to serve as civilian lieutenant governors. Bandholtz responded by appointing Captain Wallace Cadet Taylor as northern Luzon's senior inspector.

Taylor and his officers disliked Worcester's attempt to make the mountains and its peoples his fiefdom; thus, Penningroth's expedition report provided the evidence they needed of Worcester's draconian and unjust system of rule. Just three days after receiving Penningroth's document, a scathing report against Worcester's officials came from the northern Luzon PC headquarters. Written by a PC administrative assistant, its first line indicted Worcester for his previous misplaced criticism of the PC: "The District Director [Taylor] directs me to say that in the early days of Bontoc . . . Secretary Worcester criticized (PC) Lieutenant Miller for failure to prevent the Barlig war party from following him."[2] The letter then listed other examples of Worcester's criticisms of the PC in the southern islands for not controlling the local population.

This was a strange way to begin the report about the seemingly inconsequential Kalinga skirmish. The implication was clear: Worcester freely condemned PC actions while his own lieutenant governors were committing horrific atrocities. The PC's document detailed Worcester's hypocrisies and concluded with the harsh statement that because Hale used his personal army to murder civilians and burn villages, the PC would no longer provide escorts for his lieutenant governors. In short, they would no longer obey the secretary of the interior's dictatorial decrees.

Before forwarding the report to Bandholtz in Manila, Taylor added one final paragraph to the document: "It may be that higher authorities will consider the means were justified by the results but until there is some indication of an expression on the subject I will refuse to furnish escorts to lieutenant governors who take with them hordes of armed warriors for the purpose of devastating the country."[3]

Taylor directly challenged Worcester in the report. While most people walked on eggshells around the secretary of the interior, even while they secretly despised the supercilious self-appointed master of all the non-Christian peoples, it took a twice-wounded favorite of Governor-General Taft to alert the world that the emperor was wearing no clothes. Bandholtz acted quickly after reading the Bacarri report. The day after he received it, he forwarded it to Charles Elliott, the newly appointed secretary of commerce and police, seeking help in this matter for "Colonel Taylor evidently feels that the situation is serious, and instructions are requested [regarding Taylor's decision to refuse assistance to Worcester's Lieutenant Governors]."[4]

Elliott should have met with his fellow commissioner Worcester about this rift, but Worcester was in the US trying to salvage his career from the attacks of Colorado Congressman Martin. Consequently, Elliott turned to Governor-General Forbes, who was serving as acting secretary of the interior in Worcester's absence. Thus, two weeks after the Bacarri campaign, Forbes received the PC report with a one-sentence introduction: "Respectfully forwarded to his Excellency, the Governor General, acting Secretary of the Interior, for his information."[5] By doing this, Elliott was letting a fox loose in the henhouse; he knew that the governor-general would not be able to bury Hale's illegal actions, which also indicted Forbes's close friend, Dean Worcester.

Forbes passed on the documents to Pack, asking for an explanation. Pack responded with a lengthy, blistering report discrediting Penningroth's allegations, and asserted that his instructions were "carried out perfectly by my Lieutenant-Governors and that the cases of insubordination, if any, which occurred, are such as he himself [Bandholtz] can handle without reference to any other bureau than his own."[6] Pack's report was clear—his bureau was in order, and Bandholtz should look to his own house. But Pack's assertions were wrong: Early refused to respect the chain of command, Hale allowed close to one thousand civilians to accompany him, and lawless acts decimated Kalinga villages.

Pack also disparaged Penningroth's report because it included alleged exaggerations such as the burning down of Bacarri houses. Pack wrote, "These people have no houses, they are what we would term grass-shacks. . . ." Additionally, it was "ridiculous" for Penningroth to underline this part of the report with a red pencil.[7] At the end of his extensive response, he argued that Hale's effective rule included the confiscation of 262 guns from Kalinga villages. The report also included Hale's review of the Bacarri incident along with past letters (in Spanish) from lowland Filipino officials complaining about the recalcitrant Bacarri villages.

This did nothing to change the PC's stance on no longer accompanying Worcester's officials on military forays. They would have to wait for their boss's return from his trying congressional investigation. And when Worcester did return to the Philippines in the late spring of 1911, the last thing he wanted or needed was another crisis in which his authority and integrity were questioned. But that is exactly what he faced, and in his nasty state of mind he embraced the opportunity to go on the offensive. The result was a 102-page document that took Worcester seven months to compile. In it, he told Forbes that his delayed response was because he intended it to serve as a once-and-for-all indictment against the PC leadership, and Forbes would have to decide whether to support the secretary of the interior or the PC. Furthermore, Worcester traveled to Bontoc and Kalinga to investigate the situation.

While waiting for the report, Forbes himself traveled to Lubuagan during the first week of May 1911 and interviewed Hale. Four weeks later, on May 29, Worcester arrived in Bontoc to conduct his own inquiry. He was furious about the situation, and it became evident that his anger was directed toward Early.

On Wednesday, May 31, Worcester traveled from Bontoc to Lubuagan to meet with all the subprovince's headmen for a large cañao. It had been four months since the Bacarri campaign, and Hale made it clear to the Bacarri headmen that they had to show up in Lubuagan to present their side of the story to Worcester. The Bacarri elders traveled to the cañao, and an unnamed stenographer recorded the interactions. Hale began the conference by addressing the Bacarri men in their own language: "I am going to tell the Secretary of all the things we have done and the trouble we have had between us."[8] The lieutenant governor described the ugly history between his administration and the recalcitrant Bacarri villages, dating back to his initial days in Tabuk when they twice prevented suppliers from reaching American officials. He stated that he had twice traveled to Bacarri seeking to make peace but was subsequently shot at and had spears thrown at his party. Hale claimed he had no other choice but to make war on the Bacarri villages, and he detailed his destruction of the villages, confessing that he burned homes and killed men and women. He acknowledged that his men had stolen everything of value from the villages, and he was ready to return some of their blankets and jars. He also returned the jawbone of a beheaded Bacarri woman. He ended his speech by saying that Worcester would now speak to them, after which they could respond.

Worcester began by apologizing for not being the strong man he used to be so that he himself could not travel to Bacarri. He noted that he was aging and had become so important that he didn't have the time he needed to visit Kalinga. But he was unapologetic about the Bacarri massacre: "We have had a little trouble with you this last year and it was your fault. I understand that you said you wanted to have a fight. We don't thing [sic] very much of fighting. We don't get very much fun out of it, but you can always get a fight with us if you want it badly enough; if you insist on having it, if it does you any good. Now we have just had a little fight. Did it do anyone any good? So far as I can see it didn't do you any good. You lost some of your houses and things, and it seems that [men, women, and children] were killed."[9] He warned that the US had canons that he could bring to Kalinga that could shoot from one mountain to another, and "we could bring ten thousand men up here, if needed to, to stop trouble."[10] When he had finished, he invited the Bacarri men to speak. The two-sentence response from the Bacarri representative was: "We are afraid to do any more fighting. We will not fight anymore."

Worcester's blunt reply characterized his foul mood: "All right. We will do all we can to get over the trouble which we have had. These things which we are getting back to you we do not have to return. We give them back simply to show that we are friendly. You could not take them away from us. We have got them. We could keep them if we wanted to but we do not want to."[11]

Worcester was back in Bontoc on the evening of June 6, and he fired Early three days later. But he was just getting started developing a written response to the PC complaints about Hale. Finally, on Friday, October 6, 1911, Worcester sat down to type his lengthy report to Forbes, which proved more didactic than informative. He began by defending Hale's actions and reviewed every aspect of the Bacarri campaign with the repeated line that the end justified the means. He then asked the governor-general whose side he would take, Worcester's or the PC's: "Are the officers and men of the Philippine Constabulary to be required to cooperate with the Governor and the Lieutenant-Governors of the Mountain Province, or are they to be allowed to carry out the idea that the military must rule or remain ineffective?"[12]

While defending Hale, Worcester described how the PC despised his lieutenant governors because the military was so ineffective in Kalinga. He rhetorically asked, "Now what are the facts?" He pointed out that Hale had confiscated more guns in one year from the Kalinga region than the PC had in Bontoc and Kalinga during the previous decade. He then ended the report's introduction with a multipage condemnation of Penningroth and Early. If anyone deserved reprimand, it was the whistleblower himself. What was Bandholtz doing about his men who refused to take orders from a superior officer? As for Worcester, he had already disciplined his rogue official, ending his report with these harsh words: "I need hardly invite your attention to the insubordination subsequently shown by Lieutenant Penningroth who flatly disobeyed orders from Captain Harris, nor to that displayed by Lieutenant-Governor Early, who flatly disobeyed the written orders of Governor Pack and whose resignation from the special Government service has since been had at my request."[13]

Forbes received Worcester's lengthy report during the first week of October 1911, but it took him three months to reply. His brief, four-paragraph January 12, 1912, response was diplomatic, if not patronizing. He reminded Worcester that he had personally investigated the matter, even traveling to

Lubuagan to receive a firsthand account from Hale. He agreed that Hale had done nothing wrong and praised him as a model officer who used "a great deal of tack and force and that his handling of the situation has been more or less admirable."[14] Forbes also assured Worcester that he had written a directive to the PC officials requiring that they support the lieutenant governors on all future expeditions. Regarding Taylor's report, Forbes agreed that it was dangerous to let hordes of Kalinga warriors go to war with each other. Worcester himself indicated as much in past communications. Thus, Taylor and Worcester were on the same page after all. Finally, if there were any PC personnel who harbored sour attitudes toward Worcester and his men, "the quicker the officers concerned give it up or leave the service, the better."[15] To emphasize this point, the last sentence of his response read: "Penningroth has been let out of the constabulary."[16]

Worcester was unhappy with the governor-general's response, because he believed Forbes tried to mislead him with the news of Penningroth's reported dismissal from the PC. He wrote Forbes that this was the second time he had been told Penningroth had been disciplined and fired, and that it was a lie. For despite his heavy schedule and overflowing portfolio, Worcester investigated Penningroth's so-called dismissal. He learned that Penningroth had turned in his resignation on January 1, 1911, a full week before the expedition began. Additionally, Taylor accepted the resignation and wrote on January 17, 1911, while Penningroth was disobeying direct commands from Hale and Harris, that Penningroth "stands superior to all the young officers who have entered the service in this district during the past two years and his departure will be a distinct loss to the service. His services has [sic] been honest and faithful and of the superior class."[17]

When Worcester received this information, he wrote this memo to his agent, which he knew Forbes would read: "I was particularly desirous of having the record in this case [Penningroth's January 1, 1911, resignation] because I was verbally informed [by Forbes] that Lieutenant Penningroth had been dismissed from the service because of certain facts as to his record which happened to come within my personal knowledge."[18] Penningroth, on the other hand, was about to live his dream. He did indeed submit his resignation on January 1, 1911, to be put in effect nine months later. He may have willingly disobeyed orders to participate in Hale's massacre because he both respected his friend Early and was also on his way out of the constabulary. Taylor accepted Penningroth's resignation and responded with the kind words, "'Your work during two years has been of the highest order; your deportment and conduct are an example which many a man older than yourself could well imitate.'"[19]

Penningroth arrived in New York on September 12, 1911, and thirteen days later began law school at Harvard University. He graduated, passed the bar, and by 1914 had joined the Redmond & Stewart Law Firm in Cedar Rapids, Iowa. He became a senior partner in a firm that argued eighty-one cases before the Supreme Court between 1915 and 1937. Between 1924 and 1932 he also served as the city attorney for Cedar Rapids and won the 1936 Republican primary for the US Congress. The man Worcester accused of not following direct orders ended his professional career as the associate government appeal agent in the selective service between 1943 and 1947 and then as a district court judge from 1950 to 1965.

The other players in the Bacarri affair lingered on in the Cordillera. Unlike Penningroth, their ambitions were tied to controlling portions of the Philippines, and Ivy League schools were the furthest thing from their minds. They all anticipated bright futures in America's Asian colony—except for Early. When he was fired, he was given one week to pack and leave the land of the Igorots. He had nowhere to go but back to Idaho, returning once again as a failed administrator. But just before his 1911 firing, he found himself in yet another professional quandary.

CHAPTER 16

Igorots on Display

After the Bacarri expedition, Early returned to Bontoc on Sunday, January 22, convinced of the campaign's complete success, at least for his part of the mission. He wrote that throughout the ordeal all the village inhabitants were very happy to see him and work with him. For the next month, he planned ambitious building projects that would mark 1911 as the "busiest year in construction work Bontoc has ever known."[1] Yet, just three weeks after the Bacarri campaign, he found himself in another administrative mess that eventually had local, national, and international repercussions—one in which the US president became involved.

The problem began with a simple February 3, 1911, letter from Richard Schneidewind to Governor-General Forbes that included this message: "I am writing to inform you that I am taking (50) fifty Igorrots from the Mountain Province for exhibition purposes in Europe."[2] Schneidewind also mentioned that this was the third occasion he was taking Igorots to Western fairs—in fact, it was his fourth. This instance, however, differed, as the destination was Europe and not the United States. Schneidewind's motive for exhibiting Igorots was financial, and most of the Igorots he previously recruited were from Bontoc. But this recruitment trip proved different because Early, Bontoc's new lieutenant governor, determined to stop foreign entrepreneurs from exhibiting Igorots as if they were uncivilized animals. He believed these spectacles denigrated the highlanders' human dignity, and he had witnessed how previous

Igorot exhibitions proved detrimental to the participants because some had been mistreated, mutilated, and robbed by their American sponsors. Furthermore, many Igorots who returned to Bontoc from American fairs found it difficult to reintegrate into village life. Still, his primary objection to Schneidewind's plan was that Igorots were not objects to gawk at, and he would not let Schneidewind take any Bontoc Igorots to Europe. Both men were determined to succeed, and the battle lines were drawn, not in some faraway sand hill but in the mud that carpeted the Igorot villages.

By 1911, Igorots were familiar with foreign agents who offered adventurous individuals an opportunity to travel across oceans to be displayed for mostly white crowds. The first major Igorot exhibition to the United States took place seven years earlier at the 1904 Louisiana Purchase Exposition, referred to as the St. Louis Fair.

In St. Louis, the Philippine exhibit encompassed forty-seven acres and included a wide range of displays, from forest products to the exciting prospects of Philippine mining and metallurgy. A Spanish-looking Manila house and Visayan town presented a society heavily influenced by Western civilization, and 280 PC soldiers projected a native population characterized by discipline and training. While celebrating the obvious trappings of civilized Filipinos in these exhibitions, the Philippine Commission, along with leading proponents of American imperialism, had to justify America's continued work and presence in a sophisticated Asian society. It was Kipling's "half-devil and half-child" Filipino that imperialists wanted to parade before millions in St. Louis.[3] So the hardcore imperialists brought the headhunting, dog-eating Igorots down from the mountains and across the Pacific to St. Louis. The plan worked to perfection.

Truman Hunt, the man chosen to bring the Igorots to St. Louis, was strikingly handsome, and at five-foot-eight, he was taller than most of the Igorots he governed. From an Iowa-based farming family, Hunt's innate ambition drove him off the farm. By his early twenties, he had earned a degree in medicine from the University of Iowa, and following his 1887 college graduation, he married Myrtle Potter, his childhood love. Together they had a daughter in 1892. But the elation of their first child was short-lived because Myrtle came down with the measles that eventually took her life in 1893. Hunt, emotionally unfit to care for his daughter, passed her on to his mother. He then spent two years in graduate school at New York City's Bellevue Hospital Medical College.

Ambition, restlessness, and the lingering pain of a widower's broken heart contributed to Hunt's decision to join the US Army during the Spanish-American War. He was instrumental in containing a cholera outbreak in Manila, and while working in the Philippines, he fell in love with a nurse named Else. Originally from Germany, she had moved to New York City when she was eighteen and studied nursing. They married on June 9, 1902, and a year later she gave birth to a son they named Philip because he was born in the Philippines.

In June 1902, Hunt was appointed lieutenant governor of Bontoc, and served in that role until the following May when he resigned. He then took on a new assignment to organize a group of Igorots for display at the St. Louis Fair.

When he was just a boy, Hunt's mother commented that her son could talk his way out of any situation, as he was described as pragmatic and constantly on the lookout for get-rich schemes. We do not know how forward-looking he was with regard to the Igorot exhibition, but it would lead him to wealth and prominence, and eventually land him in prison.

Hunt gathered 114 Igorots, more than half from the Bontoc area, and collected artifacts found in a typical Cordillera village. It took 200 cargadores to carry the material to the lowlands, where it was loaded onto steamships.

The Igorot display was by far the most-visited Philippine exhibit at the St. Louis World's Fair. It also surpassed all the other exhibits in earnings. It cost $8,441 to construct the village, while its gate receipts totaled $200,387.[4] By contrast, the Visayan village earned $55,909.[5]

The Igorot display presented several challenges for the fair administrators. First, the Igorot men wore their everyday clothing, which consisted of a loincloth. Many were offended by the exposure of the Igorot men's buttocks. Officials ordered Hunt to have the men wear short pants. Eventually, President Roosevelt settled the issue by ordering that the Igorot men take off the pants and wear their loincloths. The Fair's board of female managers supported Roosevelt, as they found no offense in the Igorots' style of clothing.[6]

Another aspect of the display was the Igorots' diet. Dog meat was considered a delicacy among some Igorots, and the American public exhibited both fascination and abhorrence for the Igorots' public killing, cooking, and eating of the dogs that were provided to them by officials. The daily routine of preparing a dog for slaughter and then cooking it, along with displays of scantily-clothed, spear-throwing Igorot men, provided a sensation that attracted hundreds of thousands. A characteristic response to the Igorots is seen in this man's letter to his wife, "'I went up to the Philippine village to-day and saw the wild, barbaric Igorots, who eat dogs, and are so vicious that they are fenced in and guarded by a special constabulary. . . . They are the lowest type of civilization I ever saw and thirst for blood."[7]

Hunt ably managed the Igorot village and also supervised a soft drink stand that introduced Americans to Dr. Pepper, a beverage that was a huge hit in Missouri's sweltering summer months. While he made money off of sugary drinks and the Igorots, he also caught the eye of Dean Worcester, who praised

FIGURE 7.   Igorots performing at the 1904 Louisiana Purchase Exposition in St. Louis, Missouri. Library of Congress H46128.

Hunt's management of the Philippine highlanders: "'Dr. Hunt thoroughly understands the handling of such people, and has, furthermore, demonstrated his ability and willingness to live up to his agreements relative to proper care and kind treatment of the peoples which he has been allowed to take and which he returned safely to their home.'"[8] Hunt was good—good at fooling people, including Worcester.

The Igorots spent the months of April to November 1904 in St. Louis, and were now on their way home. Five Igorots did not return as they had died from various causes, including exposure to the cold. Three of the deceased's brains were removed and sent to the US National Museum (which is now the Smithsonian Natural History Museum) to help anthropologists prove that the less civilized peoples' brains were different from those of "modern" humans.

As the manager of the Igorot village, Hunt's responsibilities included properly compensating the Igorots based on their signed contracts. But while they were in the US, he refused to provide the Igorots with their promised wages because he said that he would make full restitution once they reached Manila. When they arrived in Manila, Hunt withheld $4,000 (in today's money $115,000) and ordered that the Igorots be returned to their highland villages.

His deception went beyond money. While in St. Louis, he had met an attractive seventeen-year-old woman, Sara Gallagher. He swept the young woman off her feet, and she married him just days before he returned to the Philippines. He did not tell her that he was already married and that he had effectively abandoned his wife and son in a New York City apartment.

The economic success of the Igorot shows in St. Louis motivated Hunt to gather fifty Igorots in early 1905 and launch his Igorot Exhibit Company. He planned to bring this group to various US state fairs, even though several American officials remained suspicious of Hunt's character and motives. Lepanto-Bontoc's provincial governor, William Reed, learned in early March that Hunt was about to leave the Cordillera with the Igorots, and he promptly sent a telegram to Worcester noting that "the troubles which have arisen as a result of the St. Louis Exposition and [assertions by] Igorottes that they have not received all their money indicate what might be expected from a private enterprise."[9] While a cursory investigation of these charges ensued, Worcester dismissed Reed's concerns, and Hunt was off and running with his Igorots in tow, arriving in Seattle aboard the *Empress of China* on April 19, 1905. But Hunt was not alone in displaying Igorots; his new competition came from Schneidewind.

When Richard Schneidewind was born in 1876 as the third and last child of German-born Karl and Minna Schneidewind, the family was just settling into American life in Detroit, Michigan. At twenty-one years of age, he joined the US Army, less than two months after the US had declared war on Spain. He boarded a US transport ship along with thousands of other Americans and steamed across the Pacific in time to participate in the first Philippine-American battles. But he spent his entire Philippine tour in an army hospital off Manila on the island of Corregidor, not as a caregiver, but a patient. While crossing the Pacific, Schneidewind contracted typhoid, and it took months for him to recover. Upon his July 1899 release from the army, he chose to remain in the Philippines, and sought work in Manila.

He married a Filipina, Gabina Dionicio Gabriel, on March 7, 1900. Nine months later, on December 16, 1900, Gabina gave birth to Richard Schneidewind Jr., but she tragically died just a few days afterward. Bereft of his love and with a newborn child to care for, Schneidewind leaned on Gabina's family for emotional and parenting support. He found employment in the colonial post office but was caught trying to circumvent export laws. In 1907, several years after his dismissal from the postal service, the case was explained in a report: "'About the latter part of 1901 the Schneidewind referred to was employed for some months as a clerk in the Manila Post Office. He was dismissed from that service, one of the charges against him being complicity in a smuggling scheme. . . . My recollection is that Schneidewind did not deny the charge.'"[10]

Following his firing he returned to the US, but his experience in the Philippines led him to the St. Louis Fair in 1904, where he found employment as a cigar stand manager as well as a supply officer for the Visayan village. Like thousands of others, he was impressed with Hunt and the Igorot exhibit, and he resolved to travel to the Philippines, create a touring Igorot company, and get rich producing Igorot shows.

Schneidewind paid for twenty-five Igorots to travel to the US in 1905, where they became an attraction at Portland, Oregon's Lewis and Clark Exposition. From Oregon, they traveled to Chutes Park, an area in downtown Los Angeles that also included a baseball park for the Pacific Coast League baseball team, the Los Angeles Angels. His treatment of the Igorots proved exemplary, and he looked the part of a charismatic, self-assured manager. Impeccably dressed in white linen suits, the trim, handsome Schneidewind supported a bushy mustache that covered both his lips yet remained very well trimmed. His inability to communicate with the Igorots in their language led him to hire Antero, one of Bontoc's most promising young men, to serve as his interpreter.

During May 1906, Schneidewind brought his Igorot group to Chicago, where they set up a village. Selma Eicholz, an employee at Riverview Park that housed the Igorots, caught Schneidewind's eye, and despite their twelve-year age difference, they became romantically involved. While in the midst of this budding relationship, Schneidewind learned that Hunt and his Igorots were holed up on Chicago's south side, staying underneath the rollercoaster of Sans Souci Amusement Park. When Antero, Schneidewind, and a government-appointed inspector paid a surprise visit to Hunt and the Igorots, the three men stood in disbelief. Malnourished and filthy, the Igorots ran to Antero and embraced him, pouring out their complaints. For his part, Hunt remained unapologetic for the state of his employees, and it also became clear that his evading the police and stealing from the Igorots coincided with his greater indulgence in alcohol. Given the Igorots' physical condition and their squalid housing, the government transferred them to Schneidewind's care while Hunt escaped the law once again. In a long and sordid story, he was eventually apprehended, convicted of two counts of larceny for stealing the Igorots' money, and sentenced to eighteen months in the county workhouse. But a judge then overturned the convictions and a new trial was held that resulted in a mistrial. Truman Hunt was released.

Schneidewind remained in Chicago for several months, as did the Igorots under his management. His courtship of Selma heated up with the hot Chicago summer, and in the early fall of 1906, they slipped away and traveled to

Detroit to visit his family, including his five-year-old son Dick. On October 4, Schneidewind and Selma married and publicly noted that they were immediately leaving to accompany the Igorots back to the Philippine mountains. Schneidewind promised to bring the Igorots to Detroit in the future, but for now it was time to fulfill his contract and return to the Philippines. His promotion worked; the papers' headlines regarding the wedding read: "Honeymoon to Be Spent with Band of Philippine Savages."[11]

Schneidewind spent the next six months recruiting a new group of Igorots for tours at various US sites. Along with Antero, the Schneidewinds and forty Igorots arrived in the US in April 1907. Keeping his promise, Schneidewind brought the Igorots to Detroit, and while there Selma gave birth to Carl Schneidewind. He kept his contractual agreement, and in the spring of 1908, he paid for the Igorots to return to Bontoc.

Perhaps fearing that American audiences were growing weary of the Igorots, Schneidewind turned his professional attention to Europe. Partnering with Captain Baber, an employee of Paris's Magic City amusement park, Schneidewind returned to the Cordillera along with his family to collect a group of Igorots. Antero would once again be lead interpreter, and they were now going to go to Europe. But Lieutenant Governor John Early brought the enterprise to a screeching halt, causing a domestic and international crisis.

CHAPTER 17

Schneidewind Meets His Match

Schneidewind knew there was growing opposition to his exposition shows. Bishop Charles Brent, the most respected American in the Philippines, began a campaign against putting Igorots on display for American entertainment. After Hunt's debacle with his Igorot troop, Brent wrote a pointed letter to Governor-General James Smith, imploring him to curb the practice of overseas Igorot shows.

Brent's character brought him well-deserved respect and affection, not only in the Philippines, but also around the world. His subsequent career after his time in the Philippines included the position of head of American chaplains in the European theater during World War I. He graced the cover of the August 29, 1927, *Time* magazine as he presided over the first World Conference on Faith and Order, held in Lausanne, Switzerland. He was unanimously voted the conference's president—quite a feat given that there were more than four hundred ecclesiastical leaders from scores of denominations at the meeting. Thus, his opinion carried some weight, and he was a vocal opponent of human exploitation.

Brent resolved to do even more to protect the Igorots from external exploitation. Early, his close friend, joined in that commitment, and together they sought to stop Schneidewind's practice of showing Igorots to curious gawkers. Schneidewind knew that Brent opposed the use of Igorots at fairs. He noted in his February 3, 1911, letter to Forbes that "I can expect no cooperation on the part of the Government in this matter, still I am writing this in order to avoid any appearance whatsoever of surreptitious action on my part."[1]

Unlike Hunt, Schneidewind demonstrated professionalism and transparency in his work with the Igorots and colonial officials. Forbes's pithy response to Schneidewind ended with the sentence: "There is no law under which the Government can prevent able bodied and able minded persons from going where they please."[2]

Encouraged by this answer, Schneidewind began the familiar trip to Bontoc on a steamboat to Tagudin. The sleepy town on the edge of the South China Sea, populated by Ilocano lowlanders, remained the launching pad into the mountains. Disembarking at Tagudin, Schneidewind enjoyed the warm hospitality of Amburayan's lieutenant governor, A. V. Dalrymple.

On his way to Bontoc, Schneidewind rested at Cervantes, the gateway into the Cordillera and about 40 miles from his destination. He was surprised to find a telegram from Dalrymple waiting for him—what did he need to say that he couldn't have communicated in Tagudin? The telegram turned out to be a friendly warning about what awaited the entrepreneur in Bontoc: "You will probably meet with opposition on your attempts to bring out the Iggorots."[3] Wondering how to respond to this friendly alert, Schneidewind decided brevity was in order and simply answered with one sentence: "Thank you kindly for your message, but we are acting under letter from Governor General Forbes."[4]

The trail from Cervantes to Bontoc was marked by steep inclines and declines, but it was familiar terrain for Schneidewind, and he arrived anxious to meet Lieutenant Governor Early. Their initial meeting did not go well. After Schneidewind's friendly greeting, he presented Forbes's letter, and Early responded by saying that he agreed with Bishop Brent and believed it was unethical to display Igorots. Schneidewind knew that the brewing political storm was about to erupt into a hurricane. His first major clue of Early's steadfast recalcitrance came when Antero met up with Schneidewind. Their normally warm greeting was dampened by more immediate problems. While in Tagudin, Schneidewind had sent a message that Antero should bring some horses and meet him in Cervantes. But neither Antero nor the horses met him, and so he traveled on to Bontoc, wondering why no one showed up. When they met in Bontoc, Schneidewind asked him, "Why didn't you bring the horses to Cervantes?" Antero responded that as he was about to leave Bontoc, Early found out about his connection with Schneidewind and told him that he would be detained if he assisted the entrepreneur. Furthermore, Early employed Antero as his lead assistant in the provincial census, and Early requested that he concentrate on that project.

To Schneidewind's credit, he remained calm after hearing this and returned to Early's office. He was cordially welcomed back, but Early reminded him that he intended to block any effort to take Igorots out of Mountain Province. Again, the entrepreneur produced the letter from Forbes granting him permission to take any Igorot over sixteen years old who wanted to travel abroad. After carefully rereading the letter, Early replied that he would contact the colony's attorney general and that they could continue the conversation the following morning.

Wasting no time, Early sent a message to George Rogers Harvey, the Philippines' acting attorney general. His response to Early's message was quick and to the point: "To Early, Lieutenant Governor, Bontoc. Article 489 Penal Code still effective. The exhibition of Igorrots for profit not in violation paragraph two thereof. Children must be under 16 not descendants of employers and employed in performances of character mentioned in said paragraph. (Sgd) Harvey."[5]

The next morning Early showed Harvey's response to Schneidewind, who responded that he would begin collecting Igorots for Europe. But to his great surprise, Early said, "Well you have beaten me on that but I shall use other means to prevent you from taking the Igorrots, if possible."[6]

Remaining calm, Schneidewind asked Early why he was so vehemently opposed to giving Igorots the right to choose how to live their lives. Early responded that "they are worthless" when they return from the West. As if playing a chess game, Schneidewind anticipated this response and countered with solid data that clearly disproved that thesis. He and Antero had spent the previous evening interviewing Igorots who had participated in Western exhibitions to see how they were getting along. He told Early, "[I] found that the Igorrots who had been to the States instead of living in Igorrot houses, were living in Christian houses, eating from dishes and were all well to do, not a single one of them ever having a jail sentence." He claimed that when he brought forty-two Igorots to the US, they returned with forty thousand pesos in earnings, which provided them a brighter economic future than they would have ever imagined. He strengthened his position by saying that Early himself had said that Antero "is the only one capable of doing" the census work. How then could Antero, who had spent more time in the US than any other Igorot, be called worthless?

Early appeared to relent and said, "Well, I guess you are right and if you will take the same Igorrots you had before I guess we can arrange it all right." At this point, Antero dropped out of the picture, as he feared the repercussions of going against the government. Schneidewind found an assistant in the young Bontoc man Bugti, who had been a part of Schneidewind's 1906–1907 troop, and he paid him a peso a day to gather those Igorots who had previously traveled to the US.

Bugti barely got past the town of Bontoc when he was arrested for failing to pay the road tax. He was confined to the local jail and sentenced to thirty days of imprisonment. With Bugti in jail and with Antero leading the provincial census program, Schneidewind found it impossible to find Igorots for the European fair. When Schneidewind learned that the charges against Bugti were false, he confronted Early with documents proving that the incarceration was illegal. Early responded that there must have been a misunderstanding. He claimed that Bugti was arrested for impersonating a colonial official because he reportedly implied that he was recruiting Igorots on behalf of the US government. Asking if he might meet with Bugti about this charge, he was told that he would have to return the following morning during visiting hours.

The heavy dew that Bontoc's high mountains paint on the grass, trees, and rice stalks was still visible when Schneidewind dressed and headed to Early's office the next morning. As he walked toward the office, he spied a piece of paper nailed to the office door, which was not a good sign. The brief message contained a public notice alerting all interested parties that visiting hours for prisoners were cancelled for the next seven days. Furthermore, the lieutenant governor had left Bontoc on official business and would return in the late afternoon.

Later that day, Schneidewind caught up with Early and asked him if there was any way he could see Bugti and clear up the misunderstanding. Early said that he would accept a one-thousand-peso bond (an exorbitant amount for that time and place); otherwise, Schneidewind could wait five weeks until the appointed colonial judge arrived in Bontoc to hear cases. This flummoxed Schneidewind. While outwardly calm, he exclaimed that there were 130,000 people in the Bontoc area, and he was only looking for a few individuals who would be interested in traveling abroad for a brief period. He promised that he would not take any Igorots connected with Bontoc's public or private schools. Finally, if any of the Igorots owed the government money, he would pay those debts as well as provide an advance on the road tax.

Early seemed to agree to this, and Schneidewind noted that "[Early] was very much pleased with the way we were acting in the proposition and that he believed the matter could be adjusted satisfactorily." Confident he had cleared the last political hurdle, Schneidewind visited Bontoc's government-run store and purchased items he would use and sell at the foreign exhibitions, such as handcrafted baskets, spears, shields, and axes. He brought these articles to his room at the rudimentary Bontoc hotel.

As evening came on, he was more optimistic than he had been in a long time about his future. Though venturing into relatively new territory in

Europe, how could those fairs be that much different than the ones in America? Anyway, the novelty of displaying scantily clothed wild men was wearing off in the US and Europe. But he was especially pleased that his diplomatic skills had moved the seemingly intransigent Early to allow Igorots to leave Bontoc. While thinking these things over, he was summoned to the hotel's lobby—Early wanted to speak with him. Flanked by several provincial police, Early informed Schneidewind that he would not allow any Igorot to meet with him, and so he was going to post guards at the hotel. Incredulous, Schneidewind responded that he was wasting the guards' time because he would not interview the Igorots at the hotel. But the guards were not just for the hotel; they were to follow Schneidewind everywhere, making sure that he could not recruit anyone.

The next morning, Schneidewind found Early and told him he had only one question for him: "[I] asked him [Early] if there was any way in which the matter could be arranged." Early said no and that it was useless for him to make requests to take Igorots out of Bontoc. He noted that the secretary of the interior publicly said, in the hearing of US Secretary of War Dickinson, "that the lieutenant governor was the law, that he could make laws at any and all times to suit the convenience of the office." In short, there was no authority in Bontoc to whom Schneidewind could appeal.

Pondering these implications, Schneidewind asked Early, "Well, Governor, if you make a law today and we find that we can satisfy that law, what would you do?" Without missing a beat, Early replied, "I will change it tomorrow. I have determined that you cannot take these Igorrots, [and] that I will arrest every Igorrot attempting to leave the province . . . On a Vagrancy charge, if nothing else." Word traveled fast in Bontoc, and Early's threat to arrest Igorots accompanying Schneidewind scared away every potential recruit. Early had also sent municipal police to the surrounding barrios to instruct the populace to stay clear of Schneidewind.

In this war of wills, Early clearly won the first major battle. He stood his ground, established his authority, and acted as a guardian of the Igorots. It did not seem to cross his mind that the Bontoc people were able to determine their own future. Like Bishop Brent, he believed that foreigners were subjecting the Igorots to humiliation for selfish economic gain. If only Early could have seen what would eventually happen to the Igorots in Europe, he would have fought even harder to keep them in Bontoc. And if Schneidewind would have seen the future, he would have immediately quit the war of words and wills and sprinted away from the Cordillera. But he did not have a crystal ball, and he had not risen to economic prominence by backing down from a fight. While he may have lost the first battle with Early, the war between them had only just begun.

CHAPTER 18

New Players, New Problems

As Schneidewind packed to leave Bontoc, he made a final request to the lieutenant governor: Could he spare half a dozen cargadores to carry the items he purchased from the government store? Though not one Igorot signed up for the European trip, he was stuck with scores of weapons and handicrafts that the store manager refused to buy back. Early replied that there were none to be had, but he would allow five municipal police to help carry the purchased items to Cervantes and then Tagudin for free.

One indispensable consolation Schneidewind enjoyed throughout the week's tribulations in Bontoc was that he was not alone. His partner, Captain A. M. Baber, was with him, and continued to encourage Schneidewind not to give up.

Baber and Schneidewind had anticipated potential obstacles, and so before journeying to Bontoc they had hired the Manila-based law firm of O'Brien and Dewitt, just in case they encountered problems. Consequently, before they left Bontoc empty-handed, Schneidewind sent a telegram to their lawyers succinctly laying out their predicament: "Lieutenant Governor says he will order arrest every Igorrot leaving Bontoc with me charging vagrancy. Wire advice."[1]

Manila is hot and humid in March, and the last thing these two lawyers needed in 1911 was a grueling case in faraway Bontoc. But like their clients, they would not back down from a fight. After receiving Schneidewind's telegram, they went to Thomas Carey Welch, the acting executive secretary in the Philippines, to complain about Early's recalcitrance in the face of Forbes's express permission for Schneidewind and Baber to recruit Igorots. Welch agreed that Early was obstructing justice, and they should tell their clients that they were free to take Igorots out of Bontoc. Clyde DeWitt immediately telegraphed Schneidewind, who was still in Bontoc: "Go ahead bring Igorrots out at once. See letter [by Welch] Executive Secretary wired this morning no right to interfere. Shall I come? DeWitt."[2]

Unbeknownst to Schneidewind and Baber, DeWitt had already decided to travel to Bontoc and reiterate in person the colonial government's stance to Mountain Province officials. Meanwhile, Baber and Schneidewind left Bontoc hoping to make it to Cervantes, the halfway point to Tagudin, by evening.

Cervantes was in the subprovince of Lepanto, and its lieutenant governor, William A. Miller, met Baber and Schneidewind as they entered the town. He told them that he would enforce Early's directives and also informed them that DeWitt was on his way to Bontoc, and he intended to detain the lawyer in Cervantes. Armed with this information, Schneidewind rushed to the town's telegraph office to tell DeWitt what awaited him and to stay away. While sending the telegraph, the system suddenly went dead, and the operator said the wires must have been accidentally cut. Schneidewind refused to leave until the wires were fixed, but after four hours of waiting, he gave up. The operator returned the sending fee to Schneidewind, and Baber convinced him that that they should start for Tagudin. Much to their chagrin, they noted that right after they left Cervantes the wires began working again.

In Tagudin, DeWitt and his clients mapped out their next moves. They knew that Governor Pack was visiting the PC's senior official, Colonel Taylor, in San Fernando, just 40 miles south along the coast. Baber decided that he would visit the two most important officials of Mountain Province to see if they could resolve the impasse between Early and Schneidewind. He arrived in San Fernando and received a sympathetic hearing, but was told that the problem would have to be solved in Manila by the governor-general.

The next day, Baber traveled to Manila and met with Sheldon O'Brien. As he entered the law office, he received the first piece of good news since his arrival in the Philippines. O'Brien had already called upon Governor-General Forbes and explained the illegal obstruction that his officials, particularly Early, placed on the freedom of Igorots to travel abroad. Anxious to resolve a potential lawsuit against his government, Forbes sent the following telegram to Early on February 23: "You have no right or authority arbitrarily to restrict freedom of contract or peaceful movement of Ingorrots [sic] or to prevent their leaving province. Rescind all orders infringing their rights and release all that may have been arrested in connection Schneidewind matter against whom un-doubted bona fide case of infringement of Penal Laws cannot be made out."[3]

Baber communicated this favorable turn of events via telegram to DeWitt and Schneidewind. The two men returned to Bontoc, and within a few days they had gathered fifty-four Igorots, though Antero was not one of them. Without his reliable interpreter, Schneidewind turned to another excellent Ig-orot linguist he had worked with in the past, the nineteen-year-old James Robert Amok. Identified as one of the "most Americanized of the *nikimalika* (as the Igorrotes who exhibited in America were known at home)," Amok's first and middle names were most likely given to him by the Americans who employed and educated him in Bontoc.[4]

James Amok was reportedly born on June 25, 1894, and as a teenager he worked with the missionary Walter Clapp, on an Igorot-English and English-Igorot dictionary. In his acknowledgment, Father Clapp noted his "great obli-gation [to James Amok who] assisted me by furnishing materials for this volume."[5] By 1911, Amok was certainly one of the most proficient English translators among the Igorots. Stocky and five-foot-three, he was also noted as an excellent marksman with a spear. He would eventually be a decorated World War I hero for the US.

Amok gathered the Igorots within a matter of days, and they passed their interviews with Schneidewind and DeWitt. Finally, on Tuesday, February 28, they sent a promising telegram to Baber, who was waiting for news in Ma-nila: "Ingorrots left this morning. Expect to arrive Tagudin March 1st at night."[6]

Baber sprang into action and bought tickets for the Igorots to travel to Eu-rope on the *Kioto*, as well as bedding and clothing for the trip. He also char-tered the small steamboat *Don Carlos* to transport the group from Tagudin to Manila. Finally, all signs pointed to a peaceful resolution after two and a half weeks of frustration. But though the Tagudin days were warm and bright and typhoon season was months away, a political hurricane was about to hit Schnei-dewind and DeWitt, beginning with their arrest.

CHAPTER 19

Early's Last Stand

"Conditions rotten. Every possible obstacle being thrown in our way. Cervantes quarantined no sickness. We go to Candon. They threaten arrest for employment of minors."[1] Baber and O'Brien were shocked to wake up to this March 1 telegram from DeWitt. What could have gone so wrong from twenty-four hours earlier? They had just chartered the *Don Carlos* in Manila to pick up the Igorots, but now they were unsure what to do.

Early and Miller had not given up their quest to keep the Igorots from European exhibitions. As Schneidewind's Bontoc group approached Cervantes, word reached them that Miller had quarantined all those who entered the town. Knowing that this would keep them trapped, they changed direction and took the more rugged trail to Candon, an Ilocano coastal town. But Early and Miller had their spies, and when they heard about this diversion, they sent police officers to arrest Schneidewind and bring him and his group into Cervantes.

They charged Schneidewind with abduction, and the Igorots were ordered to return to Bontoc, where they would serve as witnesses. DeWitt, the only free individual in the group, communicated all this to his colleague in Manila, and he ordered that they break their contract with the *Kioto* as they were paying one hundred pounds a day to keep it in Manila Bay. DeWitt also ordered his partner to send him money for mounting expenses. O'Brien responded that Early had already been warned that "he must avoid possible prosecution against himself."[2] Unfortunately, this warning did not curb Early's actions, so O'Brien sought out the governor-general, only to learn that he was in Mountain Province with Governor Pack.

Armed with this information, Baber telegraphed Pack, explaining the injustice of Schneidewind's arrest, and concluded the short message with this plea: "Can't the illegal prosecution of the Igorots and Schneidewind be stopped without resorting to law?"[3]

While waiting for a response from Pack, DeWitt sent a scathing summary of Early's actions to Secretary Welch. The telegram began by ridiculing Early's explanation for Schneidewind's arrest and the bogus quarantine of Cervantes. He ended it with these words: "[They] openly boast purpose [of] quarantine and Schneidewind arrest to delay us and threatens more obstacles. No unusual sickness. Quarantine only declared when our party approaching. Planned long before. Please impartial investigation."[4] Secretary Welch decided to resolve the issue in person.

Welch was hot, tired, and angry when he arrived in Tagudin, but he was encouraged that the telegraph line to Bontoc was functional and that Pack was in his office. Welch's telegram to Pack was in the form of a threatening question: "Shall I suspend Early and Miller?"[5] The message implied that Pack had failed to administer the law and was a poor supervisor over at least two of his lieutenant governors. If he would not take charge, Welch would. Ever evasive in this whole matter, Pack shot back a message to the colony's executive secretary: "I think they are acting legally but am no lawyer. Come and see for yourself."[6] Even Welch's appearance in Tagudin could not fix the problem, and so he sent a message to Bontoc demanding that Early and Schneidewind immediately leave Bontoc for Cervantes.

While waiting for their arrival (Early came alone the following day), Welch began a preliminary investigation and concluded "that all charges [against DeWitt and Schneidewind] had been trumped up."[7] He was, however, willing to hear Early's side of the story before making a final decision.

Arriving at 4:00 p.m., Early was given time to shower and have supper before the evening meeting commenced. Welch, Baber, DeWitt, Pack, Early, Miller, Kane, and Dr. Robinson (the provincial medical officer) were all present. Welch, Baber, and DeWitt represented both the political and legal authority to upend the careers of everyone else in the room, though it seemed that Mountain Province officials didn't care because they were Worcester's mavericks, and they resented outsiders telling them how to run their Igorot villages, towns, subprovinces, and province. Welch proposed a compromise: Would DeWitt withdraw his lawsuit against the officials if they would allow Schneidewind and Baber to take the Igorots out of Mountain Province? This was the crux of the matter. For more than a month the battle of wills between Early and Schneidewind centered on the highlanders. Early was convinced that the Igorots should not be displayed like animals in a zoo. For their part, Baber and Schneidewind believed that traveling abroad provided Igorots with remarkable economic opportunities. Furthermore, creating displays was their livelihood, and the laws protected their entrepreneurial business.

Early knew that Welch was acting in place of Forbes, and if he refused the compromise, he would likely be dismissed from office. But Dr. Robinson came to Early's rescue when he piped up and said that no deal could be made because one of the Igorots had a case of smallpox (though he could not produce this individual). Therefore, no Igorot could leave the mountains for the next fifteen days. Welch replied that if this was true, then no one in the room could leave the mountains for the next two weeks. This being the case, Welch said that he would send for a more senior health expert from Manila to verify Robinson's assertions. One observer noted, "On secretary Welch making this statement, the doctor jumped up and threw up both hands and said 'I raise the quarantine now.'"[8] DeWitt and Baber had won their case, and they recalled, "This closed the transaction, and the meeting adjourned, but Governor Miller, Early and supervisor Kane and the Doctor were very angry and left at once."

Before going to their hotel, Welch made it clear that no one was to go near Schneidewind's Igorots, who were camped just outside of Cervantes, or to impede Schneidewind, who was traveling from Bontoc with the remaining members of his group.

Pleased by the meeting's outcome, DeWitt, Baber, and Welch went to sleep confident that the issues were resolved and justice had prevailed. They also believed Schneidewind and the remaining Igorots would join them the next day, because he had wired them that he was on his way to Cervantes.

Americans are often surprised when they first sip Igorot coffee, as it is boiling hot, extremely strong, and flavorful. On Thursday morning, Baber, DeWitt, and Welch drank their coffee at 7:00 a.m. After breakfast, Welch left the group and began a horse ride toward Baguio. Baber and DeWitt continued drinking their coffee when a disturbing report got through to them: Kane and Robinson had ignored the previous evening's agreement and had lately ridden out to the Igorot camp. Both men wanted to dismiss the message; surely last night's agreement was clear. They had signed a piece of paper that included the promise that "no one should speak to the Igorots except Governor Pack and myself [Baber]." But they also knew how angry Kane and Early were about this.

Baber and DeWitt saddled their horses and rode out to the makeshift Igorot camp, only to find it abandoned. The only person in the vicinity was one of Early's policemen, who was supposed to guard the group. He sheepishly confessed that Kane and Robinson had roused the Igorots at sunrise and sent them back to Bontoc. To avoid meeting Schneidewind and his group of Igorots, Kane ordered them to take the long way around to Bontoc.

Without saying a word, DeWitt took off after the Igorots, while Baber returned to Cervantes and sent a message to Welch telling him to return. He then entered Lieutenant Governor Miller's office, where Pack was working. He recalled the confrontation: "[I] found Governors Pack and Early, Kane and the Doctor sitting in Governor Miller's office. When I entered the room they all laughed as they thought the joke was on me." Baber asked Pack if he recalled the settlement made the night before wherein Pack was supposed to take charge of the Igorots. Pack said no, he did not recall this arrangement, and at any rate, the Igorots told him [through Kane] that they did not want to go to Paris. Baber warned him that he had already recalled Welch, and the day of reckoning was upon them.

Baber returned to his hotel, but within an hour, Pack came calling. The prospect of Welch's return frightened him, and he told Baber that he had also sent a note to Welch telling him there was no need for the secretary to return. Several hours passed, and at noon Baber received a reply from Welch in which he said that Pack had renewed his commitment to assist DeWitt and Baber.

Together with Kane and Dr. Robinson, Pack and Baber rode to the Igorot camp, and to their surprise, they found that the Igorots had returned. DeWitt had successfully recalled them to Cervantes. Kane's mastery of the Bontoc language along with his self-assured rule had earlier convinced the highlanders to return to Bontoc, and so they were ashamed to see him. But it was DeWitt's skill as a lawyer that assured the Igorots he was the final authority as to whether they could travel to Europe. Pack then asked Kane and Robinson why they had interfered with Baber and Schneidewind's plans. Robinson claimed that he had found a sick man in the group and that it might be smallpox. "Very well," Pack noted, "Where is your sick man?" Kane and Robinson examined each member of the Igorot group before Robinson finally replied, "I guess he must have gone back." Pack then took charge and ordered all the Igorots to stay in camp and wait for Schneidewind and his group to join them. Finally, in the late afternoon, Schneidewind and Baber were reunited with the Igorots, and they made their way to Tagudin, where they boarded the *Don Carlos* just before midnight on March 12 and began their journey to Manila and then on to Marseille.

CHAPTER 20

Tragedy in Europe

Not much is known about the early months of the Igorots' participation in the Magic City Fair, but things quickly turned bad. Schneidewind was supposed to pay the Igorots five dollars a month, and for the first time, he began following Hunt's pattern of delaying payments, claiming that he had deposited the money in a London bank for safekeeping. He also sought more lucrative opportunities in England and in 1912 brought the Igorots across the English Channel to Brown's park at Earl's Court in London.

At the Earl's Court Exhibition, the Igorots built nineteen typical Bontoc houses, where they lived together. But the public did not flock to see them. Given their country's colonial past, Londoners had already had centuries of exotic primitive people to gawk at, and the Igorots were just the latest in that long line. So Schneidewind moved the Igorots to Ghent, Belgium, where they would be part of the 1913 Ghent Exposition. He convinced the tired and wary Igorots that this would be their last fair, and after more than two years in Europe, they would return to Bontoc on October 26, 1913.

Unfortunately for Schneidewind, his seven-month stay in Ghent proved a financial failure. Schneidewind claimed that the receipts were so paltry that they were "barely sufficient to pay the running expenses and food bills," and he had not paid the Igorots for over eight months.[1] At one point during the seven months in Ghent, he took half of the Igorots to Amsterdam in hopes of financial relief, but there, too, insufficient gate receipts reportedly doomed his plan. But that is not how the Igorots saw it. Amsterdam brought in a lot of money, and when they returned to Ghent, they asked Schneidewind for their salaries. When he refused their request, several Igorots found their way to Henry Albert Johnson, the American council officer in Ghent. They poured out their frustrations and claimed that not only had Schneidewind refused to pay their salaries, which were eight months in arrears, he also said that they would have to pay for their return tickets to Bontoc, which violated their original contract. When they told their boss that they did not have enough money for a return ticket, he drew up a new contract and promised that he would pay for their return after another year of touring in the US.

Johnson asked the Igorots if Schneidewind was still providing food and shelter for them, and they said yes. He then requested that they remain patient, and he promised to investigate their situation. Unlike Truman Hunt, Schneidewind would not run from the law, and he was relieved to meet with Johnson, who served as a mediator between the two parties. Johnson told Schneidewind that unless he could get the Igorots to agree to new terms and could guarantee that he would provide for their safe return to the Philippines, the US government would take charge of them. Several days later, Schneidewind met with Johnson and excitedly reported that twenty-six of the Igorots agreed that if he would pay "the sum of money respectively due each, not including arrears of salaries due, [they] would return to the Philippines at their own expense [from their savings], leaving their claims against Mr. Schneidewind to be settled at some later date."[2] The remaining twenty-nine Igorots agreed to sign another contract because they had not been as frugal as their colleagues and did not have sufficient funds to pay for their return tickets.

Johnson approved of these arrangements, and Schneidewind made good on his promise by purchasing the tickets (using the Igorots' money) with the Messageries Maritime, whose ship was to sail from Marseille to Hong Kong, at which point the Igorots would transfer to a smaller steamer for Manila. He also found a boarding house for the remaining Igorots in Merelbeke, a southern suburb of Ghent. Everything seemed to have worked itself out until Johnson received a cablegram from the US secretary of war inquiring about the status of the Igorots. Johnson must have wondered, where in the world had this come from? How could the US secretary of war have any knowledge about the Igorots in Ghent? But the situation had caught the attention of not just the secretary of war but also his boss, President Woodrow Wilson. For somehow the Igorots had typed and sent a touching letter to President Wilson.

Igorrote Village
Ghent, Belgium
Oct. 21, 1913

The President of the United States,
Our Father, I the undersign take hereby the liberty this my writing to show to the eyes of your Right Hon. Excellency to inform you the situation and the peril where your subjects are in. We are in hands of a man who take a liberty with our stupedness who doesn't know the law of the white people. The case is this your Excellency, we made an agreement with all aascorner [*sic*] the Governor of the Bontoc Province told us that he gave the privilege to Mr. R. Schneidewind for an Exhibitions in the continents. This he has to provide us for food, lodging, clothes and medicines and free fares to go back to the Philippine Islands including of salaries of five dollars each, paid every month. Now we have to claim of this gentleman eight months salaries not alone he stands in debt of some of the natives beside the salaries of more than two thousand of dollars. Any how I know sufficient of the law if two men sign an agreement and one of the two no difference which party break his agreement is no value no more for the other party. Worster still it will be for the man who took us from our native land promising us all luxuries and goodness only to blind us to go with him to try his luck, but not us; and now he sees that he is in a hole always goes deeper. Now he take the liberty with out unknowness with the law of the white people to compell us to follow him during the two and half years more extra till the San Francisco Exhibition is over and the business will be all right he will settle with us all our accounts. . . . When we were in London he told us to give our money to him and will put it in the bank for safety and so some of the natives gave him some money and he gave the receipts for their money. He said don't be afraid, if something might happen I have a property in America and in the Philippines. And even our fares for going back he will not pay. . . . Dear Excellency, our agreement two and a half years is gone and I know that the money to send us back is there in one of the English banks, I think Lloyd's Bank. So we ask you our Father to show your help and mercy to us, to save us out the hands of this man to give us back to our families and relations for support. This was the reason that we came abroad but we are disappointed, but help us to go back as our agreement is gone and that our disappointment will not come so far. There are fifty five us here men, women and children. We lost three men, one woman, and five children.

The reason we went straight to you Our Father because we can not get no help of justice to our American Consul in Ghent. When we went with our cases he sent us away with this result. The Consul told us yesterday that if our Master, Mr. Schneidewind, will left us we will be in a hole and the police will put us in jail. So better follow him till we come to Marsielle in France, then Captain will take us to the Philippines, but all the natives said that we better go to jail than follow Mr. Schneidewind because our two and a half years contract is finish, and what is the good to go with him, work, work, work, and no pay. The Ghent Exposition were we are in now will close next month, November 3, 1913, and we don't know what to do and where to go. The Consul is very good friend of Mr. Schneidewind and we can't get no help from them, they only told us we have to follow him. So we have to go to jail then when the Exposition is close as we better go to jail as we didn't come to go to jail, but we came to earn little money to support our families. Have mercy on us to send one of your men that you know, who knows about the law of European people to help us go home as we don't know where to go when the Exposition will be close. We hope that we don't ask your mercy goodness and help for nothing and that your heart really will be like a father loves his children, that is what we suppose and expect of your dear Father. Your true and unhappy children who are far from you and home unprotected in strange country.

Your obedient servants,

The Natives of Bontoc Province
Philippine Islands
James Amok
Ellis Tongai[3]

After President Wilson's office processed the letter, Brigadier General Frank McIntyre, the chief of the Bureau of Insular Affairs, wrote a personal letter to the newly appointed governor-general of the Philippines, Francis Burton Harrison. The document was the quintessential vindication of John Early, as McIntyre criticized those who permitted the Igorots to leave in 1911 while praising those who sought to protect them from the subsequent debacle. McIntyre closed the letter to his direct report with a clear directive: "The bureau will report results of the [Schneidewind] investigation requested of the State Department, but in the meantime, I would suggest that some action ought to be taken which will enable the Philippine government definitely to prevent the taking away of wild people from the Philippine Islands for exhibition purposes."[4]

While McIntyre wrote Harrison, he also reached out to Johnson demanding an up-to-date report on the Igorots and Schneidewind. This communication arrived immediately after Johnson and Schneidewind had come to an agreement on the treatment of the Igorots. When he cabled back the terms of the arrangement, Washington's response was swift and direct: "War Department will not approve twenty six Igorots remaining longer than period [of] their contract. Every effort should be made to have Schneidewind furnish transportation and live up to other provisions of contract failing in this you are authorized to arrange transportation of Igorots to Manila [Secretary of State, William Jennings Bryan]."[5]

Johnson told a stunned Schneidewind that the situation had made its way to the offices of the US president, secretary of state, secretary of war, and the chief of the Bureau of Insular Affairs. Their unanimous judgment was that all the Igorots should immediately be paid, and Schneidewind should keep his end of the contract and pay for their journey home. Johnson knew that the entrepreneur did not have the funds for any of these demands, so he told the financially broken Schneidewind that the Igorots were now the responsibility of the US government, and his business with these Igorots was over. Johnson put all the Igorots on a ship bound for the Philippines, bringing an end to a story that started with Baber and Schneidewind asking Early for permission to take Igorots to Europe. The Igorots returned to Bontoc in early 1914. That same year a law was put in place making it illegal to take Igorots to foreign fairs.

Part Four

Banishment, Politics, War, and Scandals (1911–1921)

CHAPTER 21

Early's Exile South

In his private papers, Early claims that his 1911 dismissal was based on his supervisor's hasty judgment. But Worcester's decision to fire him was not impulsive. He never respected Early the same way that he did Kane, Hale, Pack, and his other lieutenant governors whose managerial styles and racist views were like his own. By contrast, Early denounced Hale's slaughtering of Kalinga villagers, he refused to allow Kane's Chinese merchant to swindle Igorot cargadores with contraband alcohol, and he stood up to the governor-general himself in trying to protect Igorots from what became a heartbreaking debacle in Europe. In his massive 1914 volume *The Philippines Past and Present*, Worcester heaped praise on most of his lieutenant governors; Early was not mentioned. Both Olson and Kane record Worcester's antipathy toward Early, and Kane noted in an interview that "Worcester and Early were not on cordial terms. W- had E-, then in Bu of Ed, made Lt. Gov of [Amburayan]. A little later forces were to rendezvous at a certain place [Bacarri]. E's did'nt [*sic*] arrive."[1]

Given his prickly relationship with his boss, there must have been an element of relief for Early when he rode out of Bontoc on June 14, 1911. He had been in the Philippines five years, three to four years longer than he had intended. He arrived a schoolteacher and was leaving a lieutenant governor, though a disgraced one in the eyes of his superiors and colleagues. One consolation Early noted about his Bontoc departure was that the Igorots were "sorry to see me go and I believe their regret genuine."[2]

Early did not immediately leave the country, as he accepted the invitation of Bishop Brent and H. Otley Beyer to convalesce in Manila. Based on extensive subsequent correspondence, his monthlong visit with them produced deep friendships. All three wrote glowing comments about each other in private and public documents, and they all attained high-profile positions during the next two decades.

After five years of tension-filled professional work, Early decided he would take a leisurely journey back to the United States. He planned to leave Manila for Hong Kong and from there catch an ocean-crossing steamship to India. The small boat to Hong Kong barely made it to shore, as it was caught in what some consider the deadliest typhoon in the region's history. Almost 90 inches of rain fell within a week while mountainous waves threatened to sink the vessel.[3] Though passengers were told to stay below deck, the endless days of darkness in the boat's belly were too much for Early: "I could stand it no longer [and] I had myself lashed to a stanchion and let the water wash me clean."[4] The captain stripped the boat of all the wood possible to feed the boilers. Even so, the ship was seven days overdue when it crawled into Hong Kong.

From Hong Kong he journeyed through India, Egypt, Turkey, the Balkans, Austria, Switzerland, Germany, France, and England before arriving in New York. Early kept a detailed travel diary, and what stands out is, once again, his poignant criticism of Western imperial exploitation. He wrote about the great care Muslims gave the Hagia Sophia, and he praised their meticulous artwork. He also mentioned that it was the unsophisticated Western soldiers of the nineteenth century that had committed "all manner of un-Christian atrocities upon the Moslem population, candor compels us to ask when we hear of [current] Kurdish upheavals: Are we not being paid in our own coin?"[5] The poverty and unsanitary conditions in India and Egypt moved Early to question why Western powers did not do more to alleviate the degradation that their colonial policies created.

After spending a month in London, Early stepped onto the German-manufactured SS *Crown Princess Cecilie* and crossed the Atlantic, arriving in New York when the fall leaves were in full-color. He returned to the US with three immediate goals: employment, acquisition of his homestead, and marriage. Just days after his arrival, he paid two dollars to The Science Teachers and Employment Agency (STEA), which was headquartered in Boston, Massachusetts. Early began his application, dated November 21, 1911, by trimming four years off his age, listing himself as thirty-four rather than thirty-eight, the age he reached just ten days earlier. Nonetheless, his impressive credentials included employment as a school superintendent and lieutenant governor. His references included David Barrows, the soon-to-be president of the University of California, Berkeley; President O. E. Walker of the State College of Washington; and the influential sociologist W. G. Beach at the University of Washington. Early agreed to pay the agency five percent of his first-year salary and requested a placement on the Pacific Coast.

Early made his way to Washington, DC, where he completed all the necessary paperwork for the extension of his Idaho homestead contract. Prior to the fall of 1911, he had not traveled further east in the US than Missouri, and he enjoyed his East Coast tour, though he was anxious to return to Idaho.

Finally, Early's return to Minidoka initiated the final plans for his wedding. Everyone who knew Early was shocked by this seemingly sudden affair. There are no records of letters between Early and his fiancé during his years in the Philippines. But, in fact, just before he left the Philippines, he sent a note to his good friend Richard Campbell, who served as a judge in Mountain Province, telling him that he was shortly to be married to his sweetheart in Idaho. Campbell's response, dated January 12, 1912, sounded as if the wedding had already occurred: "I congratulate you heartily upon your marriage. You did the wise thing, and there are more of us that should follow your example."[6] Campbell wrote the note from Tagudin, not knowing that Early had just arrived in Idaho and that the wedding was still months away.

But Early had his eye on who he would marry before his 1906 departure for the Philippines. Recalling his first year in Idaho, one friend wrote to him, "I can't remember which one of your many former sweethearts you finally married so am uncertain whether it is the proper thing for me to convey my good wishes to your wife. I'll take a chance, however, even in the event that I don't know her."[7]

Her name was Wilhelmine Rhodes. Born in Helena, Montana, on December 8, 1883, her parents came from Virginia and slowly made their way West. Willa's older sister and only sibling Georgina was born in Missouri, a stopover her parents made on their way to Montana. In 1911, Willa was living in Heyburn, Idaho, with her mother and stepfather, Walter Pennington, a civil engineer. Georgina worked as a stenographer and had married in 1910, but Willa had not finished high school, so the best job available for her in eastern Idaho was as a telephone switchboard operator. Early knew the family well from his first days in Heyburn in 1905.

When Early returned to Idaho during the winter months of 1912, the couple chose April 30, 1912, for their wedding date. After a simple ceremony attended by a few friends, they had little time for a honeymoon, as they had made a momentous decision just before exchanging wedding vows.

In her late twenties, Willa stood five feet, three inches tall and was blue-eyed and auburn-haired. Her affable social skills made her the life of social gatherings. Her loud but charming laugh put even strangers at ease. Some noted that Willa, also called Billy, seemed to know secrets about everyone but kept them to herself. One secret that she and John kept until after their wedding was their decision to move to the Philippines. In fact, while he was putting in his teaching application with the STEA, he also wrote his friends in the Philippines asking if they could find him a new position somewhere in the islands. Not one of them encouraged him to return. A characteristic response from a former colleague was: "It does not seem that there is much future for the average American government employee in these Islands, and the sooner, therefore, that you can engage in some lucrative and agreeable occupation [in America] the better for you, and as I said before [,] the little that I can do will be done gladly and with all my might."[8]

Undeterred, Early convinced Willa that their future lay in the Philippines. Making haste to San Francisco, the Earlys booked passage on the Pacific Mail Ship *Korea*. Built in 1902, the SS *Korea* carried the Earlys across the Pacific, where John noted they enjoyed a relaxing honeymoon.

When they arrived in Manila in June, the only thing worse than the oppressive heat was Early's prospect of finding a good job. With the Democrats winning a majority in Congress in 1912 and the Republican ticket split between Roosevelt and Taft, the business-as-usual existence for colonial employees was in jeopardy—a dread that became a reality when Woodrow Wilson won the presidential election just five months after the Earlys' arrival in Manila. Adding to this professional hurdle was that it had been just a year since Worcester had fired Early. Forbes was still the governor-general and a close confidant of Worcester, who remained antagonistic toward his former lieutenant governor. Still, Early persisted and sought a job where he was evidently not wanted by the leading officials.

A biting insult among northern Luzon peoples is the Ilocano phrase *awan ti bain mo*, "You have no shame" (the Tagalog phrase is *wala kang hiya*). By returning to the Philippines, Early seemed to be a man who had no shame. Didn't he recognize that he was not wanted? Was he so desperate for a job that his only prospect was 7,000 miles away from his Idaho farm? His application with the STEA had surely produced offers. Few Americans had a resume that included a bachelor's degree and experience as both a superintendent of schools and a lieutenant governor. But something made him return to the Philippines. Perhaps it was to prove something to himself. He was almost forty years old and had little to show for making his mark in the world. As he reviewed his life, he saw that he had shared in the demise of his family brickmaking business; his get-rich scheme in the Klondike proved to be a fool's errand; his first postgraduate job resulted in his dismissal from the Almira School District; his bet on a newspaper business in Heyburn, Idaho, lasted less than a year; and he had been fired from his most significant professional job as Bontoc's lieutenant governor. If he returned to the Philippines because his previous years there represented his glory days, he was back for more. He found that his dreams would have to wait for ten years.

When Early arrived back in Manila, he visited the Department of Education and found that there might be some work for him in the central portion of the archipelago; someone wanted him away from Manila and the entire island of Luzon. Early was offered positions in the regions of Capiz, Romblon, and Negros Oriental. All three places were in the Visayas—the thousands of islands between Luzon and Mindanao. Economically challenged and often forgotten in national politics, the Visayas must have felt like exile for Early, but he flourished there for the next decade.

Between 1912 and 1914, Early served as a principal in a Capiz high school. Located on the northern coast of Panay Island, the sparsely populated province of Capiz was one of the first regions where Spain attempted to establish its permanent presence in the archipelago. Its capital, Roxas City, was on the coast, and the province's economy under Spanish rule was mainly coastal fishing because the inland was filled with dense jungles and swamps.

Early wrote that his immediate challenge in Capiz was to clean up his predecessor's mess. In particular, the classrooms were chaotic and there was an extremely undisciplined student population. He restored order using a firm and caring hand, and within two years his school was described as a "model of decorum."[9] Early's good work in Capiz was noticed by the colonial director of education, who then promoted him to superintendent of the entire province of Romblon in 1914. His new portfolio increased his administrative responsibilities as well as his personal and professional challenges.

Romblon was just north of Panay, and it was unique in that it was a small archipelago comprised of twenty islands. While the water and mountain barriers kept Early from easily overseeing all the province's schools and teachers, the greater challenge was the ethnic and cultural divides between Romblon's inhabitants. Populated by indigenous tribes, along with those Tagalog, Visayan, Bicalano, and various minor dialect speakers, the islands forced Early to grapple with his students' numerous cultures. Nonetheless, the director of education assigned him to supervise Romblon based on both his success in Capiz and his previous experience with Mountain Province's numerous cultural and geographical challenges. Word was getting out that Worcester had blundered in firing Early.

Early's big break after three years of semi-obscurity in the Visayas came in the form of an offer from his old friend, Bishop Charles Brent. During a 1913 visit to New York, Brent enlisted a good number of influential friends to establish an organization called Upbuilding the Wards of the Nation. Its focus was to educate and improve the infrastructure of the long-neglected inhabitants in Sulu, the islands between Borneo and Mindanao. Its elite board members included Admiral George Dewey, Mrs. Henry Cabot Lodge, Mrs. W. Emlen Roosevelt, Josiah Strong, Mrs. William H. Taft, and Major General Leonard Wood.[10]

With this support, Brent returned to the Philippines and tasked Reverend R. T. McCutchen with finding a suitable location for a college for the Moros, Sulu's largely Muslim population. Price not being much of an issue, McCutchen secured fertile land outside the city of Jolo in January 1915 and was pleasantly surprised by the numerous local volunteers who helped to build the new buildings.[11] Riding the wave of momentum on this project, Brent turned to the one man he knew who could bring the project together—John Early.

From his Manila-based office, Brent spent much of June 5, 1915, writing a five-page letter to Early. He got right to the point in the document's opening sentence: "I offer you the position of Superintendent of the Moro Agricultural School."[12] The position included a renewable five-year contract, a promised annual increase to his starting salary of $1,850, at least one-month annual paid vacation, and fully paid regular vacations to the United States. Brent told Early that the Moros eagerly anticipated the opening of the new college. He also hinted at how the job would forever place Early in the history books: "The work is unique. It is the first effort in history to do work of this sort among the Moros of Jolo. . . . The School will become just what you are capable of making it. You will be furnished with facilities necessary and funds for the prosecution of the work. There are no limits to the usefulness before us. I would look for the development of an institution as distinguished as Silliman Institute."[13]

This represented both a challenging and promising professional advancement for Early, so Brent was shocked that after Early's initial acceptance of the generous offer, he changed his mind and declined the position. Upon receiving this news, Brent replied in a letter, "It was a disappointment to receive your letter of Aug. saying that you would be unable to undertake the work at the Moro Industrial School in Jolo. I have counted on your ability to help us in this difficult and interesting task."[14] What was even more disconcerting to Brent was that Early revealed the dark secret that kept him from accepting the job—Willa was not well. She had not adapted to the rigors of the Philippines, and the isolation of Romblon had brought her mental state to the breaking point. Early hoped that by staying in Romblon rather than moving to the further frontier of Sulu, she would recover. Willa was relieved that her husband refused the Sulu job, but as the summer of 1915 progressed, she grew worse, until her mental state was untenable. Early explained all this in his letter to Bishop Brent, and Brent's gracious, sympathetic reply included the kind words: "Of course I understand what holds you back and appreciate your difficulty . . . [I hope] that your wife will soon recover her full vitality."[15]

But things did not get better for Willa. She did not care that the world was in chaos during that summer due to World War I; she had to find some peace of mind. She refused to stay in the Philippines and bought a one-way ticket to the US, leaving her husband alone in Romblon, their marriage now hanging by a thread. Once she made it to America, she retreated to her hometown of Butte, Montana.

As for John Early, he remained in Romblon, now alone with his Bontoc memories of glory to fill his evenings. In 1916, he and his fellow teachers were transferred from the Bureau of Education to the Classified Civil Service Employees due to new administrative codes. The window of opportunity for American employment as colonial educators was rapidly closing. There were 2,623 American compared with 6,363 Filipino government employees in 1913. Six years later these figures had dramatically shifted so that there were just 760 American and 12,047 Filipino employees.[16]

No correspondence between Willa and John during the two years of their separation survives, and he makes no reference to this in his memoirs. But there was some good news for the Earlys during their separation. Walter William Marquardt was appointed the Director of Education in the Philippines. Marquardt, a strikingly handsome Dayton, Ohio, native, first arrived in the Philippines as a rank-and-file teacher in 1909. He quickly climbed the professional ladder, to the point that he now held the colonial education system's top position. During his first years in the islands he made numerous visits to Mountain Province and highly respected Early's work ethic, hospitality, and care for the Igorots. It was time for Early to call in a much-needed favor. Though she had not yet graduated from high school, Early wondered whether Marquardt would extend a job offer to Willa, who had decided to rejoin her husband. She knew how to read and write. Could she at least be considered for a provisional job? Marquardt's response must have been positive, because in March 1917, Willa wrote to the Bureau of Insular Affairs requesting permission to travel to the Philippines on a government transport ship. The request was approved, and Willa left San Francisco on May 5, 1917, to try her hand again at her marriage and the Philippines, as well as a new profession.

Even before she was reunited with her husband, paperwork came through so she could take a job for which she was unqualified. Marquardt sent in an April 20, 1917, document appointing Willa a temporary teacher of domestic science with an annual salary of 2,000 pesos. Just a few months later, he revised Willa's salary to 2,400 pesos. But the next two years did not go well for her despite her acquisition of an enviable profession and salary. She learned that a title and salary did not automatically come with an educator's much-needed skill, disposition, knowledge, hard work, and experience. In April 1918, Early sent several of his Romblon teachers to the national teachers' conference held in Baguio City. This weeklong annual conference included sessions on pedagogy, curriculum, and other tips for more effective teaching. He sent his wife along with others who needed pedagogical improvement. But she never showed up for the training. Several of the Romblon teachers diplomatically wrote their boss from Baguio saying that they had last seen his wife in Manila, and she was not at the meeting. Willa was, in fact, failing in the classroom and once again losing her mental stability. While Europe was finally at the precipice of peace after four years of bloody fighting, she was lost. She could not stay in the classroom nor in the Philippines, and so she once again left her husband and returned to America in 1919.

Despite his personal crisis, Early's professional prospects were on the rise. In 1918, Marquardt appointed him superintendent of schools for the entire province of Negros Oriental. The fourth-largest of the more than seven thousand islands in the Philippines, Negros was divided into two provinces—Occidental for its western position and Oriental on the eastern side. Oriental was just a few miles from the island of Cebu, so Cebuano served as Oriental's main language, and the province was important for its sugar plantations. With its rich soil, importation of over five hundred carabaos (water buffaloes) from southern Vietnam, and two engine plows, just one town in Oriental produced over eleven million pounds of sugar in 1907.[17] Dominated by a handful of plantation owners, the island's immense gap between planters and workers was evident in the dilapidated schools, particularly schools near the plantations. Marquardt wanted this changed, and challenged Early to take control of the situation.

Early immediately recognized Oriental's immense educational challenges. He implored the planters to use their economic windfall brought on by World War I to support the province's educational infrastructure. Their wealth had dramatically increased because Europe's land that was formerly used for sugar crops was so decimated by trench warfare that between 1913 and 1920, the global sugar supply decreased by 20 percent. But the Negros hacienda owners had mostly used their increased income to import luxury automobiles for themselves, and they had not focused on the educational needs of the island's children.

Early surveyed the education system in Negros Oriental and concluded that the struggling high school in the provincial capital, Dumaguete, characterized the overall malaise most islanders felt toward schooling. The high school building, built in 1907, had not received any maintenance for ten years, and its second floor was demolished because it was unsafe. After more than a decade, it still did not have enough resources to offer a senior year of high school. Building on the economic growth of Negros, Early wrote, "This boom time furnished the golden opportunity for permanent improvements in schools. I seized the opportunity to build substantial concrete buildings wherever they were needed. . . . The planters in their generosity thought nothing of contributing into the hundreds of pesos for pianos, libraries and that sort of thing."[18] Local papers claimed that "Early exerted every effort to increase production in school gardens and agricultural clubs."[19] He approached a major planter for donations, and the landowner "signed a check for 170.00 [pesos] to purchase complete sets of textbooks" for twenty-one fifth-graders.[20] By 1921, every town in Negros Oriental had Early's imprint on its education system. This came to the attention of important colonial officials, further changing Early's professional trajectory.

Things were also brighter in his personal life. Willa once again stabilized mentally and physically and decided to give her marriage and the Philippines yet another chance. On January 22, 1920, Early wrote his Manila-based boss requesting transportation for his wife. On the US side of the Pacific, Willa wrote to their influential friend Marquardt, also requesting a US transport ticket to the Philippines. Marquardt had been promoted to the Washington, DC–based position of agent for Philippine public instruction, and his portfolio included choosing the applicants for Philippine assignments.

In Willa's initial letter to Marquardt dated March 16, 1920, she notes at the outset that she had been in the care of a specialist who helped her get back on her feet. She ended her letter with a fatalistic view of her impending return to the islands: "I have enjoyed the year in the States, but the call of the East is to be heeded after all."[21]

Willa sent a follow-up note, which was more personal and a bit more desperate in tone. In it she asked if Marquardt would give her another chance at teaching. She tacitly acknowledged her previous professional failures. While trying to regain her physical and mental well-being in Portland, Oregon, she had also attended Portland's Benson Polytechnic High School, and while she still lacked a high school diploma, she believed that if given another chance, "I feel certain I can carry on the work much more satisfactorily than before."[22] Marquardt lost no time in sending Willa a positive response; his respect for and debt to her husband still remained in his thoughts as he closed his letter to her: "The news you are returning to the islands makes me wish that I was going too. Be sure to give my very best regards to my old friends."[23] She was granted free transportation, and by May 1920 she was back with her husband in Negros Oriental. Marquardt provided her a temporary teaching appointment, as she still failed to qualify as a regular teacher.

Together again, and with John making significant progress building schools throughout Negros Oriental, life was good. But with the passage of each month, it was John who sorely felt the need for a change. In April 1922 he decided to retire and asked to be relieved of his responsibilities at the end of the school year. During the last days of June 1922, the Earlys said goodbye to their friends and colleagues and made their way to Manila. Their best, if not only, ticket back to the US was through the circuitous route of the Australia-Oriental shipping line. They boarded the SS *Changsha*, which took them to Borneo, Australia, New Zealand, Tahiti, and then to San Francisco. Early was certainly due for a break from the rigors of his profession. Out of the last 192 months, he had spent only 6 of them in the United States. He intended to make a final proof of his Idaho farm, buy 10 acres of farmland in California, and move to the Pacific Coast, but it was not to be. Even before arriving in the US, he was making plans for an immediate return to the Philippines, because he had received a letter from the new governor-general that would make his dreams come true.

CHAPTER 22

Changes in Mountain Province

Like the Spanish before them, American colonial officials claimed that the Igorots were a major reason they needed to govern the Philippines. Taft, Forbes, and Worcester—all Republican officials—shared this view, and they dominated Philippine politics from 1901 to 1913. They believed that the divide between the Philippine lowlanders and highlanders was so wide that a forced amalgamation would prove ruinous for the Igorots, and they planned to preserve the highlanders' culture through continued geographical and political separation. They were also confident that education and increased social services would prepare the mountain people for the modern world. Igorots would also move away from a subsistence lifestyle to commercialized agriculture through the exportation of coffee, tobacco, and silk, three commodities that were not too difficult to transport down the mountains.

Two impediments to their plan were that Igorots were often taken advantage of by lowland and Chinese merchants, and they were content to live outside of a larger national economy. A commercialized agricultural scheme increased annual weeks of labor and disrupted social rhythms and relationships. As late as 1911, Forbes still believed that this plan would work if American officials protected the Igorots: "The Sales Agency . . . will conduct markets in each province at which these products can be sold or exchanged at fair rates for the things most urgently desired by these people [Igorots]. Now they get fearfully robbed . . . for the scoundrelly traders, usually Chinamen, never let them get any sort of price for their tobacco, coffee and other products. Paternalism is needed here."[1]

But America's colonial policies toward Mountain Province changed when Woodrow Wilson won the 1912 presidential election. As a Democrat, he hoped to disentangle the US from its imperial foray in the Philippines, and he appointed fellow Democrat Francis Burton Harrison to replace Forbes as the new governor-general in October 1913.

Dean Worcester knew his dictatorial rule would not be tolerated by Wilson and Harrison. As secretary of the interior and a member of the Philippine Commission since 1899, and the only member who served continuously since its creation, Worcester was arguably the most influential and most despised American in the Philippines. Rather than suffer the indignity of losing his job, Worcester resigned in June 1913, but agreed to stay on until September.

Harrison chose Winfred Denison to replace Worcester, and in April 1914 Harrison and Denison, accompanied by fifty soldiers and guides, took their first inspection tour of the Mountain Province. Their approach to the Igorots radically differed from their predecessors, who were known to travel with no protectors and relied on their personalities to legitimize their authority. Worcester and Forbes used to dance with the Igorots. Harrison, on the other hand, "seldom ventured into the countryside—and then only with trepidation. Once, on a visit to a tribe of Igorot aborigines, he was seen washing himself with carbolic soap after shaking their hands."[2]

Harrison and Denison's Mountain Province tour was cut short by the international crisis of a potential war between the United States and Mexico, but they still came to several conclusions following their visit. First, Worcester's policies were a complete failure. Denison wondered at the stupidity of using the paradigm of Native American reservations for the Igorots. The model did not work in the US; why would it work in the Philippines? Second, they saw very little, if any, difference between the Igorots and lowland Filipinos. They were taken aback by a policy that differentiated between the two peoples. In short, Harrison wrote, "I can see no very essential difference between the non-Christians of the Mountain Province and the lowland Filipinos."[3] Finally, they both believed that the secretary of the interior's portfolio was too large to give adequate attention to the Igorots, and so they created a new position whose exclusive attention would be for the non-Christian peoples of the Philippines. The position was called the delegate of the secretary of the interior for the non-Christian people.

Worcester kept track of these changes from afar, scoffing at this new approach and arguing that the new position should be offered to A. O. Zinn,

Worcester's longtime private secretary. When Zinn turned down the job, it was extended to Charles C. Batchelder, who gladly accepted it. Worcester derided the choice, saying that Batchelder had spent less than a month in the Philippines and "among the list of qualifications recorded as possessed by him there is nothing to show that he had ever seen a Philippine wild man."[4] Batchelder's marching orders were to break down the barriers dividing Igorots from the rest of the world. To this Worcester replied, "The first necessity, in getting rid of an obstacle, is to recognize its existence. It is encouraging to find that the secretary knows that the wall is there, as this has been repeatedly and emphatically denied."[5]

Worcester's criticism of Batchelder was both unwarranted and rooted in ignorance. In 1889, Batchelder graduated magna cum laude from Harvard, where he served as editor of the *Crimson*. He was particularly drawn to the courses of William James and was described as "singularly gifted" in psychological research.[6] Described as a driven visionary, Batchelder believed any challenge, mental or physical, could be met with positive thinking. At one point, he wrote that the mental healing espoused by Christian Scientists works "just as well with a pagan religion as with the christian [*sic*] one . . . [because the] emotional nature of man, which controls mental healing, is intimately connected with his higher aspirations, and belongs rather to the domain of religion than to that of medicine."[7]

Batchelder spent only two years in his role as delegate, but there is much to learn from his approach and assessment of Mountain Province's past and future. His marching orders were to integrate the Igorots with lowland society and to bring an overall improvement to the mountain peoples. He met with Worcester's lieutenant governors, toured the province, carefully read the past decades' worth of annual reports, and concluded that Worcester's policies were not complete failures; they had actually laid a foundation that Batchelder could build upon.

After Batchelder's initial investigations, he bemoaned the lack of medical, social, and educational resources among the Igorots. During his two years in Mountain Province, the number of doctors, schools, and sanitary inspectors dramatically increased. He understood that cultural norms that caused health hazards, such as keeping pigs under and around the house, could only be changed from within the community rather than by an outside entity. He also made unpopular personnel decisions that were long overdue. In particular, he set his sights on removing Lieutenant Governor Hale from his long-held position as Kalinga's paramount power. The self-proclaimed God of Kalinga continued to rule by fiat, causing enormous problems for the PC and every other entity that challenged his authority. To be sure, Kalinga enjoyed unprecedented peace due to Hale's rule, and he remained protected by Worcester because they shared a similar political philosophy. But Hale took his privileges further into the economic sphere, establishing centers where rice was bought and sold at a set price. Worcester had previously warned Hale that this practice needed to change, but he convinced his boss that monopolizing Kalinga's economy protected its inhabitants from unjustified price hikes as well as unscrupulous outside merchants. His monopoly continued. To guard his political and economic privileges, Hale also hindered a group of Belgian Roman Catholic priests from establishing missions and schools in Kalinga.

Governor-General Harrison refused to accept Hale's explanation for his rice monopoly, and he ordered him to close his stores by January 1915. As a follow-up, Batchelder met with Hale in February 1915, and Hale assured him that neither he nor any of his wife's relatives were involved in buying or selling goods in Kalinga. But just days after this meeting, Hale began building a store in the Kalinga town of Balbalan, which would be run by one of his wife's relatives. Armed with this new information, Batchelder plainly asked Hale why he should remain Kalinga's lieutenant governor given his overt insubordination. An embarrassed, if not contrite, Hale responded, "I did not intentionally disobey the Secretary of the Interior or misinform him. . . . I have not been well for some time. I am tired . . . and need a rest, as I am afraid that both my memory and judgment have suffered."[8] This confession did not save Hale from dismissal. He left Lubuagan but stayed in Kalinga, buying a large farm in Balbalan just 20 miles north of Lubuagan.

Hale's dismissal shocked the Kalingans as his rule had defined the region over the past eight years. Despite his abrasive personality, he had many supporters, especially conservative Americans who longed for the old system of inordinate deference given to the white man. In the media, the conservative *Manila Times* reported, "It is generally conceded by old-timers that the charges against the Governor [Hale] have been trumped up . . . [by] a certain class of Filipinos who have been unrelenting in their effort to get his head ever since the New Era began."[9]

Hale, however, was not about to go gently into that good night. He had little respect for his replacement, Samuel Kane. This is a bit surprising in that they had certain similarities: both were Worcester's appointees, acted above the law, were instrumental in Early's firing, and married local women. But Hale was fluent in the Kalinga language, and Kane was not. All the local authorities in Kalinga's towns had been appointed by Hale and were loyal to him. They continued to go to his house when there were disputes. Thus, the Manila-based officials ordered him to stop acting as the supreme authority in Kalinga and to support the newly appointed lieutenant governor and the PC. Hale responded that he had no intention to change and "if [I am] further annoyed by these milk-sops in Manila, [I will] lead a party of spear and bolo men down there and clean them out."[10] Harrison had no choice but to expel Hale from Kalinga, and he ordered PC Captain A. H. Gilfillan to take his men to Hale's farm, disarm him, and escort him out of Kalinga with an order that he not return. Gilfillan was the perfect man for the job as he was both diplomatic and firm. Hale accepted his exile and bought some property in Tagudin. He stayed there just a couple of years before joining Worcester in the southern Philippines, where he worked as a foreman on Worcester's massive cattle farm.

Harrison recalled this incident after he left the Philippines, but with a more favorable view of Hale, describing both Hale and Kane as "often absolutely alone and surrounded by warlike men who had always in the past been re-garded as savages, and had until then defied the white man, they worked steadily and unafraid along the paths of honor, justice, and reform." Harri-son's compliment and assessment of Hale sounds very much like Worcester's view, but there was a caveat to Harrison's admiration for these lone rangers: "The only mistake made on the part of the Government was in leaving some of them so long at their lonely posts; in several cases they broke in nerves or health, gradually undermined by the influences of solitary life and unlimited power."[11]

Hale's expulsion allowed Batchelder to support the Belgian missionaries' entrance into Kalinga. By 1915, the missionaries had a proven track record, with fifty-four schools scattered throughout Mountain Province that en-rolled over three thousand students, and they extended their successes into Kalinga.[12]

Batchelder's initial theories about Mountain Province changed over time. For example, he initially believed that the region was overpopulated. In 1915 the province contained 387,388 inhabitants. By the end of Batchelder's term in 1918, that number had increased to 408,070.[13] The naive Batchelder ap-proached the supposed overpopulation by encouraging the Igorots to move to the lowlands. He promised they would receive farming lands and medicine to combat malaria. But then Batchelder learned that Igorots were mystically linked to their homeland. Writing in the prestigious *Annals of the American Academy* in 1924, he recalled that the supposed overpopulation was not a prob-lem at all. Rather, there was a cultural and historical dependence on subsis-tence agriculture centered on rice and camote. He sought to change this by introducing new vegetables and fertilizers. Batchelder's assessment of his suc-cesses were mixed at best: "The result of this was that the [diversified] food supply became adequate, as many of the new plants could be raised on the unirrigated hillsides, and the sale of the coffee brought in a certain amount of cash from the lowlands . . . other industries taught in the schools, also added to their incomes. While these experiments were only on a small scale, they were carried on along scientific lines under expert advice, and merit study by those who are engaged in solving economic problems in the tropics. Unfortunately, they were discontinued when the American administration was terminated, and practical autonomy introduced."[14]

Batchelder and Denison's tenures in the Philippines were cut short for two very different reasons. Denison's replacement of Worcester was in line with a career on a meteoric trajectory. At nineteen, he had graduated from the prestigious Phillips Exeter Academy in New Hampshire. He then enrolled at Harvard, where he eventually became the editor-in-chief of the *Harvard Monthly*. In 1900, four years after his graduation, he began practicing law in New York. Six years later he won an appointment as an assistant US district attorney for New York. In a highly publicized case, Denison successfully prosecuted a fraud case related to sugar imports. The case brought him national attention, and in 1909 he left New York to accept a new position as assistant US attorney general in Washington, DC. In 1913 he took his next significant professional leap as secretary of interior in the Philippines. Much was expected of him, as was mentioned in a journal article: "Mr. Denison may know in advance little of the Philippines. But he knows a great deal about high ideals and some principles of public service."[15]

Of all President Wilson's Philippine appointees, Denison had the largest shoes to fill. Noted for an indefatigable work ethic, he looked forward to his new job. Unfortunately, Denison's life took a precipitous downward turn during his early months in the Philippines, and he never recovered. In his first year in Manila, he became deathly ill. Doctors could not properly diagnose his illness, but they assumed he had contracted a tropical disease. Less than a year after arriving in the Philippines, Denison was forced to resign his position, and he returned to the US, taking a position in New York City's Stetson, Jennings & Russell law firm. After just two years in that job, Denison teamed up with a fellow Harvard alumnus, James Curtis, to open their own firm in New York's Woolworth Building.

But Denison's health nightmare grew darker by the day until, on the afternoon of Wednesday, November 5, 1919, he put on his overcoat and walked to New York's Pennsylvania subway station. On the crowded platform, he put his overcoat over his head and jumped in front of an oncoming subway train. His legs severed and body crushed, he died instantly. An inventory of his pockets revealed that the lifelong bachelor carried just one object—a gold watch with the inscription: "With best regards and best wishes from the Directors and assistants of Bureaus, Department of the Interior, Philippine Islands, Manila, September 25, 1915."[16]

As for Batchelder, he continued to thrive following his abrupt Philippine departure. He left the Philippines unexpectedly after a new law was passed in 1916 that replaced the Philippine Commission with an elected upper house, placing Igorot policies in the hands of Filipinos for the first time. But before leaving the Philippines, Batchelder concluded that Worcester's system actually turned out to be the best among the highlanders: "Some one person should be put in entire charge of the Mountain Province, and he should be required to travel constantly, so as to supervise what is going on in person. He should be given full control. . . . The authority in the Mountain Province should be concentrated in the hands of one person. . . . [The Igorots] are used to having all authority in the hands of one official, and the multiplicity of officials confuses them."[17] One wonders whether Batchelder, a self-confessed progressive liberal, would have had a different view of Hale at the end of his time in the Philippines. Batchelder went on to a distinguished career in the US government, serving in China, India, and other places around the globe until his death on May 4, 1946.[18]

CHAPTER 23

Colonial Policies

Harrison, Osmeña, and Quezon

Abraham Lincoln's 1860 election victory ushered in an unprecedented run of political dominance by one political party. Once in the executive office, the Republicans made it a political fortress that the Democrats found almost impossible to dislodge. Between 1860 and 1912, ten men were elected to the office of US president, and only one was not a Republican. The 1912 presidential campaign took place in the context of more than twenty-two years of unbroken Republican executive rule.

The Republicans should have easily continued their hold on the office with their incumbent candidate William Howard Taft. The affable Ohioan certainly enjoyed the credentials needed for a second term. As the first governor-general of the Philippines, he was groomed by Teddy Roosevelt, who rewarded Taft's Philippine service with a 1904 cabinet appointment as secretary of war. Though his great ambition was an appointment to the US Supreme Court, Taft knew that his party had him in mind as the 1908 Republican presidential candidate; Roosevelt also advocated for his friend's nomination, and Taft defeated the Democrat and perpetual loser William Jennings Bryan, who ran for president four times and lost four times.

Taft's 1908 victory signaled business as usual in the Philippines. He had coined the phrase "little brown brother" to refer to Filipinos, supported Dean Worcester's policies, and appointed Cameron Forbes as governor-general, thus perpetuating America's control of its Asian colony. It was also during Taft's presidency that Early joined the Mountain Province government.

Republican domination of the executive office and its concomitant colonial policies did not mean there were no opposing voices. From the beginning of American rule in the Philippines, Democrats railed against imperialism and advocated for indigenous rule. Filipino leaders also galvanized their political parties in opposing American rule, and the US Democrats found natural Filipino allies who sought independence. In 1912, neither group was optimistic that much change was on the horizon. But their savior came from a most unlikely source—the leading proponent of American exceptionalism, Teddy Roosevelt, who split the Republican ticket and thus assured Taft's defeat.

Wilson's 1912 victory presaged changes in Washington that included a new approach to governing the Philippines. In Manila, thousands of Filipinos braved a downpour as they paraded through the streets celebrating the sentiments expressed by a local journalist: "[Wilson] will preside over our triumphal entrance into the promised land after redeeming us from the long captivity to which the Imperial pharaohs reduced us."[1]

Surprisingly, American colonial policy was hardly mentioned in the 1912 presidential campaign, though the Democratic platform advocated for "an immediate declaration of the nation's purpose to recognize the independence of the islands as soon as a stable government can be established."[2] Wilson reiterated his party's position in a public speech, claiming that the Philippine Islands "are at present our frontier, but I hope we presently are to deprive ourselves of that frontier."[3]

Before making decisions about the Philippines, Wilson turned to an old friend from his Princeton years, the political science professor Henry Jones Ford, for advice. After spending more than two months in the Philippines, Ford typed an eighty-page report that provided little new insight into the Philippine situation. He advised Wilson to promise future independence for the Philippines and continue the transfer of official duties and offices from Americans to Filipinos. He was impressed by what America accomplished during its first decade of rule, and Forbes gladly accepted the praise, aware that his professional future hung in the balance.

Wilson forwarded Ford's report and recommendations to the newly appointed secretary of war, Lindley M. Garrison. At a loss in understanding the whole Philippine situation, Garrison turned to his aide Felix Frankfurter to decipher the report and draft a Philippine plan for Wilson's administration. At its heart, the new policy advocated an aggressive approach to the transference of government authority to Filipinos. Wilson remained reluctant to replace

Forbes, as he believed he had demonstrated remarkable leadership. But keeping Forbes in the Philippines was untenable because he opposed a rapid transfer of authority to Filipino politicians. Obviously, Wilson needed a governor-general who agreed with the new policies.

Unlike earlier years, the Philippine governor-general position was no longer the coveted office that led to the US presidency. In 1899, Roosevelt desired the office of governor-general "above all others" before settling for the vice-presidency, and Taft's tenure as America's first Philippine governor-general eventually led to his successful presidential campaign.[4] But Democrats viewed the job as ending American rule and handing it off to Filipino officials. After a brief search, President Wilson chose Francis Burton Harrison to replace Forbes. At forty years old, Harrison had already spent a quarter of his life in the US Congress as a Democrat representing New York. Handsome and wealthy, Harrison exuded confidence.

Originally from Virginia, Harrison's ancestors included Thomas Jefferson, and his father served as Confederate President Jefferson Davis's secretary. Perhaps Harrison's only blemish that Catholic Filipinos might have whispered about was that he married six times. For Filipino politicians, the important conviction Harrison possessed was that the US should hand over the reins of Philippine politics to Filipinos. Indeed, his timeline for the transfer of power was even too aggressive for the two most prominent Filipino politicians of the time, Sergio Osmeña and Manuel Quezon.

History is easiest told with broad brush strokes centering on a few individuals—usually prominent politicians or other cultural figures. This is the case with the early political history of the Philippines. Drawing upon the political ideology of its nation's founders, American colonial leaders intended to impose their style of democracy on the Filipinos. They initially courted Filipino politicians sympathetic to American rule and helped them to establish the Federalista Party. But forcing democracy on an entrenched nepotistic system based on centuries-long patronage of the poor masses to the economic elite was overambitious and unrealistic.[5]

Taft and his colleagues nurtured rudimentary aspects of democracy in the first few years of American rule. The first Philippine national election held in 1907 populated the newly created National Assembly, a legislative body akin to the US House of Representatives. The Philippine Commission served as the de facto upper house or senate. The governor-general held veto power over any bill the National Assembly passed. Still, the 1907 election was quite a feat as it represented "the first parliament ever freely elected in Asia, [and] it was a tribute to the liberalism of US colonial rule."[6] But the American-nurtured Federalistas were trounced by the more independent Nacionalista

Party, which garnered fifty-eight of the eighty seats; the Federalistas only won sixteen seats.

If elections reflect the will of the people, then voters demonstrated their overwhelming desire for a speedy independence. This was the basic platform of the Nacionalistas, and they received national prominence in the electorate. It also helped that this nascent but dominant political party included two young charismatic leaders who became the faces of national politics for the next three decades.

Sergio Osmeña was born in Cebu in 1878 to an unwed fourteen-year-old. Despite his illegitimacy, Osmeña was taken in by his Chinese-Filipino relatives,

FIGURE 8. Sergio Osmeña (*left*) and Manuel Quezon, two past presidents of the Philippines. They worked closely with the various governor-generals—all except General Leonard Wood. National Library of the Philippines Collections.

who supported his education. He was bright, serious, and revered for his integrity. After elementary school, he moved to Manila, where he eventually received his law degree from the prestigious University of Santo Tomas and earned the second highest score on the 1903 bar exam. A devoted husband and father to thirteen children, Osmeña was elected speaker of the first National Assembly.

Osmeña's Nacionalista colleague, Manuel Quezon, also attended the same Manila-based schools, and the two spent their formative years together, though their origins radically differed. Quezon's father was a Spanish soldier who married the local schoolteacher in Baler, a town in eastern Luzon's Tayabas province. While Quezon's family did not have the wealth that the Osmeñas enjoyed, it did possess the patronage and prestige that came with their Spanish blood. During and in between his studies, Quezon participated in the turn-of-the-century battles for Philippine independence. With his Spanish background, he initially supported the Spanish against the indigenous nationalist movement. He then switched sides to join Aguinaldo in the fight against the occupying American forces. Finally, he allied himself with the Americans, particularly with Harry Bandholtz, the preeminent military leader in Tayabas and the future commander of the PC. In 1906, both Osmeña and Quezon were elected governors of their provinces—Cebu and Tayabas, respectively. Together these men, then in their late twenties, rallied the Nacionalista Party to an impressive National Assembly election in 1907.

While Osmeña led the newly elected assembly, Quezon chose a different route for national prominence and self-advancement. Two Filipinos represented the Philippines in America's House of Representatives, and though they were not allowed to vote, they were spokesmen for their country in the US. The governor-general appointed one representative, normally an individual in step with the American colonial policy, while the National Assembly chose the other. Quezon sought and won the National Assembly appointment and remained in Washington, DC, from 1909 to 1916.

Quezon charmed Washington. Strikingly handsome, articulate, and subject to changing his views more often than Osmeña, Quezon praised the US for its work in the Philippines in his initial speech to Congress. However, he contextualized his praise with a plea to understand a people's desire for liberty: "Ask the bird, sir, who is enclosed in a golden cage if he would prefer his cage . . . to the freedom of the skies and the allure of the forest."[7]

Quezon played the political game to perfection. He worked both sides of the aisle but knew the Democrats were more open to Philippine independence. He was reportedly an important influence in the appointment of Harrison as the Philippines' governor-general. But Quezon gave his special attention, time, and charm to William Atkinson Jones, the Democratic Congressman from

Virginia who chaired the Committee on US Insular Affairs, the agency that oversaw the Philippines.

Jones, like most of his Democratic colleagues, was eager to grant the Philippines independence. Working with Quezon, he introduced a bill that guaranteed the Philippines sovereignty in eight years, with an American commitment to keep its military in the archipelago for twenty years while the newly independent country built up its own armed forces. The proposed legislation also changed the government structure. As it stood in 1912 when the bill was introduced, there was a three-legged Philippine political paradigm: the executive branch (governor-general); the Philippine Commission, a few men (almost all Americans) appointed by the US president; and the National Assembly. The Jones Act proposed to change the system, doing away with the Philippine Commission and replacing it with an elected senate. The governor-general would still have veto power over the new bicameral legislative body.

While the Jones Bill achieved support in the House of Representatives, the Senate would not allow it to see the light of day. That changed when Woodrow Wilson won the 1912 presidential election. Jones and Quezon anticipated a more favorable reception to the bill from Wilson, but the bill languished due to multiple barriers. Even Wilson did not want to set a specific date for granting full sovereignty to America's Asian colony. The final compromise that led to its passage was that in exchange for the elimination of the Philippine Commission, the bill provided no specific date for Philippine independence. The preamble simply noted that the US would grant independence to the Philippines once a stable government was in place. Such nebulous language at the very beginning of the bill guaranteed that it would be some time before the Philippines was fully independent. Nonetheless, the Philippine Commission was abolished, and compared to every other Southeast Asian colony, the Philippines had the greatest measure of indigenous authority. After the bill passed, Quezon rightly believed this was his opportunity to achieve paramount political attention in the Philippines. He left Washington, was elected president of the new Philippine Senate, and maneuvered his way past Osmeña in anticipation of a future presidential election.

Chapter 24

World War I and a Troubled Yet Vibrant Economy

It was not exactly Lincoln's Emancipation Proclamation, but for many Filipinos the August 1916 passage of the Jones Bill represented a promised freedom that was over three hundred years in the making. Parties were held, speeches were given, and parades of people celebrated. It had taken four years for the bill to make it through the US Congress, but there was finally a law that explicitly stated America's intention to grant the Philippines independence. While not in the bill itself, the preamble read: "Whereas it is, as it has always been, the purpose of the people of the United States to withdraw their sovereignty over the Philippine Islands and to recognize their independence as soon as a stable government can be established therein."[1]

The more immediate implication of the Jones Law included the transfer of all legislative authority into Filipino hands, as the commission was replaced by the Philippine Senate. Governor-General Harrison remained the executive official, and since his 1913 arrival, he had worked to transfer authority and positions from Americans to Filipinos. He introduced an extremely attractive retirement policy for Americans in the insular government. By the time the Jones Law passed, there were only 27 Americans in provincial positions (or 13 percent of officials in the provinces), and less than 1 percent of municipal officers were American.[2]

In June 1916, the three-year cycle of elections for the Philippine Assembly took place. Osmeña and Quezon's Nacionalista Party, with a platform advocating independence, won seventy-five of the ninety seats in contention. Quezon ran for the newly created Senate, and under his leadership, the Nacionalistas secured an even greater victory than in the National Assembly, as they won twenty-two of the twenty-four seats.

Former classmates and colleagues, Osmeña and Quezon's previously amiable relationship turned sour as they both coveted the party's top position. At one point, Quezon threatened to resign from the party and create a new organization. One prominent scholar of the era noted, "Tension between the Filipino leaders remained close to the surface during the first year of the new government, and all of Harrison's diplomatic skills were employed to prevent an explosion."[3] To placate both men, Harrison created a Council of State in January 1917 that would serve as an advisory group, and both Quezon and Osmeña became part of the nascent organization. Of even greater importance, later that year the Philippine legislators authorized the creation of the Board of Control, consisting of the governor-general as well as the president of the Senate (Quezon) and the House speaker (Osmeña). This new board authorized the buying and selling of government shares in national enterprises. In short, these three individuals "exercised effective control over the government's enterprises," and they took advantage of this situation.[4]

The passage of the Jones Bill coincided with the midpoint of the unprecedented global conflagration of World War I. Nothing so influenced Harrison's tenure as governor-general as the effects of World War I on America's archipelago colony. There were two in particular: Philippine economic growth and financial nepotism.

Along with an appreciation of America's military protection, Filipinos' overwhelming response to America's entrance into World War I was solidarity. More than a month before America declared war on Germany, Harrison, with support from Quezon and Osmeña, ordered the confiscation of German ships in Philippine docks and bays. After Wilson's April 2, 1917, request that the US Congress declare war on Germany, Filipinos took to the streets for parades and pronouncements of support for America. The Philippine Senate passed a bill calling for a militia made up of all able-bodied Filipino men between eighteen and forty-five years of age. Harrison requested that he be given the opportunity to lead the Filipino army of twenty-five thousand in the European theater, noting that he planned to appoint Quezon as a brigade commander. Harrison's requests were quietly ignored, as the War Department saw more problems than advantages in using Filipino soldiers. In response, the Philippine Legislature authorized the construction of a submarine and a destroyer for the war effort. The war bonds quota for the Philippines were easily sold, and a general sense of camaraderie that only a war can bring characterized Philippine-American relations. It also helped that the war was an economic windfall for the Philippines.[5]

In 1915, prior to America's entrance into the war, Harrison increased internal taxes due to a global shipping crisis. Additionally, he introduced new levies that led to unprecedented revenue for the insular government. By 1918 the Philippine government collected 31 million pesos in taxes compared with 9.7 million the previous year. Exports also increased. Between 1913 and 1915, Philippine exports averaged 100 million pesos annually; in 1918 they exceeded 270 million. Huge increases in exports, internal revenue, and the selling off of German businesses, along with the use of eight confiscated German ships, created a red-hot economy.[6]

Unfortunately, mismanagement of wartime economic growth proved to be Harrison's greatest political legacy. The seed of the Philippines' postwar economic calamity was the 1916 establishment of the government-controlled Philippine National Bank (PNB). With initial assets of twelve million pesos (from the increased taxes), the bank was led by H. Parker Willis. An economic expert and professor at Columbia University, Willis hoped to assist Filipinos in achieving their independence.

While fiscally conservative, Willis encouraged loans to Filipinos involved in agriculture. He also extended long-term loans secured by resources not immediately transferable to cash. With Willis's guidance, the PNB became the Philippines' largest commercial bank, with assets increasing to 249 million pesos by 1918.

Along with the war years' economic growth, the Philippine Legislature decided to liberalize policies so that the government could invest in or create companies. These government-led companies included the National Petroleum Company, National Cement Company, National Iron Company, National Coal Company, Manila Railroad Company, and National Development Company. The National Development Company, which served as an advisory and support organization for entrepreneurs, was given fifty million pesos. Individuals also profited from the government's largess. Quezon, for example, was elected the president of the Manila Railroad Company in 1917 and stayed in that role until 1921. The enterprise was a major economic liability, yet Quezon had six bills passed in the Senate to prop up the fledgling company. He also used his position to hand out free railroad passes while the trains crisscrossed Luzon, where Quezon was most popular.

Not to be outdone, Osmeña insisted that Venanacio Concepción be appointed the PNB's vice-president. Harrison and Quezon reluctantly approved this request. Concepción was from the Visayas, Osmeña's political stronghold. A military general during the Philippine Revolution, Concepción had no background in finance, banking, or general economic principles. What he did have, for Osmeña, were connections to Visayas' sugar and coconut plantation owners. When the economically savvy Willis returned to the US after guiding the PNB in its first two years, Concepción was handed the bank's presidency. It proved disastrous. He loaned millions of pesos to coconut and sugar mills as well as other industries profiting from the turmoil of World War I. With Concepción at the helm, backroom deals and clandestine loans soon exceeded the PNB's reserves.

When World War I ended, the global demand for Philippine exports plummeted, prices fell overnight, and Philippine businesses lost money even when they had products to export. In 1921, Philippine exports garnered 176 million pesos, 58 percent below the export revenue of 1920 and considerably lower than the 270 million of 1918.

With the PNB in an all-out crisis, the War Department hired Francis Coates Jr., who managed the Federal Reserve Bank of Cleveland, to review the PNB's books and policies. His subsequent 1920 report to Harrison was a blistering indictment of its leadership and policies: "There is not one experienced or trained banker on the staff . . . [and] very, very slight surveillance and control is exercised over the main office in Manila and practically none elsewhere . . . there probably exists no parallel case in any banking institution in the world."[7] Because of Coates's report, the US sent a team of auditors, who produced an even more damning report on the PNB: "The investment made by the Philippine government in the Philippine National Bank has been completely lost . . . examination reveals that the bank has operated during almost the entire period of its existence in violation of every principle which prudence, intelligence and even honesty should dictate."[8]

Adding to the sordid economic mess was Harrison's misuse of the revenue boom from 1916 to 1919. During these years of fortune, Secretary of the Interior Rafael Palma pleaded that a portion of these additional resources be used for municipalities and social programs, but the politicians, under Harrison's guidance, were obsessed with industrializing the Philippines at the expense of rank-and-file citizens. Consequently, this placed a strain on health services and left a lasting stain on Harrison's administration. The 1918 smallpox epidemic was just one of the many costs of his social service neglect.

At the turn of the twentieth century, the Philippines experienced a smallpox pandemic. American soldiers and members of the Philippine Commission concentrated on bringing it under control, with immunizations of children carried out by public school teachers. The vice-governor was responsible for overseeing this because public education was part of his portfolio. The commission's conscientious attention to this crisis almost eradicated smallpox from the islands, which garnered it international praise. However, following the passage of the Jones Law, Harrison and the insular legislature removed the immunization program from the American vice-governor's portfolio, and it floundered due to neglect. In 1918, while the world lived in dread of the influenza epidemic, a smallpox pandemic reappeared in the Philippines, taking the lives of fifty thousand, the great majority of them children. Harrison blamed others for this tragedy, but it demonstrated his lack of leadership, the misappropriation of financial resources, and his hands-off approach to governing.[9]

The economic and health debacles of Harrison's administration would not come to light until 1919 and 1920. Up until then, things seemed eternally bright for the trio of Harrison, Quezon, and Osmeña, especially on November 11, 1918, the day Germany surrendered, ending World War I. With the international crisis over and Woodrow Wilson proposing a new world order in his Fourteen Points, the three men believed that this was their moment to secure Philippine independence. The Philippine Legislature approved a plan to immediately send a commission to Washington made up of over three dozen people to present their case for independence.

Just two days after the armistice was signed, Harrison asked President Wilson to receive the Philippine delegation. The president had other things on his mind as he was preparing to leave for Paris, so the War Department requested that the Filipino officials postpone their visit. But they persisted, and led by Harrison, Osmeña, and Quezon, the delegation met with the joint House and Senate committees on the Philippines. Quezon insisted that the Philippines was ready for independence. Harrison echoed this message, claiming that "there exists today in the Philippine Islands a stable government . . . elected by the suffrages of the people, which is supported by the people, which is capable of maintaining order, and of fulfilling its international obligations. [It should be granted independence at the] earliest moment."[10] In 1919, the Senate Committee on the Philippines was led by the Republicans and, in particular, the senator from Ohio, Warren G. Harding. His cool reception to this request previewed the coming conflict between the Republicans and Filipino politicians.

CHAPTER 25

Marriages and Scandals

While the Harrison-led postwar delegation may not have achieved its objectives in Washington, it did provide a surplus of sensational news regarding two of its leaders: Quezon and Harrison. Quezon's numerous liaisons with women on both sides of the Pacific, as well as on ships while crossing the ocean, are legendary. The one-time president of the UN General Assembly noted that "One cannot evaluate the Quezon charisma or his effect upon people without taking into account his frank and unselfconscious pursuit [of] women. He was a congenital womanizer with nature on his side [and] engaged in several notorious affairs with American wives of military officers stationed in Manila."[1] While in his early twenties, Quezon married a poor rural beauty, but he later had the marriage annulled. A few years later he was convicted of attempted rape but escaped any penalty through the aid of his American advisers. So it was with some surprise that after ten years of speculation as to where his marital affections would land, he chose to marry his cousin Aurora Aragon Quezon a few days after leaving for Washington. They married at the American Consulate in Hong Kong on December 17, 1918, with his fellow delegates as witnesses.

Harrison's personal life was even more sordid. Married six times, Harrison was on his second marriage when he was named governor-general. His first marriage, which produced two daughters, was to Mary Crocker, the eldest daughter of California's railroad millionaire Charles Frederick Crocker. Mary died in 1905 due to injuries sustained in a Long Island automobile accident, and Harrison subsequently became despised by Mary's friends due to his immediate pursuit of the beautiful Mabel "Louise" Judson. Just four years earlier, Louise had married Dr. Roland Cox Jr., a prominent New York City surgeon, but by 1906, she and Harrison were spotted together in Cuba.[2] One disparaging comment about Harrison in the California press appeared in 1911: "Harrison married Mary Crocker, one of San Francisco's greatest heiresses, and when she died he inherited the bulk of her immense wealth. He is sharing the enjoyment of that wealth today with the woman he married in hot pursuit after his first wife's death . . . who, it was said, long before her marriage was wearing some of Mary Crocker's emeralds."[3] In fact, Harrison was considerably well off even before he had married Crocker, due to his family's prosperity, but he became fabulously wealthy after inheriting Crocker's fortune.

After marrying Harrison, Louise appeared content to live a luxurious life as the wife of a rich congressman. She cared for Harrison's two daughters, and they all accompanied him to the Philippines in September 1913. There are differing accounts about what happened to Harrison's second marriage. One theory is that Louise did not like the Philippines and asked her husband to leave. As one writer put it, "As was the case for many American women [Louise] did not suffer the Manila climate easily . . . and urged Harrison to give up the Philippine post."[4] But more reliable and numerous sources indicate that Harrison began a less-than-clandestine affair with a younger American woman who was married to an American military officer stationed in the Philippines. The gossip about the affair and all those involved became public through several newspapers. Louise was in Europe at that time and was on her way back to the Philippines when she received word from Harrison that he did not wish her to return. Though they were a family—she had given birth to their three sons—the governor-general wanted freedom from domestic constraints. She returned to the US, moved from her home in Brooklyn to southern California's Coronado Island, and began divorce proceedings, citing cruelty and desertion.[5]

Back in Manila, a surprising new love blossomed in Harrison's life. The romance had its roots in the first months he was in Manila when the Harrisons hosted extravagant parties in the governor-general's mansion. Through these events, they became acquainted with Clarence and Margaret Wrentmore.

Clarence George Wrentmore (1867–1934) was born and raised in a suburb of Cleveland, Ohio. He graduated from the local college and then moved to Ann Arbor, where he earned several graduate degrees. In 1893, he began his academic career as an instructor of drawing in the same year that Worcester was appointed an instructor at Michigan. Wrentmore's reputation as a brilliant engineer propelled him to the position of associate professor of civil engineering, but around 1910 he requested a two-year leave of absence to serve as the head of the Bureau of Public Works for Manila. He enjoyed the Philippines, and on May 11, 1911, he was in Baguio, where he wrote his alma mater and former employer, "Gentleman: I have the honor to tender my resignation effective at the end of the current college year, from my position as Junior Professor of Civil Engineering and the University of Michigan."[6] Whether from humility or other motives, Wrentmore's pithy resignation note did not include his reason for leaving the University of Michigan faculty, which was his appointment as dean of the University of the Philippines College of Engineering. Well-respected by his colleagues, Wrentmore and his wife Margaret savored their life in Manila. And when the newly arrived Harrisons sent out invitations to their parties, they invited the Wrentmores, who came to the gatherings along with their two daughters: Betty, who was thirteen, and Margaret, who was eight. At the time, no one could have guessed that both of these girls would one day marry Francis Burton Harrison nor the pain he would inflict on each of them.

In 1918, the Wrentmores welcomed home their seventeen-year-old daughter, Betty, after her first semester at the University of California, Berkeley. Unbeknownst to them, Betty had fostered a deep infatuation for Harrison from the time she was thirteen. Now, as a striking seventeen-year-old college student, she caught Harrison's eye. She soon became his constant companion, taking daily horse rides with him when the weather permitted. Their liaisons in the governor's mansion and other secret hotel rooms embarrassed her parents, who tried to end the affair by sending Betty back to the US. But Harrison and Betty had already made secret plans to marry.

Gossip about their continued relationship was confirmed when Harrison arrived in the US with the Philippine Commission in the spring of 1919. He had been away from the US for more than five years, and he ostensibly had returned to support Quezon and Osmeña's appeal for Philippine independence. His personal motives were to reunite with Betty, obtain a divorce from Louise, and remarry. Betty was now eighteen years old, and he was forty-five. He announced their engagement and made sure the papers picked up the news. He had an uphill battle, as Mrs. Wrentmore was dead set against the marriage. The issue became national news when Betty met with reporters and gave her side of the story. Her picture graced newspapers as did her defiant insistence on following her heart: "Mother doesn't realize that I am grown up. She apparently believes that this is just a case of 'puppy love' on my part and that I'll soon forget all about Governor Harrison. This is not so. I love him and he loves me. Why, I have made him my hero ever since I was thirteen years old. My mother also thinks it is wrong to marry a man who is divorced. I think it is better to be divorced half a dozen times than to live with someone one hates or is unhappy with. We shall certainly be married in May."[7]

Betty and Harrison rendezvoused in Chicago, and they married the day after his divorce from Louise was finalized. They returned to the Philippines one year later and were able to reconcile with Betty's parents. Harrison reportedly bribed his way back into the family's good graces by using his position to appoint Mr. Wrentmore to a project that would pay him twenty-five thousand dollars. The press commented about this, "The job, according to the news story, carried with it very little work, and is regarded on the islands as one of the best sinecures ever handed out." Both the governor and Wrentmore were loudly criticized for this nepotistic "sop."[8]

Harrison's tenure as governor-general ended in 1921, and he and Betty moved to the elaborate sixteenth-century Scottish castle of Teaninich, where they continued to live off the inheritances from his family and first marriage, and he spent time hunting and fishing. In early 1925, Betty invited her younger sister Margaret to visit them. Margaret, at the time an eighteen-year-old freshman at the University of Michigan, left school to visit her sister, who seemed to be living a dream life in the huge castle. Betty and Harrison were in their fifth year of marriage, but all was not well. Harrison began an affair with Margaret, and the following year Betty sued for divorce while living in Paris, citing abandonment. Three months later Harrison married Margaret at his private villa in Morocco. She was nineteen; he was fifty-four.

In the first years of their marriage, Margaret gave birth to a son, Norvell Burton Harrison. Six years later, in 1933, Margaret shared the same fate as her sister. Harrison had tired of his fourth wife, and a newspaper article reported that, of all things, Betty tried to bring peace to the marriage. She failed, and the couple divorced.[9] The following year their father Clarence Wrentmore died after a brief illness at sixty-six years of age.[10]

In 1935, within a year of his divorce from Margaret, Harrison married for the fifth time, and the next year Quezon and his colleagues bestowed on Harrison the honor of being the first American to gain Philippine naturalized citizenship. He then served as an adviser to Quezon and subsequent Philippine presidents, including Osmeña, whom Harrison disparaged in private communications with Quezon. Harrison's fifth marriage also ended in divorce, and he married for a sixth and final time in 1949. That marriage lasted until his death in 1957.

Harrison's extravagant and reckless personal life produced at least eight children from five different marriages, along with numerous broken hearts and ruined lives. In particular, Margaret was left listless after Harrison discarded her six years into their marriage. Her one consolation was that she had a son from that union, though they were virtually abandoned by Harrison. Tragedy struck again for Margaret in April 1941 when thirteen-year-old Norvell died in a Tucson, Arizona, car accident. A broken Margaret could not cope with yet another heartbreak, and several weeks later she shot herself in the head in a Coronado hotel room, ending a life scarred by a man who lived for himself at the expense of those around him.[11]

One might overlook Harrison's personal life if it had not affected his professional work. But numerous sources confirm that he neglected his duties as governor-general in pursuit of women and sexual pleasure. In particular, the Igorots wondered why he had visited them only once during his eight years in office.

CHAPTER 26

Wilson's Parting Shot and the Republicans Return

Woodrow Wilson staggered to the end of his second term with a very different conclusion to his presidency than he had envisioned or expected. The only US president to earn a PhD, his dissertation was apropos for his future career: "Congressional Government: A Study in American Politics." Presidents are usually characterized by confidence, but Wilson was particularly assured of his keen insight into human nature and history's ebbs and flows. He was the first Democratic president since Andrew Jackson to serve two consecutive terms and just the first Democratic president since Andrew Johnson. But Wilson's presidency is viewed by many as a Shakespearean tragedy. Two years into his first term, his beloved wife Ellen died of kidney failure, which sent him into a six-month depression that coincided with the outbreak of World War I. In 1915, he subsequently married Edith Bolling Gait, a sprite and intelligent widow who brightened his world.

Reelected in 1916 with the campaign slogan "He kept us out of the war," Wilson visualized putting the world back together through global peace. After America's 1917 entrance into the war, the country's global economic prominence allowed him a preeminent position at the Paris Peace Conference during the first half of 1919. At the meeting, his Fourteen Points served as his guiding principle. Unfortunately, Wilson was physically ill during his months in Europe, and he made foolish political deals so as to get the victors to accept his pet project, a League of Nations in which diplomacy and understanding would replace rifts and conflicts. He left Paris believing "at last the world knows America as the Savior of the world."[1]

But while Wilson built diplomatic bridges in Paris, he burned them in Washington. Despite his involvement in winning the war, Wilson's popularity was rapidly falling. In the 1918 midterm elections, the Republicans picked up twenty-five seats in Congress, and both houses had a Republican majority, which only previewed the Republican landslide victories two years later. In the 1920 presidential election, the Republican candidate Warren G. Harding defeated the Democrat James Cox, carrying thirty-seven of the forty-eight states and 404 of the 531 electoral votes. Even more astonishing, Harding captured sixteen million popular votes versus the nine million of his opponent. This was also the first presidential election in which women voted.

Harrison and Filipino politicians witnessed the implosion of Wilson's presidency and the Republican resurgence with serious apprehension. With Republicans in solid control of Congress and the White House, they rightly feared a retreat from the past eight years of increased Philippine control in America's colony. But Wilson would not leave office without complicating Philippine policy for his successor. In his final annual address to Congress on December 7, 1920, Wilson's last point addressed the Philippine situation: "Allow me to call your attention to the fact that the people of the Philippine Islands have succeeded in maintaining a stable government. It is now our liberty and our duty to keep our promise to the people of those islands by granting them the independence which they so honorably covet."[2] With this statement Wilson asserted that, according to the 1916 Jones Law, the Philippines should immediately be given its freedom. This bold statement placed Harding in a difficult position because if he did not grant Filipinos independence, he would be in violation of the Jones Law and the ultimate betrayer of liberty. Of course, Harding could point to Wilson's hypocrisy. For six of the eight years of his presidency, Wilson enjoyed a Democratic majority in both houses, and he had the opportunity to grant the Philippines independence; now, he was leaving the matter to his successor. Harding privately commented that Wilson made him "the object" of this message and that it was meant to "embarrass" him.[3] It is possible that Wilson was so ill that he did not keep abreast of the Philippine situation, because just three weeks before proclaiming the Philippines' stability, Harrison—the loudest proponent for Philippine independence—wrote to Frank McIntyre, the chief of the Bureau of Insular Affairs, that financially the Philippines was "worse at the present moment than it has ever been before."[4]

Harding would not take Wilson's bait to make a pronouncement on the Philippines. While serving in the Senate, he had chaired the Committee on the Philippines between 1919 and 1920, and had met with Harrison, Quezon, and Osmeña's independence mission in the summer of 1919.

As the incoming president, Harding's first move on the Philippine question was made on January 6, 1921, two months before his inauguration. Seeking counsel on the issue, he invited former Governor-General Cameron Forbes to visit him in his Marion, Ohio, home, hoping that Forbes would accept a second Philippine tour of duty. Eight days after receiving the invitation, Forbes appeared on Harding's Ohio doorstep. The president-elect reportedly began the meeting by flattering Forbes, telling him he was the only person who could straighten the crooked economic and political situation Harrison had created. While both Forbes and Harding agreed that Harrison should not stay on one hour longer than necessary, Forbes cautioned Harding against the simplistic view that the Wilson administration had ruined the Philippines, and he pointed to the positive changes in the Philippines over the past eight years. He also said that he would do all he could to help, but the ten years he had spent in the Philippines had taken a severe toll on his health, and he believed another stint in the Philippines would possibly result in an irreversible health crisis. He cautioned that it would be disastrous for Harding to reverse the increased role Filipinos enjoyed in the islands' political, social, and economic spheres, and suggested that Harding consider Generals Leonard Wood or John Pershing as the next governor-general. Both soldiers had served in the Philippines and were highly respected among the American populace. Finally, Forbes recommended that Harding send an investigative mission to the Philippines that could write a report on the colony's current situation. This would follow President Wilson's pattern after he won the 1912 election. Forbes ended the meeting with the promise that he would accept a lead role in a fact-finding mission if it were offered him; Harding thanked him for his advice, and they left each other on good terms.

Having struck out on his first choice for a new governor-general, Harding turned to his next-preferred candidate, General John Pershing. Best known as the commander of American forces in Europe in World War I, Pershing had both a remarkable military career and a recent personal tragedy. An 1886 graduate of West Point Academy, Pershing's first assigned duty was in New Mexico Territory, where he fought several battles against the Apache. He distinguished himself in the Spanish-American War and fought the Moros in the southern Philippines, leaving the archipelago in 1903. President Roosevelt took a liking to him and placed him in diplomatic and other assignments meant to advance his career. In 1905, Pershing married Helen Warren, the daughter of the influential Senator Francis Warren; this too helped him leapfrog more seasoned and deserving military colleagues. Pershing's seemingly charmed life came to a crashing halt on August 27, 1915, when a fire broke out at the San Francisco Presidio where his wife and children lived while he worked in Texas. Helen and their three daughters died in the fire; only their son survived the conflagration. Pershing responded to the tragedy by burying himself ever more deeply in his military career. His commitment resulted in President Wilson's appointing him as US commander of American forces in Europe throughout World War I. He returned to the US a hero, and he appeared to be the perfect choice as the next governor-general. But like Forbes, Pershing turned down the offer, citing health issues.

General Leonard Wood was the third and riskiest option. As Harding mulled over the gamble of asking Wood, he did not know the profound implications this would have on the life of John Early.

PART FIVE

Sweet Dreams and Nightmares Come True (1922–1932)

CHAPTER 27

The Wood-Forbes Mission

On the first day of spring, 1921, John W. Weeks, President Harding's secretary of war, met with General Leonard Wood and Cameron Forbes. His instructions were brief and clear. The president wanted them to conduct a thorough on-the-ground investigation as to whether the Philippines passed a three-point test for independence: Is the Philippine government properly and effectively administered? Are the non-Christian minority people properly cared for? Is the country's defense adequate to repel foreign aggression?

On that same day in Washington, Forbes met with his old friends from Manila, Mr. and Mrs. de Veyras. When he was governor-general, Forbes had helped Mrs. de Veyras's family avoid economic collapse with a generous loan. They told Forbes that Quezon was vehemently opposed to his return to the Philippines, but they hoped Forbes would not only lead the fact-finding mission but also consider returning to his role as governor-general. They also mentioned that Quezon was cautiously optimistic about Wood's appointment on the fact-finding mission because he had served as the governor-general of Cuba when that island gained independence.

When Wood and Forbes arrived in Manila on May 4, 1921, Quezon wrote Harrison that he and the other Filipino officials gave them a cool reception. This was not true, but he hoped the lie would stroke Harrison's ego. Quezon had in fact sent a cablegram to his friends in the US before Forbes arrived noting that it would be "very embarrassing" for him to deal with the former governor-general "especially because knowing Governor Forbes as I do I fear that he would make it impossible for me to have even official relations with him."[1] Quezon did not mention that he still owed Forbes three thousand pesos from an earlier loan. Despite all this, Wood and Forbes were pleasantly surprised by the warm reception they received at Manila's pier. Led by Quezon, the officials offered all their resources to assist the mission. To discredit the de Veyras's narrative and gain Forbes's confidence, Quezon showed Forbes a cablegram from Mr. de Veyra that noted they had "done everything possible to eliminate Forbes [from the mission]." Forbes was deeply hurt by the "treachery" from a couple who professed loyalty and faithful friendship. He broke off his relationship with them for the rest of their lives.[2]

There was another surprise waiting for Forbes. He had envisioned a leisurely two-month journey through some of the islands' major urban areas to ascertain the country's general well-being. Wood had other ideas. He planned a grueling schedule that included visiting every province, major city, and the majority of the archipelago's municipalities (counties). Wood's plan prevailed, but two months into their mission, he insisted that Forbes take several days of rest as he was on the edge of a "breakdown." When they had completed their investigation, they sent a message to Secretary Weeks, noting, "We have examined 47/48 provinces, have visited 449 [out of 800] municipalities, and covered 15,000 miles on foot, horseback, boat, motor car and rail. Everybody has been given an opportunity to speak. A great number of memorials have been received."[3]

While many issues surfaced concerning the Philippine situation, Wood and Forbes focused their report on the chaotic fiscal situation of the colonial government, which was on the verge of collapse. Wood sent a message to Secretary Weeks less than a month into their mission that "cash reserves are now about ten percent of legal requirements. If bank [Philippine National Bank] should fail, it would mean practical bankruptcy of insular government."[4] Writing to Bishop Brent about the same matter, Wood claimed that "the situation here is one of very great gravity."[5]

In early June, E. J. Westerhouse, the director of the colony's Bureau of Public Works, wrote to Harrison that he dreaded what would be uncovered if the mission should investigate the National Bank: "Concepcion's [bank president] record will read like the reminiscences of a drunken sailor."[6] Three weeks later, Concepción was arrested for breaking laws related to banking. Even Quezon acknowledged that he and Harrison were partially responsible for the National Bank debacle, though both profited from its mismanagement. Writing to Harrison, Quezon noted, "Had it not been for the Bank your administration would have been unassailable. . . . You and I saw that the bank would be our Waterloo."[7] Based on their investigation of the fiscal situation, Wood cabled Secretary Weeks that "Economically, the Filipino people are unable to maintain an independent government under present conditions."[8]

Their interviews also uncovered aspects of Harrison's professional and personal life. Initially they dismissed the sensational and sordid stories, but the overwhelming evidence and numerous reliable American and Filipino witnesses convinced them that the accounts were true. The mission's officials sought to downplay Harrison's foibles, but he had many enemies in the American community due to his policies that transferred almost all official positions from Americans to Filipinos. Indeed, there was a tinge of anti-Americanism in Harrison's worldview. This partially explains why he moved to the United Kingdom after he left the Philippines rather than return to his home country. His transfer of authority into Filipino hands was indeed helpful in fulfilling America's professed goal to withdraw its control from the islands. Unfortunately, his method was to favor and empower a few high-ranking politicians while he basically withdrew into a world of ceremonial roles and the darker compulsions of human nature.

Numerous officials, including Captain Seeber, the former chief of the Manila police; Senator Osmeña; Attorney General Araneta; attorney Francisco Ortigas; and Supreme Court Justice E. Finley Johnson painted a lurid picture of Harrison's personal and professional life. He was unrestrained in his pursuit of sexual encounters with women, particularly married and teenage women. One businessman, E. Womack, corroborated the stories about Harrison in an interview with Wood: "The Governor's morals were so bad, especially his tendency to follow up young girls, that he was regarded as a pervert."[9] Harrison's record was not a secret. Taft wrote to Wood just before the mission departed for the Philippines that Harrison "has been a disgrace to us by his domestic and personal indecencies and has seriously affected our standing among the Filipino people."[10] Even Osmeña, with whom Harrison and Quezon formed the government's economic enterprises, severely criticized the former governor-general's immorality, and Quezon also reportedly acknowledged Harrison's "flagrant immorality and neglect."[11]

But for Forbes, the most disturbing aspect of Harrison's tenure was his failure to properly manage his constituents. There were provinces that he never visited, others that he only passed through on a train ride, and many that he had visited only once in his eight years in office. He particularly neglected Luzon's highlanders, whom he reportedly disliked and visited only once. He despised their "unsanitized" lifestyle. Forbes sarcastically noted about Harrison's love of hygiene more than his care for Igorots: "Quite close to godliness."[12]

Harrison's champion was Quezon, who repeatedly wrote to the former governor-general expressing the sentiment, "I love you and admire you."[13] He also worked to make Harrison the first American to be granted naturalized Philippine citizenship. When Harrison returned to the Philippines in the 1930s, Quezon employed him as an advisor. He would continue to draw a salary as an advisor to multiple Philippine presidents, though a close reading of his diaries reveals his days and nights were filled with playing bridge and golf and attending parties. He publicly denigrated American culture and presented European society as preferable. His January 1, 1936, diary entry shows a man who knew he was living a life of amusement and not one of examination: "Doria [Harrison's fifth wife] and I had 'New Year's talk' and agreed that I was not really welcomed out here, and my services in the Government were not actually needed—that Quezon was exceedingly kind and loyal to me, but that my presence was likely enough a source of embarrassment to him. That we (D&I) would stop living in a dream world, that we would slow up social efforts and really try to enjoy ourselves."[14] But he continued in his dream world, divorcing Doria to marry a younger Spanish woman, his sixth wife, and using his naturalized Philippine citizenship to serve as an adviser to Philippine presidents after World War II.

Forbes and Wood concealed Harrison's profligate legacy in their final report. Their evaluation did include criticisms of the banking system and the overall economic health, or lack thereof, of the Philippines. They also had something to say about their visit and interviews with the Igorots, comments that would forever alter John Early's plan to quietly retire in California.

CHAPTER 28

Governor-General Wood

While Wood and Forbes made their way through the Philippine barrios, municipalities, and provinces in the summer of 1921, Quezon crossed the Pacific for a US visit. He confided to Wood that he was mentally and physically drained and needed to escape the pressure of Manila, though he publicly claimed that his US trip was to "sound out Harding on his plans for the colony."[1] Harding gave Quezon good and bad news. The good news came first: the US had no intention of retreating from its policy of granting the Philippines independence in due time, and it would continue Harrison's practice of placing Filipinos in positions once held by Americans. But Harding also said some alarming words. First, he intended to follow the 1916 Jones Law. This should have cheered Quezon, given how hard he had worked to formulate the bill and guide it into law. But he and Osmeña, with Harrison's acquiescence, had usurped much of the executive authority spelled out in the law and transferred it to the legislature, and to themselves in particular. Quezon now faced a reckoning for Harrison's detached leadership. He was also privately disappointed that Harding was pressing Wood to become the Philippines' next governor-general. Wood was Harrison's complete opposite, as he was woven from the same ideological cloth as Teddy Roosevelt, William Howard Taft, and Dean Worcester. In short, he was an indefatigable worker, paid attention to details, and believed in American exceptionalism. He would not be a weak executive filling his days with amusements or illicit affairs. Quezon returned to the Philippines determined to hold onto the authority that he believed rightly belonged to the legislative branch.

Wood reluctantly accepted Harding's appointment, and on October 15, 1921, he was installed as the interim Philippine governor-general. He wanted to include interim in the title because he planned to stay on for just one year before accepting a job as provost of the University of Pennsylvania.

Just days after Wood's installation, the Philippine legislature passed a resolution that it was satisfied with Wood's appointment and pledged its cooperation with him. While Wood appreciated the gesture, he did not care whether his professional decisions pleased a particular audience. For example, Manila's American community was appalled when Wood did not replace the members of Harrison's cabinet. He also regularly consulted with Osmeña, asking his opinion on several personnel appointments. While Wood surmised that this would anger Americans in Manila, he was surprised that Quezon in particular was disturbed by Osmeña's influence over the new governor-general.

Generally, American officials in Manila held a higher opinion of Osmeña than Quezon; however, this was not the case with Harrison, who belittled Osmeña in his private papers and blamed him for numerous problems. Though Harrison, Osmeña, and Quezon formed the politically powerful Board of Control, behind closed doors Osmeña was ridiculed by his two partners. Now with Harrison gone and a no-nonsense American executive in place, Quezon made his move to supplant Osmeña. His first volley criticized Osmeña for collaborating with Wood to fill official positions. He "charged his rival [Osmeña] with authoritarian domination of appointments to the government and of the legislative process." He labeled this leadership style as "'unipersonalism' and one-man rule."[2]

The divide among the Nacionalistas had little to do with the Wood-Forbes Report, although most Filipino officials were disappointed, if not outraged, by it. They viewed it as an evaluation of Filipino competence in self-rule, and if it represented a report card, they had failed. The Filipino politicians asked Harding to reserve judgment on the document until they could provide a rebuttal. He agreed. Meanwhile, even before the Philippine delegation met with Harding, one of the Philippine resident commissioners, Isauro Gabaldón, gave a lengthy speech to the US House of Representatives declaring, "My answer to the Wood-Forbes report is to demand anew, and with more emphasis than ever before, the immediate granting of independence. . . . I protest against that report, because it is inaccurate, unfair, misleading, unrighteous, uninformed and unenlightened."[3]

Led by Osmeña and Quezon, the Filipino delegates made their way to Washington to plead their case. It must have been an awkward trip for the two

Filipino leaders as Quezon's push for political power had split the Nacionalistas, and he had created the new Colectivista Party. They left the Philippines on the eve of the June 6th elections, which witnessed a slight victory for Quezon's new party.

After meeting with Harding, Quezon and Osmeña returned to the Philippines to pick up the scattered pieces from the national elections. Quezon believed he now enjoyed the most political influence. He flexed his political muscles when Wood proposed to name a member of the minority party to his cabinet. Quezon publicly declared that his Senate would not confirm a cabinet member who was not a member of the ruling party. This proved to be just the beginning of Quezon's turbulent and acrimonious relationship with the governor-general that only concluded with Wood's death.

Emboldened by his stand against Wood's proposed appointment, Quezon, without asking Wood, called a meeting of Wood's cabinet in early November 1922. He told them he wanted them to consider "'their duties and freedom of action in their own departments and their relations with the Legislature.'"[4] Following that meeting, the cabinet met with Wood on November 9 and asked if they served at his pleasure or Quezon's. Taken aback by the question, Wood asked why they would have anything to do with Quezon, and they told him about the clandestine meeting. Wood quickly summoned Quezon to the governor's mansion and admonished him to review the Jones Law and stay within its bounds, which placed the cabinet in the purview of the executive branch. Wood also told him that he had received orders to disentangle the government from big businesses.

Quezon would not back down. He initially agreed to sell off the government-controlled businesses, including the sugar factories and the Manila Railroad Company (MRR). A distinguished economist reviewing Quezon's relationship with the MRR concluded that "during his presidency of the MRR, Quezon had recklessly squandered the railroad's resources by issuing passes and creating jobs to further his political fortunes . . . [Wood then] ordered an audit of the enterprise, which eventually attributed the vicissitudes of the MRR to 'political influence.'"[5] The Board of Control agreed to privatize government-owned businesses. Wood began seeking buyers, thus fulfilling his pledge to Secretary Weeks to get the government and politicians out of the major business enterprises. Wood was pleasantly surprised by Quezon's agreement to disentangle himself from major businesses, but he had a surprise waiting for him.

Quezon told Harrison about how he had hoodwinked Wood by agreeing to sell off the government's Portland Cement Company though "he never intended to do so . . . [and when] Wood sent for him and presented him with the contract which he (Wood) had already signed . . . Quezon told him he had changed his mind, and that he took that privilege because Governor General Wood did it so often himself!"[6] This growing hostility became public on July 3, 1923.

During Harrison's tenure as governor-general, municipalities were always late paying their taxes to the colonial government. Typically, they would ask for an extension from the secretary of the interior, who would approve the delays with Harrison's acquiescence. During Wood's first year as governor-general, he excused this delay but warned municipality officials that chronically late payments were not fiscally responsible and instructed them to adhere to future deadlines. Thus, in the spring of 1923, when the first municipality requested permission to delay paying taxes, Wood denied the request. Quezon responded with a letter to Wood and asked the national papers to publish it. The letter not only filled the Philippine papers, it was also splashed on the headlines across America. Quezon accused Wood of acting as a dictator, arguing that municipalities should be able to decide when they wished to pay taxes. He ended the letter with a direct criticism: "There is a growing feeling among our people that the views of Filipino officials have little, if any, weight with you."[7] A looming showdown between Wood and Quezon was on the horizon, and it would center on John Early.

CHAPTER 29

Vindication

Governor-General Harrison did not like or appreciate the Igorots. Despite his minimal interaction with them, he asserted that he saw very little difference between the highlanders and the lowland Filipino Christians. Whatever differences there were he blamed on Worcester for keeping the Christian and pagan peoples separated.

His ignorance of historical and cultural differences between the Christian, Spanish-influenced lowlanders and the animist, independently minded mountain peoples was fortunately tempered by Section 22 of the Jones Law, which ordered the establishment of the Bureau of Non-Christian Tribes to assist the secretary of the interior in the "general supervision over the public affairs of the inhabitants of the territory represented in the legislature by appointive senators and representatives."[1]

Unfortunately for the Igorots, Harrison and his advisors did not prioritize the well-being of those in Mountain Province. When the Jones Law was passed, E. A. Eckman was commendably governing Mountain Province. His extensive professional experience dated back to 1901, and he had held numerous key positions in the province, including as an officer in the PC; lieutenant governor of Lepanto-Bontoc, Bontoc, and Benguet; and mayor of Baguio City from 1911 to 1913. In January 1913, he was appointed governor of Mountain Province, but Harrison replaced him with Joaquin Luna, the brother of the famous Philippine painter Juan Luna and the noted general Antonio Luna. In

1904, Joaquin Luna became La Union's governor, and then from 1908 to 1916, he represented La Union in the Philippine Assembly. The Jones Law called for the establishment of a senate, and Harrison let Luna know that he intended to appoint him the senator representing Mountain Province. As such, it would behoove Luna to spend some months in Mountain Province, so he was appointed as its governor for the summer months of 1916. In October 1916, Luna was replaced by Aquilino Calvo. It was a mistake for all involved. Of Calvo's four-year disastrous tenure as governor, Harrison simply wrote: "Dr. Calvo's administration was a failure."[2] Several journalists reported that Calvo's 1916 appointment was the means to remove him from the Philippine Senate, where he was unwanted due to his irrational behavior punctuated by an uncontrollable temper.[3] Once he got to Mountain Province, several of his lieutenant governors came to the quick conclusion that Calvo was mentally unsound and "a bit crazy."[4] Bontoc's deputy governor, Joaquin Ortega, became the object of Calvo's paranoia. Writing several years later, Ortega noted that within just a few months of Calvo's arrival, the new governor became convinced that Ortega was trying to replace him. Numerous complaints against Calvo made their way to Manila, and he spent his four-year tenure in a paranoid frenzy trying to hold onto his power.

Harrison had to fix this situation before the Wood-Forbes Mission, and so in 1920, Harrison replaced Calvo with Joaquin Luna. But the damage was done. When Mountain Province's elders learned that Wood and Forbes were going to visit the Philippines to assess the colony's situation, they wrote a letter that noted, among other things, "We do not believe that we are ready for independence for which our representatives and senators are clamoring . . . unless we [Igorots] are given some time to prepare ourselves for self-government we stand a good chance of being exploited by our Christian brothers. . . . We sincerely believe that we have expressed in the foregoing statements the opinion and wish of the majority of the inhabitants of the Mountain Province."[5] Fifteen elders signed the letter and attached their fingerprints to the document. Another observer noted that when Colonel Frank McCoy and Professor Otley Beyer of the Wood-Forbes Mission met with the Igorot elders in the presence of hundreds of people, including Filipino officials, they said, "We don't want these Filipino officials up here. We don't want them about. If we must have officials, give us the Americans back again."[6]

When Wood and Forbes visited portions of Mountain Province, trailing reporters penned stories with headlines such as: "Filipinos Divided: Many Don't Want Independence, Non-Christian Tribes Nearly a Unit against Change in Government";[7] "Filipinos Not All Agreed on Independence: Wood-Forbes Mission Finds Christians in Favor, Pagans Opposed";[8] and "Filipinos Are

Friendly with United States: Non-Christians Fear Independence, Want American Rule Kept."[9]

Indeed, when Forbes traveled to Bontoc, the elders requested the return of American officials until the Igorots gained enough educated indigenous leaders to govern the province. But then Forbes was stunned when he met with Ifugao elders at Payawan. Sitting with their Tagalog senator, they requested immediate independence. Forbes was fine with their wish but wanted to understand why their statement didn't align with everything else he had heard from the other Igorots. But it was later reported that "they had received instructions from the [Senator] that when questioned that they would state that they desired independence."[10] Ifugao's lieutenant governor, Dosser, was the most revered official in Mountain Province at the time on both sides of the independence issue, because he remained neutral as to political alliances. He had lived with an Igorot woman in his early days in Ifugao and eventually married a Filipina from the lowlands. Even Harrison reflected on Dosser's importance in Mountain Province, as well as the fact that the early American lieutenant governors were responsible for the modicum of civility there:

> The American officials in the Philippines who laid the foundation of the present edifice of peace, order, and progress in the Mountain Province displayed the best qualities of our race. The best-known active field agents among them were William F. Pack, Jeff D. Gallman, E. A. Eckman, Major O. A. Tomlinson, P.C., Eugene de Mitkievicz, John H. Evans, Leo J. Gove, Samuel E. Kane, W. F. Hale, C. W. Olson . . . and Major William E. Dosser, P.C. Often absolutely alone and surrounded by warlike men who had always in the past been regarded as savages, and had until then defied the white man, they worked steadily and unafraid along the paths of honor, justice, and reform. . . . To the Filipinos the service is not attractive, far away from gaiety and association with their own people.[11]

Even Dean Worcester, when asked to comment on the current situation in Mountain Province during the Wood-Forbes Mission, pointed out that Dosser was the only remaining faithful official in the area: "As you know, success in this matter [working among the Igorots] is very strictly a question of the personality of the men who carry on the work. The old trained men who got such admirable results have all been eliminated with the single exception of Dosser in Ifugao, and he has largely lost his influence through carrying out of undesirable orders given by higher authority. . . . I have been the recipient of many messages from headmen in the mountains begging for the elimination of Filipino officials and return to the old regime."[12]

Igorots desired self-rule, and to them this meant noninterference from both Americans and non-Igorot Filipinos, as Calvo's bungling of his duties made them wary of lowland officials. In a sense, American officials were the devil they knew; and if Dosser, Wood, Forbes, the Igorot headmen, and other historical documents are to be believed, the highlanders sought the return of an American provincial governor.

Reports began to circulate that the Igorots desired the return of John Early. Despite his humiliating 1911 dismissal, the Igorots remembered him as their former protector. His professional experience among the Igorots included his refusal to participate with American officials in a massacre against the Kalinga people, his attempt to keep Igorots from joining the tragic European fair experiences, his defense of the Igorots' land rights, the protection of his constituents from exploitation as cargadores, his use of Igorot traditional laws as a primary guide for keeping law and order, his development of brick structures in Bontoc that could weather seasonal typhoons, and his establishment of an effective system of rural education.

Some Filipino politicians dismissed the multiple sources and letters that requested Early's return to Mountain Province. If the Igorots wanted an American governor, why not choose Dosser?[13] He was on the scene and was well-known. But Dosser had multiple strikes against him. First, he was viewed as an outsider on multiple social fronts. He had reportedly gone through an Igorot ceremony in which he took a local woman as a common-law wife but then later married a more sophisticated lowland bride. His new wife went out of her way to prove that she did not have one drop of Igorot blood running through her veins. She wanted to be an outsider among the Igorots. Furthermore, while serving as Baguio's mayor, Dosser was at times excluded from American-only gatherings due to his wife's race. Finally, he was complicit in carrying out Calvo's ineffective policies in Mountain Province.

For his part, Early was remembered in both local, national, and international documents as an individual who respected Igorot culture. He attributed many of the conflicts with the Igorots to Western hubris and expressed in speeches and written documents the fundamental truth that all peoples were equal. Given his previous advocacy of human rights for the Igorots, it is not surprising that the highlanders sought his return.

Early did not know that he was being discussed as the Igorots met with the Wood-Forbes Mission. At the time he was preparing to retire and had received permission to return to the US. His past decade included monumental professional and personal trials; yet through it all, there remained two constants for him: his consistent attention to educating Filipino youth, which steadily moved him up the administrative ladder; and his presence in the Philippines. Most

Americans—whether business folk, missionaries, or colonial officials—left the Philippines at least once every four or five years. Since 1906, Early had left only once for about half a year. His reputation as a rock-solid stalwart who was committed to his profession increased during that decade. If 80 percent of success is showing up, then Early was wildly successful. His 1911 humiliation had the opposite effect Worcester intended. Early did not let his dismissal define his career or life. Still, ten years with no rest had taken its toll on Early and he needed a break. In his memoir he wrote that his scheduled vacation in 1917 was postponed "because of war activities in which I was engaged on behalf of the Philippine government." Five years had passed since that scheduled vacation, and he wrote, "I had begun to feel the need for vacation very badly."[14]

Just before leaving Manila, however, Early was stunned to receive a letter from Governor-General Wood. It had been more than a decade since Early was noticed by a governor-general, and that was when Forbes scolded him for being overprotective of the Igorots who Schneidewind wished to display in Europe. Thus, it must have been a shock for Early to receive Wood's letter. The document's content was even more surprising and thrilling:

July 7, 1922

My dear Mr. Early,

Although you are still engaged in interesting and constructive work, I imagine you often hark back to your early days in Bontoc. My assistant, Colonel McCoy, and your old friend, Dr. H. Otley Beyer have recently returned from a long trip in the Mountain Province and have been putting me in touch with the present conditions there. They have told me of your successful work there and the energy and interest you showed in the natives and their development and how you started the making of brick in the town of Bontoc and built a schoolhouse and other brick buildings there that still show your good and solid work. *But even more than the evidences of your energy is your winning the lasting goodwill of the Bontocs and their frequent expressions of it throughout the province.* I congratulate you on such fine performance and I hope the next time you come to Manila you will drop in to see me so that I can talk over the present conditions in Bontoc with you.

With my good wishes and please add my remembrances to Mrs. Early. Very Sincerely Yours,

Leonard Wood[15]

There it was. All his shame, failures, indefatigable energy, and defense of the Igorots against colonial exploitation—everything was vindicated in that one document. He was an Irish brickmaker's son who had learned his father's craft and shared it for the betterment of the Philippine highlanders. He was a late-blooming college graduate whose courses in sociology debunked notions of Western superiority and guided his actions and policies toward the Igorots. Unafraid of adventure and hard work, Early's 1906 decision to volunteer for the reportedly most difficult teaching assignment and his insistence that Igorots be given the same rights of protection and fair treatment had won for him "the lasting goodwill of the Bontocs . . . throughout the province."

Wood was so impressed with Early that he had decided to appoint him the governor of Mountain Province. But Early did not wish to cancel his trip to the US, and he needed to complete his commitment to his Minidoka homestead farm. Wood intervened. In a letter to the chief engineer for the US Reclamation Service, he explained Early's absence from his farm for ten years. He concluded the letter: "In view of his long service to the Philippine Government, it is requested that final crop proof will be expedited in his case so that he may return to duty early in 1923."[16]

The Earlys returned to the Philippines at the beginning of spring 1923, and Governor-General Wood requested that John be appointed as superintendent for schools in Mountain Province while Willa enjoyed her first permanent job in the Philippines. They owed a great deal to W. W. Marquardt for his intervention in securing Willa a position for which she was not qualified. They were able to thank Marquardt at a dinner held in his honor at Baguio City's Teachers Camp on Saturday, May 19, 1923. There were twenty guests, and limerick cards were placed at each setting. John's read: "In football they christened him Jack (He'd a kick like a mule as full-back). The old scout's a winner, The lusty old sinner, On the trail he's a whale with a pack." Willa's read: "There was once a fellow named Titian. Painting 'beauts' was his sacred mission. If 'Billie' he'd seen, He'd have fallen I ween—Dropped his brush and all inhibition."[17]

Wood initially appointed Early superintendent of Mountain Province schools, but he intended to install him as governor to reestablish American executive oversight of the Igorots. The reappointed Luna was more effective than Calvo, but the Igorots complained that he rarely visited them. Even Governor-General Harrison admitted that lowlanders did not want appointments to serve among the Igorots.

In his 1923 annual report, Wood noted, "[The] Mountain peoples as a whole desire continuance of American sovereignty. They also desire American local governors, and because of old hostilities running back for centuries are peculiarly averse to having their government too much Filipinized."[18] One year later, he wrote to his superiors, "Generally speaking, both Moros and non-Christians [Igorots] desire American governors because of old antipathies between them and the Christian Filipinos."[19]

These reports set the stage for Wood's decision to appoint Early as governor. He reportedly offered Governor Luna several other prestigious positions, but in the end, Luna resigned his post and did not remain in government service. His departure was more of a dismissal than a voluntary act, and Quezon and his colleagues were justifiably outraged with the situation. Nonetheless, on May 1, 1925, Wood appointed Early as interim governor of Mountain Province. While this was sweet vindication for Early, the appointment became a political battleground between Quezon and Wood.

CHAPTER 30

Political Deadlock

Quezon and Wood's relationship continued to deteriorate. Quezon's grievance against Wood bolstered his party's standing across the archipelago, and he claimed that not only was Wood an overt racist and dictator, but he also intended to reverse Harrison's policies of the Filipinization of the colonial government. On the other hand, Wood asserted that he planned to increase Filipinization but was bound to the Jones Law paradigm of leadership.

Late in the 1923 legislative session, Quezon offered Wood this quid pro quo: the legislature would appropriate funds for Wood's civilian advisers if he restored the same privileges cabinet secretaries enjoyed under Harrison. Not only did Wood reject this offer, he also asked the War Department if he could use a line-item veto on the Philippine legislature's proposed fiscal budget. When the answer came back yes, he promptly rejected the annual one hundred thousand pesos appropriated for the Commission on Independence. These funds paid for the numerous trips Filipino officials made to the US as lobbyists for Philippine independence. Quezon also used these monies to fund US excursions for his supporters. Wood believed these trips were junkets that allowed politicians to take ocean cruises and holidays in Washington. Quezon challenged Wood's line-item veto authority in the courts and called for a boycott of all American-imported products. Losing the legal appeal, he retaliated by pressuring the legislature to reject all of Wood's cabinet appointments. When it did this, Wood simply waited for the session to end and reappointed the same men on an interim basis. They could serve until the Senate reconvened in the fall of 1924, when it would assuredly reject the nominees once again. Quezon responded to the interim appointments by calling the legislature into session in mid-July.

Quezon's last stand was to prevent Wood's governmental appointments, which culminated in a major fight over John Early's May 1, 1925, appointment. Early began his duties as interim governor (until the Senate would be in session) and noted that the province was "in not very good condition."[1] He was fifty-one years old, and it had taken half a century for him to reach what he thought would be the pinnacle of his career.

But Quezon had no intention of approving Early's nomination, and on October 1, 1925, the Seventh Philippine Congress (1925–1928) rejected the appointment. One month later Wood reappointed Early as interim governor. The game went on for the next three years, with the Senate rejecting Early's appointment and then Wood reappointing him in an interim position at the end of the legislative session. It would take an untimely death to change this situation.

Wood's health had slowly deteriorated during the first years of the 1920s, and he often claimed he did not have time to follow doctors' orders. But after years of delay, he underwent the first of two much-needed hernia surgeries on September 22, 1926. His painful three-week recovery initially kept him in Manila, but in November he traveled to Baguio to recuperate in the cool, pine-forested Cordillera mountains. His spirits dramatically changed with the scenery and climate. He also continued to grow closer to the Earlys, with whom the Woods spent a great deal of time while in Baguio. Returning to Manila for Christmas, Wood wrote an end-of-the-year letter to Early, closing with, "Mrs. Wood joins me in all best wishes for a Happy New Year and many of them for you and yours and the people whom you are governing so well. With kindest regards, sincerely yours, Leonard Wood."[2]

The spring of 1927 brought with it the second hernia surgery, and the Woods again traveled to Baguio, where they remained until early May. But just when Wood regained his health, another disaster struck. On their May 7 return to Manila, as they were about 40 miles from the city, their chauffeur swerved to miss a pony-pulling cart and flipped the car over as it hit a pile of gravel. Mrs. Wood's ankle was broken, and Wood was "badly shaken up."[3]

Amid these misfortunes, Wood's long-standing chronic issue reemerged. For decades, he had dealt with an angioma brain tumor that most often remained dormant but would then begin growing, making it difficult for him to function. He had undergone previous surgeries that cut away portions of the tumor, allowing him to carry on his duties. His 1910 surgery for the tumor brought immediate relief and a diminution of the pre-surgery symptoms, but over time the tumor had again grown to a dangerous level. In 1925, the tumor's growth began affecting Wood due to a semi-paralysis of his left leg and arm. Dr. Harvey Cushing, a leading neurosurgeon, had operated on Wood in 1910, and he promised that another surgery would return Wood to normal physical functioning. In 1927, Cushing was at Harvard, so Wood had to make his way back to his boyhood home for the operation.

Wood left the Philippines on May 28, 1927, and trouble seemed to follow him. After a stop in Kobe, Japan, the vessel experienced a sudden "roll [which] flung him against a chair, breaking three ribs and tearing loose some of the muscles."[4] He could barely walk after that, and every breath was an agony. A more accurate report indicated that the SS *President Madison* had "lurched and threw him against the rail," breaking two of his ribs.[5] Following this accident, Wood remained in a weakened condition even after the SS *President Madison* docked at Victoria, British Columbia.

President Coolidge, vacationing in South Dakota, asked Wood to meet him at his summer house there, and so they spent the days of June 23 and 24 together discussing the Philippine situation. The press reported that Wood's apparent physical frailty "handicapped him considerably." Though he assured reporters that he planned to be back in the Philippines in September, many closed their stories on the Wood-Coolidge meeting with the note that though "he seemed determined to continue his work there . . . Wood is advancing in years and it is not known what effect the injuries he received have had on him."[6]

Coolidge publicly reiterated his support and admiration for Wood as the governor made his way to New York to spend some time with his friend Henry Stimson. He eventually arrived in Boston, where Dr. Cushing awaited him. In the seventeen years since his last operation on Wood, Cushing had learned a great deal about brain surgery. For example, he realized the advantages of using local anesthesia so that the patient could communicate with the doctor during surgery.

Based on his two prior experiences, Wood knew that the surgery would take a few hours, so they planned to start the operation at 8:30 a.m. on August 6. He had every confidence in Cushing and did not consider this a serious or dangerous procedure—Wood was also a surgeon. He gave no special directions to his wife should anything go awry, and he made no will. The surgery was proceeding relatively well except that there was an enormous amount of blood loss, so much so that at one point Wood lost consciousness. Anticipating this, Dr. Cushing had several volunteer medical students in the room, and over the course of the procedure, three students provided their blood to the governor.

By 2:00 p.m., Cushing wanted to stop the operation and resume the following day, but Wood insisted that Cushing finish the job. He continued several more hours, and just as he was about to call the surgery a success, he took out the last piece of the tumor. Unfortunately, a bone hid the fact that the tumor was attached to the large vein that runs through the middle of the brain. Cushing's action opened the side of the vein, and an enormous amount of blood came gushing out of the lesion. By 4:30 p.m., Cushing believed he had found and plugged the cut with cotton. After several hours he reopened the wound and removed the cotton, but by 8:30 p.m.—twelve hours into the surgery— Wood's blood pressure plummeted, and he lost consciousness. He died at 1:50 a.m. In his notes following the surgery, Dr. Cushing, who was known for his inordinate self-confidence, wrote, "Thus died a gallant gentleman from a combination of too much courage and poor judgment on the part of the surgeon."[7]

Wood's unexpected death altered US-Philippine relations, and it changed Early's life and his relationship with Philippine legislators. Early was in his third year as interim governor with little change in sight, and his primary, if not exclusive, political ally was now gone. Many understood his precarious political situation, and he claimed that some legislators approached him for corrupt favors in return for confirmation. He declined such requests. His more immediate task was an August 13, 1927, public speech at Baguio's Auditorium, which was directed toward Filipinos and Americans. He began with the sobering words, "General Wood is dead. That message prostrated us Sunday afternoon. All our groping minds could grip was we will never see those kindly eyes kindle nor hear the encouragement of his voice . . ." After reviewing Wood's life and accomplishments in some detail, Early ended his address with the only reference to his personal relationship with him: "As a man, we all love him and who can speak of the man who holds his soul—there are no words. The future may give us [Early] some rewards, but nothing to equal his simple 'I wish I had more like you.' It has made the trails easy, the rivers safe, the Apayao jungles pleasant. His reward is ours while memory lasts."[8]

There is no indication that Early knew what was ahead of him, but he currently occupied a position higher than he could have ever hoped for. Then, to the astonishment of all, the new governor-general became Early's personal and influential friend. They became intertwined due to a congressional hearing that took place before the new governor-general left the US for his post.

CHAPTER 31

"We Felt It Was Our Duty to Confirm Him"

Isauro Gabaldón y González woke up to a snow-covered Washington, DC, on Wednesday, February 1, 1928. With a bushy mustache, a large head, and a fleshy face, he took after his Spanish father more than his Filipina mother. Educated in his father's hometown of Tébar, Spain, Gabaldón then entered Madrid's Universidad Central. After earning a law degree, he moved to his Philippine home province of Nueva Ecija, northwest of Manila, and became its governor in 1906. He then entered national politics, which eventually led to his position as one of the two Filipino resident commissioners in the US Congress.

Gabaldón did not want to get out of bed and face the day, but he did, making his way to the congressional room where the Committee on Territories and Insular Possessions was scheduled to debate and vote on S. 2787, the Belo Bill, which gave the Philippine governor-general authority to, among other things, appoint the governor of Mountain Province without needing the Philippine Senate's approval. Also up for debate was an annual appropriation of $125,000 for the governor-general to employ special advisers of his choosing. While Gabaldón vehemently opposed the bill, that was not the primary cause for his depressed affect and mood at the committee meeting.

Senator Frank B. Willis, the committee chairman from Ohio, brought the meeting to order at precisely 10:30 a.m. Willis, a strikingly handsome fifty-six-year-old, was climbing the ranks in the Republican Party and was in the midst of a campaign run for president. He would be dead the following month from a brain aneurysm at a political rally.

Willis started the meeting by explaining the urgency of passing the bill. Henry Stimson, the newly appointed Philippine governor-general, was on his way to the Philippines, but before leaving he told Willis that the governor-general's job would be easier if the Belo Bill would be approved by the committee before he arrived in Manila, and "needless to say it would be a still greater assistance if [it] can be passed promptly."[1]

While Gabaldón may have appreciated Stimson's desire to expedite the bill's passage, he charged Senator Willis with ramming it through the committee. For one thing, Gabaldón's fellow commissioner, Pedro Guevara, also a lawyer and brilliant writer, had suffered a heart attack the evening before the committee meeting and remained in serious condition, which was the primary reason for Gabaldón's sorrow. Gabaldón had spent the previous day with Guevara and needed his colleague to present a proper argument against the bill. Furthermore, Gabaldón rhetorically asked how a fitting discussion could take place when "as it is, there are only two on your [American] side out of thirteen members composing the committee and myself alone on the other."[2] Willis would not budge from his determination to push the bill through. It was up to Gabaldón to speak against it.

In a brilliant speech cut short only by a time limit imposed on him, he explained why Filipino politicians were justifiably concerned that the bill would further diminish their authority and push the Philippines further away from independence. He argued that Americans should trust Philippine legislators. To prove his point, he mentioned how the case of John Early proved the Philippine Senate's integrity, for, after rejecting his appointment several times, it reversed its decision, coming to the conclusion "after proper and thorough investigation that it did not [initially] act correctly."[3] He explained that the senators were insulted when Wood asked the Mountain Province governor, Joaquin Luna, to resign. Yes, Luna was not a highlander, but he was the brother of two national heroes. They could agree that Luna's predecessor, Governor Calvo, had made a mess of things, but Luna effectively managed the Igorots. So, the senators' response was a three-year refusal to confirm Early. But then Gabaldón insisted that their rejection of Early had nothing to do with politics; rather, the politicians simply did not "know him [Early] and we did not think he would make a good governor."[4] When Wood persisted in appointing him as interim governor, the Senate sent a delegation to interview Early and review his work. Gabaldón claimed Early had so impressed the politicians that at the following session the Senate unanimously confirmed his appointment. To emphasize the difficulty of the situation as well as Early's impressive character and work,

Gabaldón closed this portion of his presentation with these words: "You can see how embarrassing it was for the Philippine Senate to confirm the appointment of an American who had replaced a distinguished Filipino. There was every political consideration for disapproving this appointment, but when we learned of the success of Mr. Early as governor of Mountain Province, we felt that it was our duty to confirm his appointment and we did not hesitate to reverse ourselves."[5]

These complimentary words about Early did not hide the reality that politics played a part in the Senate's refusal to confirm his appointment. Wood first appointed Early on March 1, 1925, but the Senate only confirmed his appointment during the last days of August 1927, just days after Governor-General Wood's unexpected death. Was Early's appointment the Senate's postmortem gift to Wood?

Early received many congratulatory messages following his confirmation, but none was more heartfelt than a lengthy September 12 letter from Gouverneur Frank Mosher, the Episcopalian Bishop of the Philippines who had replaced Brent. Before coming to the Philippines, Mosher had spent twenty-four years as a missionary in China. He was born two years before Early, and they both shared the pain of losing their mothers when they were young boys. They were also similarly described as possessing endless energy and a vision for providing a better future for the Igorots.

Mosher began the letter by explaining that his delay in sending his congratulations via telegram was because he didn't want anyone to wonder if "it made a particle of difference one way or the other whether you were confirmed or not." He also complimented Early on his diplomacy and how his personality, policies, and achievements made it so "there is unquestionably a confidence and a trust in you and a liking for you personally such as overcomes their consistency [of rejecting Wood's appointees]."[6]

Another congratulatory message came from Charles Olson, the former treasurer of Mountain Province, who had kept a diary that commented on Worcester's 1911 dismissal of Early. Early surely enjoyed writing a lengthy response to Olson. He reported that his two former antagonists—Kane and Hale—sought to make a living through work on Worcester's ranch in the southern Philippines, but both were fired due to their "deficiencies."[7] Kane was working for a hotel in Baguio and survived by receiving support from his wife's lover in Manila. Hale moved to Manila, where he worked for a rope company. Of greatest surprise was what had happened to former Governor William Pack. Early claimed Forbes told him that Pack had sworn off alcohol and had become a minister, which, Early added, "strengthens one's faith in the omnipotence of God to hear such things."[8]

Olson must have smiled when Early addressed his sweetest reversal of fortune: "I saw quite a bit of Mr. Worcester before he died. . . . Mr. Worcester revised his opinion of me upward before he died and downward of the gentlemen who libeled me when I was here as Lieutenant Governor."[9]

In his first three years as governor, Early witnessed unprecedented advances among the Igorots. His 1926 and 1927 provincial annual reports are the most cited from the era of American rule. He delivered numerous speeches explaining the innate genius of the Igorots' morality and sense of justice. His growing reputation and the affection directed toward him were captured in a letter to Early from a prominent Igorot: "Please let me have the consolation and satisfaction of expressing in words and on a piece of paper a strong feeling that I resisted to express by acts when I came to see you in Baguio. . . . All of us whom you have bestowed special favors and shown special interests when we met each other feel that we have something binding in common, and we instinctively think of you, talk about you, and murmur words of prayer for you. Please feel that you have so many friends in the Mountain Province who are worshiping you."[10]

Between 1925 and 1928, Early resembled a horse finally set free of its stable. He plunged into the daily rhythms of hiking throughout the province, meeting his constituents (no matter what their requests or station in life), and instituting policies for social, educational, and medical advancements.

As 1927 came to a close, life was good for Early: Worcester had apologized to him, the Philippine Senate acknowledged its earlier error in not confirming such an effective and gracious nominee, and he savored the opportunity to tirelessly serve the people he loved. It would seem that life could not get better. But then it did. The following year a man came into his life who would become both a powerful professional ally and one of Early's closest friends.

CHAPTER 32

Henry Stimson

On November 15, 1935, the status of the Philippines changed to that of a Commonwealth, and the American governor-general's position was replaced by Manuel Quezon, the first elected president of the Philippines. Between 1901 and 1935, there were sixteen American governor-generals including one who later became a US president and Supreme Court judge (Taft), the first cousin of a US president (Theodore Roosevelt Jr.), a man who barely lost the nomination for a successful Republican presidential contest (Wood), and a famous tennis player whose name still graces a major tournament (Dwight Davis). But of all these officials, Henry L. Stimson was the most distinguished. He served in the cabinets of four presidents as either secretary of war or secretary of state. As secretary of war during World War II, he told the newly sworn-in president, Harry Truman, about the secret production of the atomic bomb. One biographer notes that "Stimson was almost alone in having responsibility for every stage in the atomic-bomb project—from the theoretical research that made it possible to the operational decision to drop it on a certain target on a particular day."[1]

Stimson was born on September 21, 1867, in Manhattan, New York, to a wealthy family and a father who was one of the city's leading surgeons. At the age of eight, Henry and his six-year-old sister, Candace, lost their mother to a kidney illness. In his state of abject grief, Stimson's father sent him to the Phillips Academy, an elite boarding school in Andover, Massachusetts. Stimson excelled there and went on to earn an undergraduate degree at Yale and then a law degree from Harvard, after which he promptly moved back to Manhattan and joined a firm headed by Elihu Root, one of the primary architects of America's foreign expansion. Stimson concurred with and praised Root's imperial vision, and by 1895, he had become a partner in one of Wall Street's most influential and prestigious law firms: Root, Clark & Stimson.

Though not keenly interested in politics, Stimson acquiesced to the pressure placed on him by the New York Republican Party machine and ran for governor in 1910. As expected, he lost the election but was rewarded for his efforts by being named President Taft's secretary of war in 1911. His portfolio included the Bureau of Insular Affairs, which administered the Philippines.

Following Taft's 1912 presidential defeat, Stimson returned to his law practice and increased in national prominence by his participation in World War I, where he served in France as an artillery officer. Various US presidents sent him to foreign lands to negotiate treaties and his influence within the Republican Party grew. He still practiced law in Manhattan, but became one of the earliest and most vocal voices warning that Japan's expansion in East Asia should be curtailed.

During the summer of 1926, the Stimsons took a leisurely journey across the Pacific at the invitation of their longtime friend Leonard Wood. Stimson's Philippine visit was not solely a vacation, as Wood sought his advice on how to break his paralyzing relationship with Filipino politicians, particularly Quezon and Osmeña. In typical Wood style, he packed Stimson's itinerary with semi-arduous trips. A lifelong outdoor and fishing enthusiast, Stimson hooked a barracuda in the waters surrounding Cebu. Wood then took him to the Moros' remote villages.

Back on Luzon, the Stimsons were thrilled to escape the oppressive heat as they made their way to Baguio. The Colonel, as he was known, thoroughly enjoyed Baguio and expressed his admiration for Early's work among the Igorots.

While he was in Manila, Stimson met with Osmeña and Quezon and told them not to expect immediate Philippine independence. He also indicated that he would like to see some type of ongoing connection between the US and the Philippines. Following the Philippines visit, Stimson toured Kyoto, and his appreciation for its beauty reportedly spared it from the atomic bomb.

Upon returning home, he updated President Coolidge on the Philippine situation, and he praised Wood's work and policies. He wrote articles published by *Foreign Affairs* and *The Saturday Evening Post* in which he heaped praise on Wood while blaming Filipino politicians for the political impasse.[2] Given Stimson's alliance with imperialists like Root, Taft, Roosevelt (with whom he was particularly close), and Wood, it is surprising that he became one of the most popular and admired governor-generals in the Philippines.[3]

When Governor-General Stimson walked onto the Manila pier on March 1, 1928, he faced a significant challenge. The past two executives were ineffective— Harrison because of his laziness and profligacy, Wood due to his inability to work with Filipino legislators. Stimson needed to put the colonial train back on its governing track.

In his inaugural speech in Manila, Stimson referred to the Filipinos as "my fellow-countrymen."[4] Unlike Wood, who refused to meet with a Filipino official without a white witness, Stimson enjoyed numerous one-on-one meetings with Quezon, Osmeña, and other Filipino politicians. He often said that "the only way to make a man trustworthy was to trust him."[5] Though he held the same racist views as Wood and Roosevelt, Stimson decided to attend Manila's mixed Filipino-American Episcopal church rather than his "segregated Presbyterian congregation."[6] The Stimsons made the governor-general's palace open to all, and as Mrs. Osmeña told Mrs. Stimson during one of her many visits, "The best improvement that you have made in the Palace is that you have opened its doors again to the Filipinos."[7]

Stimson also paved the way for the executive transition from an American governor-general to a Filipino president. He had many more plans for the Philippines, but his tenure in the islands lasted just one year—almost to the day. The 1928 presidential election placed Herbert Hoover in the White House, and he tapped Stimson to be his secretary of state. But for the year Stimson was in the Philippines, the most significant personal change in his life was a deep and abiding friendship with John Early, and everyone knew it.

Stimson's formative years at the very formal Philip's Academy, Yale, and Harvard, along with his innately reserved personality, made him appear to be cold and aloof. Critics picked up on this and later reported, after his 1910 loss of the New York governor's election: "His cultured accent, his uneasy platform presence, his cold personality, almost every detail of his manner . . . gave his electorate an impression of a young aristocrat who condescends to rule, and who, though he may be a good ruler, condescends. . . . The opposition press called him 'the human icicle.'"[8] Even Quezon, who claimed that Stimson was the Philippines' most effective governor-general, did not develop a close friendship with him like he had with Harrison. But Stimson's relationship with Early defied his normal remoteness. Walter Robb, who was arguably the most influential American journalist in Manila during the American colonial period, put it best: "Stimson cultivated a coldness toward men, but to this man [Early] he utterly melted."[9]

The friendship between the two men seemed unlikely. Stimson was the scion of a family whose Ipswich, Massachusetts, roots began when George Stimson arrived in the colony around 1636. Henry's father occupied a prominent social position as an accomplished surgeon in Manhattan. Early's parents, on the other hand, were nineteenth-century Irish immigrants, and his father was a disgraced, bankrupt brickmaker. Stimson attended America's finest schools, joined Manhattan's top law firm, and quickly became a partner. He was also quite wealthy. In 1903, at the age of thirty-six, he bought 100 acres in West Hills on Long Island, where he built a distinguished summer home. On the other hand, Early graduated from the Washington Agricultural College, an institution that was so new when he attended it that its future was in doubt. His only chance to own property was a homestead covered by sagebrush and bereft of water.

But there were deeper aspects to Stimson and Early that cemented their friendship: both men were around eight years old when their mothers died, neither had children, and they were intolerant of immoral conduct. Throughout their careers numerous reports noted that they reprimanded employees for making disparaging comments about women or boasting about sexual exploits. They were straitlaced and not given to promiscuity or excessive alcohol. Finally, Stimson and Early were professional to the core. Their prodigious reports are characterized by detail and thoroughness.

It is a well-known axiom that we never get a second chance to make a first impression. Stimson's standard of behavior, decorum, and refined speech were at such a level that he often discounted individuals after initial meetings due to their language or behavior. Early's chance with Stimson came two years before his appointment as governor-general. On the evening of Thursday, August 12, 1926, Stimson invited Early for dinner at Manila's Malacañang Palace. This occurred during the Stimsons' visit with Leonard Wood. Stimson's diary notes that the conversation went late into the evening. The primary topic was the welfare of the Igorots and Early's two-year tenure as the province's interim governor. Early presented demonstrable progress over the past two years and explained that his interim status was due to the Senate's ongoing battle with Wood. Stimson noted in his diary, "Met with Gov. Early at dinner at Palace and had long talk over conditions in Mountain Province. Fine upstanding American."[10]

Two years later, when he arrived as governor-general, it took Stimson just a few weeks to put his advisory team in place. Initially, he tapped two men to implement his vision for what he hoped would heal the country's political and social wounds while maintaining the Republican Party's policy of keeping the

Filipinos under American rule. These two men, Halstead Dorey (1874–1946) Blanton C. Winship (1869–1947) were both World War I heroes.

Following his church attendance and lunch, Stimson worked on Sunday afternoons with his two top aides. But on Sunday of June 17, 1928, John Early became part of Stimson's inner circle, and they became a professional foursome. They spent that particular afternoon filling open positions in the government and discussing provincial boundaries. For this, Stimson turned to Early for guidance and advice and asked the governor to submit a report the following day that he could share with General Douglas MacArthur, who had been given command of the Philippines that summer. Stimson's three advisers often met in Baguio, as Early had a province to govern while Dorey and Winship were geographically flexible.

During his second month as governor-general, Stimson traveled north for an extensive inspection trip among the Igorots. This was his first opportunity to witness Early's governing policies and philosophy in action. Stimson, Mabel (his wife), and Dorey left Baguio on Monday morning, April 16, heading north to meet the Earlys. As soon as their vehicle passed Trinidad, the road became barely navigable. By noon they had reached Haight's Place. The story behind this rest stop resembled one in a Victorian novel. During the Philippine-American War, an American volunteer soldier named G. F. Haight was close to death due to tuberculosis and was advised to journey into the high mountains with the hope that the cool air might revive his deteriorating body. He made it 30 miles north of Baguio before losing all his strength. In his exhausted state, he was slowly nursed back to health by an Igorot woman whom he eventually fell in love with and married. Now back on his feet, Haight realized that the Cordillera's climate and elevation (over 6,000 feet above sea level) was conducive to growing vegetables. He used his savings to buy seed, and with his wife made a profitable business selling vegetables in Baguio's larger market. With their profits they built a large house that accommodated travelers making their way in and out of the Bontoc and Ifugao areas.

After lunch at Haight's Place, Stimson's party continued north until they hit a spot approximately 7,000 feet above sea level. Experimenting with a shortwave radio, they picked up a strong signal coming out of Leningrad and enjoyed a wireless concert that evening.

The next morning their transportation mode changed from car to horseback, and at 11:30 a.m. they reached the mountain peak of Mount Data, where Governor Early awaited them. They spent the afternoon and evening at a rest house, and the following day they rode into Bontoc, where Willa had prepared a feast for them.

For the next two days, Stimson met with the Igorot headmen and officials. His diary entries reflect how tremendously impressed he was by the work of the Igorot officials and Early's governance. The brick hospital, administrative buildings, and modern jail facility were a testament to Early's work as lieutenant governor between 1910 and 1911. On Thursday, the Igorot headmen presented their requests to Stimson, and he was pleased to hear what they were: they asked for more medical personnel, and forestry laws that were fair to those planting and cutting trees.

Stimson decided to make a more arduous journey into Ifugao territory. Leaving Mabel with Willa in Bontoc, he asked Early and Dorey to join him. For the next four days, the three men made their way into numerous hamlets and spent some time in Banaue. The monumental rice terraces so impressed Stimson that he wrote a three-page description of the region. Early's stamina during the hikes impressed Dorey and Stimson, as did the familiarity and affection the Igorots extended to Early during the evening fire chats. During their hikes, Early repeatedly requested that Stimson's administration implement a reforesting program in Bontoc, Kalinga, and Ifugao as well as a preservation plan for all of the Cordillera's existing forests. Stimson's diary on the Banaue experience ended with the words, "Governor Early will send me a rough description of three forest reservations—one Mt. Data, two—Mt. Polis and the Polug Range. I will see Fischer about them before I go down to Manila so that he may take the necessary steps."[11]

Those four days in Ifugao cemented Stimson and Early's relationship. From that point on, Stimson consulted regularly with Early on numerous matters, and they vacationed together, both in the lowlands and highlands. The two met eight of the twelve months Stimson was in the Philippines, and their wives also corresponded regularly. While most of their interaction centered on official business, there were numerous examples of late-night personal conversations—something rare for Stimson. He noted "a very pleasant" dinner and evening with the Earlys on October 12.[12] The Mountain Province governor regaled the group with stories of his first days in Bontoc and his adventures while serving under Worcester. Stimson recapped each story in his diary; many were comical, but some more sobering. The last story of the evening (mentioned in other documents) was the darkest one. In 1909, Early and three cargadores climbed Mount Kabunian, a challengingly steep mountain just south of Bontoc and west of Ifugao in today's Benguet Province. He described the experience of navigating "certain cliffs which must be gotten around on ledges two or three inches wide where one must use his hands to cling to roots and jutting points of rock to keep him from going a thousand-foot drop to the bottom of the cliffs." As night fell, a powerful typhoon descended on the surrounding mountains and valleys, leaving Early and his companions cold and scared. Stuck near a small landing, Early told the Igorots not to venture off in the storm, and in the morning they would make their way off the mountain. When morning arrived and the rain diminished, Early found that all three cargadores had died of exposure: "The cold wind and horizontally driven rains which made the shelter even of a rock ledge impassible were sufficient to account for their deaths." Early made his way down the mountain, only to be greeted by a group who claimed that the cargadores' deaths were due to the fact that "they had violated the dwelling place of spirits."[13] Though Early finished his tale by praising the faith and spirituality of the Igorots, Stimson noted that the story left them with a sense of dread.[14]

Stimson spent the 1929 New Year holiday with Early in Baguio, and their friendship grew to the point that Early received a letter from a former colleague in Negros who claimed, "Another news item brought by this mail . . . is that 'Governor John C. Early, of the Mountain Province persistent rumor makes the next Vice-governor!'"[15]

But as Stimson and Early took long walks in Baguio in the first days of January 1929, it is unclear whether they knew how the next two months would radically change their lives. Both men loved what they were doing. At one point, Stimson viewed his role as governor-general as the capstone of a career in public service, though in many ways his career was just beginning. In just a few weeks he would become the US secretary of state and eventually the secretary of war throughout World War II.

As for Early, he was at his highest professional position, and in a few weeks US newspapers referred to him as "the best governor in the Philippines" and the next Philippine governor-general. But at the precipice of being remembered in perpetuity, his life took a dark turn—so dark that he would be forgotten in US and Philippine history.

Chapter 33

Dark Days

Baguio City's cool pine-scented breezes made the first days of 1929 a time of reflection, relaxation, and anticipation for Henry Stimson and John Early. The city's fecund soil produces exotic flowers while the rains stay away in January, and the early morning fog gives way to deep blue skies. Stimson was not anxious to leave the mountain air for Manila's oppressive heat, and his diary for that year's first week is punctuated with comments about long walks with Early. They enjoyed each other's company and spoke as if 1929 would be a year of great accomplishment and advancement for the Philippines in general, and Mountain Province in particular. But both were hiding important secrets and information from each other. Perhaps they hoped to go on pretending that life could continue as it had for the past few months. They understood that their friendship and Baguio's beauty were unbearable because they could not make time stand still.

Stimson's secret was on the verge of exposure, and many saw it coming. Its immediate cause was the November 6, 1928, US presidential election that swept Secretary of Commerce Herbert Hoover into the nation's highest office. Hoover's dominating victory (he lost only eight of the forty-eight states and won 444 of the 531 electoral votes) gave him a mandate to continue pushing the Republican agenda, which included the ideology of American exceptionalism. His most important cabinet choice was that of secretary of state. Japan was flexing its military and colonial muscles in Manchuria, and a rising German politician in Bavaria was poised to further change Europe and the world. He had already taken the title Führer as the Nazi party's supreme leader.

Having served as President Coolidge's secretary of commerce, President-elect Hoover knew firsthand the importance of professional relationships between the president and cabinet members. Hoover's relationship with the president during his six years of service in the cabinet was prickly. When asked if he would support Hoover, President Coolidge replied, "For six years that man has given me unsolicited advice—all of it bad."[1]

There were many viable candidates for the important post of secretary of state, but Hoover chose Stimson because he had, among many other achievements, helped negotiate a critical peace in Nicaragua's 1927 civil war. His work in the Philippines was also universally praised, and he had experience as President Taft's secretary of war from 1911 to 1913. Initially, Stimson only told Mabel about the offer, but then American papers began catching on to the story during the second week of January. The *Austin American* ran a story on January 14 noting that a surprising new development in Hoover's cabinet "was the entry of Henry L. Stimson, governor general of the Philippines" as the potential new secretary of state.[2] Even when his selection became apparent in the first days of February, Stimson remained silent about his potential new role. Finally, on February 6, Stimson released this press statement: "It is true that at the request of the President-elect of the United States I am about to leave the Philippines in order to take up another duty. What the nature of that duty is I prefer to leave to Mr. Hoover to announce."[3]

Early's secret was also becoming difficult to hide. In fact, we do not know when he himself found out about it. There were rumors. People would later tell Early they knew something was wrong. He looked a bit more tired than usual, and his solid six-foot frame seemed to be shrinking. He was always on the move, so some thought that he just needed some rest. Since his May 1906 arrival in the Philippines to January 1929, Early had spent 249 out of 265 months working full-time in the islands, and he had been governing Mountain Province for five years. The professional and physical burden of his past twenty-three years would tax anyone's mental and physical strength. Still, there was something noticeably different about Early's gait and affect. There were also other symptoms: severe abdominal pains, blood in his stool, and greater fatigue. He initially thought that his professional pressures were manifesting in ulcers. But it was worse than that. After a clandestine visit to the colony's most respectable physicians, they all agreed on the diagnosis—an advanced and terminal case of colon cancer. While the doctors kept this diagnosis to themselves, per his request, Early must have wondered about the disease's timing.

Here he was, on the cusp of becoming the colony's vice-governor or even governor-general after failing at almost every endeavor in his life, and now he had to die.

Early confided this news first to Willa and then to Stimson. At the same time, Stimson told Early that he had been recalled to the US by the new president-elect but that he had a plan to help Early. As the son of a prominent surgeon, Stimson followed advancements in medicine. The growing reputation and buzz around Dr. George Crile and his Cleveland Clinic included tales of operations and postsurgical radiation treatments that provided cures for even the worst cancers. Stimson believed Early's cancer was not necessarily terminal—the miracle cure was just across the Pacific. On February 16, he wrote a memo to Early requesting that he join him on his return trip to the US so they might collaborate on the 1928 governor-general's annual report. He also requested that Willa accompany them. Most observers assumed that Early was traveling with Stimson because he was the governor-general's chosen successor.

On the afternoon of Saturday, February 23, 1929, the Earlys and Stimsons made their way to Manila's pier and boarded the Dollar Line's *President Pierce*. Over ten thousand people lined the dock to say farewell to Stimson, a scene that so moved him that he repeatedly recalled it in his diary and letters. The ship's initial stops in Hong Kong and Japan were punctuated by numerous state dinners as officials believed Stimson was the next US secretary of state.

The *President Pierce* docked at San Francisco on March 21, and reporters congregated around both Stimson and Early. A picture of the Earlys was published in the *New York Times Mid-Week Pictorial* with the caption: "One of Our Pro-Consuls John C. Early, Governor of Mountain Province, P. I., arrives in San Francisco on the President Pierce."[4] The picture is a sobering sight. Willa is leaning against the ship's rail, holding an umbrella with her right hand. Standing slightly behind her, almost towering over her, John Early is dressed in a handsome, if a bit baggy, suit. But it is the expression on both their faces that draws viewers into a mood of deep melancholy. The Earlys are both staring with an expressionless gaze into the distance. They are a couple with neither smiles nor frowns. They are a couple whose once bright future was now in grave question, and the photo tells that story. Many reporters wrote that Early was in the US because Stimson wanted Hoover to appoint him as the Philippines' next governor-general. Despite denials from Stimson, the media continued the narrative, with comments such as, "There are persistent rumors that he [Early] is going to Washington to meet Hoover as a probable successor to Stimson."[5]

But Early was in such a weakened condition that after stepping off the *President Pierce*, he went directly to San Francisco's Letterman Hospital. After two

FIGURE 9.   This is one of the last photos of John and Willa. His once-tight suit now hangs on his body due to his multiple surgeries and his three-year battle with cancer. John C. Early Papers, Bentley Historical Library, University of Michigan.

weeks of medical tests and hospital rest, he and Willa traveled to Cleveland to consult with one of America's most famous surgeons.

John Early and Dr. George Crile shared the same birthday, November 11, though Crile was nine years older. He was born in central Ohio in 1864 as the fifth of eight children and was raised on a 340-acre farm. When he was ten, Crile joined 7,000 other children who enrolled in the Coshocton public school system. In his early teens he worked as a teacher, and at eighteen he became the principal in Plainfield where, in that capacity, he accompanied a local physician in visiting patients. Enthralled with medicine, he diligently studied the sciences and gave his college's commencement address, entitled "Influence of Science."[6] In 1886, he moved to Cleveland to attend Wooster Medical School. He graduated as the valedictorian and then was offered an internship at the university hospital.

A 1935 article from the *Cleveland Clinic Journal of Medicine* addressed Early's specific disease of carcinoma of the rectum. The article's first sentence illustrated the confidence and optimism Crile and his Cleveland Clinic colleagues had with regard to curing patients: "The primary object of any operation for cancer of the rectum or rectosigmoid must be the eradication of the disease."[7] The article closed with encouraging statistics: "In a series of 127 cases in my experience there have been 14 deaths, and mortality of 11 per cent. In 52 per cent there has been immunity from recurrence for five years or more; in 63 per cent the patients have been free from cancer from three to five years; and in 70 per cent there has been no demonstrable recurrence under three years."[8]

Such statistics made Stimson believe that Early's case was not hopeless. Thus, in his earliest days as secretary of state, he took time on April 10 to dictate three important letters: one to Major General F. Le J. Parker and the other two to John and Willa Early. In his lengthy letter to Parker, Stimson apologetically noted that he had misplaced a written order he had given to Governor Early on February 16 while they both were still in the Philippines. The letter requested that Early return to the US with Stimson to help write his 1928 annual report on the Philippines. But the underlying motive for Stimson's request, which was unknown to almost everyone, was to supply Early with free transportation back to the US to seek treatment for his cancer. Early also needed to continue drawing a salary as he had no savings to draw upon. Stimson indicated in his letter that John and Willa were entitled to their salaries until the annual report was completed, and they should be compensated for their traveling expenses, including their daily per diem. Toward the end of his letter, Stimson noted that his aide, Captain Eugene Regnier, would fill in some personal details about Early's situation. Regnier, a dashing military man, worked with Stimson in the Philippines and became a controversial figure, as he was the first military aide to serve as a secretary of state. Stimson concluded his letter with highest praise given to Early and a veiled reference to Early's illness: "Early is the best provincial governor in the Philippine Islands today and has deserved so well of his country in every respect that I think in this personal emergency he should be so thoroughly well-treated. He has rendered devoted service to the Philippine islands for twenty-three years and has had no leave whatever for six years. . . . I hope you can arrange for this matter, and I want to help in every way that I can."[9]

After dictating this letter, Stimson wrote Early telling him he was needed in Washington and that his salary, along with his $7.50 a day per diem, would continue until the report's completion. Willa received a similar letter from Stimson asking that she accompany her husband and informing her that she too would enjoy the same compensation.

On May 7, Early received confirmation from the Bureau of Insular Affairs that a check for his salary and per diem was deposited in the checking account it had opened on his behalf, using a copy of his signature from past correspondence for authentication. This important financial information was addressed to "My dear Governor Early care of Dr. Kriles Clinic, Cleveland, Ohio."[10]

Early was in poor shape and he placed his hope in Dr. Crile. The new protocol for colon cancer, which had saved patients who were considered lost causes, was surgical removal of the visible cancer followed by two rounds of intense radiation treatment. In 1929, the myth of radiation as a cure-all for cancer persisted, and it was not until the early 1930s that a reassessment of radiation treatment tempered earlier hopes. Doctors learned that radiation did not eliminate metastasized cancer and that one effect of radiation was that it could actually produce cancer in some patients. As Dr. Siddhartha Mukherjee explains in The Emperor of all Maladies, "The complex intersection of radiation with cancer—cancer-curing at times, cancer-causing at others—dampened the initial enthusiasm of cancer scientists. Radiation was a powerful invisible knife—but still a knife. And a knife, no matter how deft or penetrating, could only reach so far in the battle against cancer."[11]

But Early had beaten the odds his whole life, and he believed he could overcome the disease that had spread to the point where he could barely walk. The initial surgery in Cleveland went well, and so a casual observer would be taken aback by the letter, written on May 25 from Washington, DC's Wardman Park Hotel, that Willa Early received from Mabel Stimson. Mabel began the letter: "I only learned last night all that you and the governor had been through since we parted in San Francisco . . . Oh how wonderful it was that you were not impaired in that terrible disaster which shocked the whole world. It must have been pretty terrible to be so near it and so hard for you and Governor Early—I cannot bear to think of the anxious days you are living through and hope with all my heart that the skies will brighten and all the clouds roll away."[12]

The tragedy she referred to was not Early's cancer and surgery. While that was a crisis, it was not something the whole world knew about. The tragedy was a fire that took the lives of 123 people at the Cleveland Clinic, where Early was a patient.

About an hour before noon on May 15, 1929, the heat from a lightbulb in the basement of the Cleveland Clinic ignited x-ray film, producing toxic gas, fire, and explosions. Those who inhaled the gas were dead within just a few minutes and had grotesquely colored faces. The deceased included physicians, nurses, staff, and patients.

Early survived the tragedy, but he now faced radiation treatments that at times brought post-operation patients to the brink of death. He remained in Cleveland through the first part of the summer and received a great deal of correspondence, particularly from friends who were learning about his condition. He had managed to keep his illness so quiet that even his closest spiritual mentor, Bishop Mosher, did not send a cable until June 15, with the brief but heartfelt words, "Your illness just known. Entire mission distressed and pray [for] your recovery. Mrs. Mosher and I send love and sympathy to you both."[13]

News of Early's surgery traveled throughout the Philippines and especially in Mountain Province. On July 29, Bontoc native A. Faculo, who Early mentored and who became deputy governor of Apayao in 1935, wrote a detailed letter to Willa. The final paragraph referenced her husband's disease: "I hope that by this time the Governor is on his way to recovery. The people of Bontoc, young and old philosophers, have been very anxious about the Governor's state of condition when we learned that he was in the hospital there."[14]

Ever the optimist, Early wrote to Stimson in mid-July that he was about to be declared cured after the second round of treatment. Stimson was overjoyed and noted that he would find a position for Early in the US, but that he should concentrate on making "every possible effort to complete the cure which has been so auspiciously begun."[15]

But Early was more sober in his self-assessment with the Bureau of Insular Affairs. In a letter to its Purchasing, Distribution, and Accounting Department, he requested travel funds for a return trip to California. He explained that he had just completed his second round of radiation treatment and atypically admitted, "I am quite a bit weakened by the x-ray treatment and wish to avoid as much hot weather as possible."[16]

In early August, the Earlys left Cleveland and traveled to Willa's hometown of Butte, Montana, where they stayed with her stepfather W. W. Pennington. Their arrival in Butte was newsworthy, and a *Great Falls Tribune* article appeared on August 15. Despite the reporter's provocative and leading questions, Early maintained even-handed responses about life among the highlanders. He explained that Igorot society, rule of law, and dress were as morally correct as those of the US. Rather than a group of tribes hungry for blood and head-taking, he presented the Igorots as peoples defined by generosity, particularly with regard to hospitality. He also mentioned his fluency in various highland dialects. When asked whether the US should give the Philippines independence immediately, Early refused to give a response. The article did not mention

Early's health, describing him as "tall, heavy set and alert in action" and his reason for being in the US was official business in Washington. At the end of the article, however, Early hinted that he had his mortality in mind: "He [Early] has nothing but high praise for the people over whom he rules. 'It is very likely, if all fairs well, that we will spend the remainder of our lives on the islands.'"[17]

After their time in Montana, the Earlys traveled to Berkeley and spent time with David Barrows, UC Berkeley's former president. On September 4, he wrote to Stimson that his health was greatly improved, due in part to his stay in the fresh air of Montana. Stimson responded on September 20 with delight, but they both knew that his October examination results in Cleveland would determine his personal and professional future. Stimson wrote, "I certainly hope that the report of the October examination in Cleveland will be all that you hope and expect. At all events, as my father used to say, do not let us quarrel with the hopeful signs of convalescence."[18]

Early's final physical exam was scheduled for October 31. Together with Willa, he boarded the train in San Francisco and once again traveled across the US. While he surveyed America's vast interior from the train window, he must have recalled how the train journey was taking him back to his origins. His parents had emigrated from Ireland to Ohio, then to Missouri, and finally to Minnesota. He was born just four years after the continent was connected by railway.

Other important developments related to his future were in the works while they made their way east. The new governor-general of the Philippines, Dwight Davis, had written a letter to Stimson with an idea. Given that Early was severely weakened by cancer, might it be possible that he would have sufficient strength to serve as a special advisor to Davis on the non-Christian Philippine population? To be sure, there would still be some travel involved in the position, but considerably less than that required of a Mountain Province governor. This new position was available due to the Belo Bill that Stimson insisted the US Congress pass while he was serving as the colony's governor-general. Davis noted that he was well-aware of Stimson's "very high opinion of him [Early], which is confirmed by everything I hear here."[19]

On November 1, the day after Early's exam, Stimson wrote him and asked if he would consider Davis's offer. It included a considerable increase in salary and a much less strenuous portfolio. Stimson diplomatically explained that the proposal was contingent on the doctors' prognosis, and he ended the letter claiming he knew that Early preferred life in the Philippines but understood his health would determine his future. Before receiving Early's reply, Stimson responded to Davis's suggestion in a November 2 cablegram: "Strictly confidential for Governor General: Reference your letter of October 1st concerning

Early. Think suggestion admirable and that he would be highly useful. Reports about a month ago indicate his health decidedly improved. Will ascertain present condition and notify you."[20]

Ten days later, Stimson cabled Davis a definite response, saying that Dr. Crile "has pronounced Early cured," and Early was looking forward to his new role as adviser. Stimson reiterated his approval of the plan: "Personally I think such a selection would be ideal not only with respect to advice as to northern province but also on account of his long experience with general Philippine questions and his broad tolerant attitude."[21] Tolerant attitude was code for Early's deep respect for the innate racial equality and dignity of Filipinos in general, and the Igorots in particular.

From Cleveland, the Earlys traveled to Washington, visiting with the Stimsons while completing official documents for their return to the Philippines. They traveled by train to California, and the government picked up all the expenses provided Early remain a colonial official for the next two years. He hoped that he would be able to see 1932.

Though the doctors declared Early "cured," he remained in a severely weakened state. In a December 13 memo, Colonel William Keller, chief of the Surgical Service at Walter Reed General Hospital, gave specific instructions on Early's transportation care. He wrote that he was still recovering from an "extensive abdominal operation" and a severe "colostomy wound." His precarious condition required treatment throughout each day on the train, and he needed to take rest stops along the way and stay in hotels where he could properly address his wound.[22]

America's top officials were looking out for Early, and he needed their assistance. Whether he was aware of it or not, Dr. Crile was lying to Early. He was not cured—his physical hell was just beginning.

CHAPTER 34

Advisor to the Governor-General

Readers who made it to page forty-seven of the January 2, 1930, *Oakland Tribune* saw an article claiming that John C. Early was the most prominent passenger leaving the following afternoon for Hawaii and Asia. It reported that Early was on his way back to Manila after months of work in Washington, DC, "conferring with government officials."[1] In truth, Early could barely walk as he boarded the SS *President Jefferson* on January 3 and watched San Francisco fade away. He was reasonably certain it was his final glimpse of America. After stops in Hawaii and Yokohama, where he was mentioned in local papers, he arrived in Manila to work with the new governor-general, who seemingly "'never enjoyed a day of his stay'" in the Philippines.[2]

Governor-General Dwight F. Davis's short tenure in the Philippines (1929–1931) is largely misunderstood and underappreciated. Although he was often referred to as the "urbane patrician," one reporter attempted to debunk Davis's supposed haughtiness: "When a young man survives the double disaster of being born rich and being educated at Harvard [and] became one of the greatest tennis players the world has known. . . . Whatever he may turn out to be, young Mr. Davis is not one thing. He is not a snob."[3] This journalistic assessment of thirty-two-year-old Davis captured much of his life to that point. He was born in 1879 to a prominent and wealthy family that included a maternal grandfather who served as the mayor of St. Louis.

But Davis never relied on his family's money or influence. An indefatigable worker, he earned his way into Harvard, and while there he won the amateur singles and doubles titles in tennis. Upon graduation, he donated his trophy for future amateur champions—the tournament and trophy still bear his name. He moved from Harvard to St. Louis, where he earned a law degree from Washington University. He distinguished himself in the local government by his effective and innovative tenure as St. Louis's parks commissioner, insisting that inner-city parks include baseball fields for children. On November 15, 1904, Davis married Helen Brooks. The following year, they embarked on a world tour and visited the Philippines to spend time with a friend from his Harvard days, Cameron Forbes. They enjoyed their time with Forbes, but Helen suffered greatly from Manila's heat and humidity.

During World War I, Davis volunteered for service in France and earned the Distinguished Cross. He returned to the US, moving to the nation's capital to seek a political position. He was appointed assistant secretary of war in 1923 and then became President Harding's secretary of war in 1929. One of his colleagues in Harding's cabinet was Herbert Hoover, so when Stimson met with President-elect Hoover, both men were aware of Davis's effective governance, and they agreed to appoint him the next governor-general. He had hoped for a different position, such as ambassador to England or France, but he accepted the Philippine appointment, though his wife would not join him due to the tropical weather and her fragile health. His domestic situation in Manila was tremendously enhanced by Alice and Cynthia, his elegant adult daughters, who enthusiastically entertained crowds at Malacañang along with their cousin, Alita. The three women, like Davis himself, eschewed snobbery and enjoyed working and playing with Filipinos from all economic stations. One local journalist noted that "Alice has the Islands' heart."[4]

Of all the Philippine governor-generals, Davis most effectively worked behind the scenes. He avoided publicity and sought to shift the spotlight to local and national officials. He quickly won over skeptics who assumed he was another rich, privileged scion in the mold of Harrison or Forbes. In his first year, he visited forty-two provinces, with plans to visit the remaining seven the following year. He published detailed reports and dutifully fulfilled public promises made to rank-and-file citizens. In an early address to the legislature, he called for economic improvements and spoke of potential financial improvements for all Filipinos. He made sure that he prefaced his remarks by praising the House and Senate leaders, crediting them with the country's stability. In the middle of his speech he said, "I want every member of the Legislature to feel that he is always welcome to Malacañang."[5]

As Early made his way back to the Philippines, he wondered how he would get along with Davis. He enjoyed a cordial relationship with Leonard Wood and warm friendship with Stimson, but what about Davis? Furthermore, Early hoped that a restful, leisurely Pacific crossing would revive his health, but he seemed to grow weaker with each passing day on the ocean. At some point he became convinced that his days of hiking into remote Igorot villages were behind him. As Davis's aide, he would work more closely than in the past with the governor-general. He needed this job because he was reportedly financially destitute. This situation came to light when Early's former supervisor, Governor William Pack, sent a letter dated December 4, 1929, to the Bureau of Insular Affairs requesting that he be appointed the new governor of Mountain Province—a position he held two decades earlier. Pack said he had learned that Early had "incurable cancer," and he wanted to fill the void.[6] A January 10 BIA response assured Pack that Early was "cured" and on his way back to the Philippines.[7] He replied four days later that he was happy for Early because "I don't think he has any too much laid aside for a rainy day."[8]

On Early's first Friday back in the Philippines, January 31, 1930, he typed the hardest message of his life to Davis, "Sir: On account of my physical condition not permitting me to make the trips of inspection required for the proper performance of my duties as Governor of the Mountain Province, I feel constrained to tender my resignation from that position. Very respectfully, J.C. Early."[9] Davis responded that he had no choice but to accept Early's resignation: "Under the circumstances stated, I can not do otherwise than accept it [Early's resignation], but I do so with regret, having been informed of the efficiency and tact with which you have performed the duties of that position and of the satisfaction of the people of that province with your administration."[10] The following day, Davis offered Early the position of advisor with an annual salary of 12,000 pesos ($6,000), a very generous compensation. As a teacher in 1906, he had annually earned $1,200, and even his salary of $4,250 as governor was considerably less than what he would have received as aide to the governor-general. He accepted Davis's offer, and despite his health issues, he hit the ground running, undertaking three extensive tours of the southern Philippines before making his way into Mountain Province. From the first of February to the end of May, he spent just three weeks in Manila.

Early's extended stay in Mindanao during his first months as Davis's aide resulted in lengthy and detailed reports on the region's social and economic landscape. Three themes emerged from these reports. First, the non-Christian tribes, particularly the Bogobo, were gradually being pushed off their lands by both legal and illegal means. The Bogobo occupied some of the richest agricultural land in the area, which was coveted by both the government and private businesses. Timber and copra (dried coconut) exports were the economic staples of Mindanao, and access to rich soil was needed for related businesses to flourish. Early recommended that the government place restrictions against encroachment into tribal lands. In short, he suggested the creation of reservation-type structures to protect the non-Christians from exploitation. Early insisted that these should differ from America's Indian reservations in that the Mindanao tribes would enjoy the fertile land rather than fallow terrain.

A second focus of Early's reports highlighted the Japanese population and businesses in Mindanao. He gave the exact number of Japanese in the province of Davao (10,025) as well as each one's occupation. His overt admiration for this community included praise for its organization and work ethic. His reports provided an excellent window into what the Japanese accomplished throughout Southeast Asia between the two World Wars. From their growing dominance in textile exports to the Dutch East Indies, to their increased transport of Malay rubber around the world, Japanese companies built a widening economic network in a world spiraling into a deep depression. He studied the amount of Mindanao's hemp production for the first half of 1930 and concluded that only four of the eleven companies involved in the industry were Japanese (the others included five American, one British, and one Chinese business), but the four Japanese companies produced 63 percent of the hemp.

The third major topic in Early's report was the inability of everyday Filipino farmers and entrepreneurs to succeed in Mindanao due to political corruption and the bloated number of government officials and agencies. During the first part of 1930, the provincial governor was on leave due to an ongoing investigation, the treasurer was laid up with a broken leg, and the third member of the provincial board was "a slow-witted man not at all fitted for civic employment and seemingly lacking in a sense of responsibility to the people for his acts."[11] Early lamented that the private roads built by the Japanese were a quarter of the cost of the government roads, that private companies had built 450 kilometers of road compared with the government's 50 over the past twenty years, and that though outnumbered twelve to one, the Japanese had superior schools and hospitals. In hopes that something might change, Early wrote, "Unless government becomes effective, unless [a] Filipino [farmer] obtains the same care and direction as the Japanese he is beaten before he starts."[12]

After three exhausting trips to Mindanao between February and May, Early traveled to Baguio at the beginning of June. He needed rest and time to process his time in the south before writing his reports. It was on the very cool Thursday morning of June 5, 1930, that he took time to type a personal letter to Candace Stimson, Henry's sister. They had grown close since her visit with them in 1928; in fact, the Earlys had spent time at her home in New York just the year before. As he stared at the mountains surrounding his cottage, he wrote with a tinge of nostalgia about their walks in those hills just two years earlier: "Baguio is bathed in June beauty now and there is no beauty like June's, and no June so perfect as a Baguio June, so we are intoxicated even though we drink orange juice at cocktail parties."

He encouraged Candace to once again visit the cool air of Baguio, though his final paragraph was serious: "I am improving in health and spirits since coming up here and have about decided to fool the medical paternity which gave me two years to live."[13] In fact, Early's health was becoming a matter of national importance since his name was soon to come across the desks of President Hoover and Secretary of War Patrick Hurley.

CHAPTER 35

Vice-Governor

Eight months into his tenure as governor-general, Davis sent an eighty-five-word cablegram to Hoover and Hurley alerting them that the Associated Press was reporting that vice-governor Eugene Gilmore planned to resign effective June 1, bringing his eight years in the Philippines to an end. Davis strongly expressed that the appointment of a new vice-governor was critical: "Cannot overestimate the importance of best possible appointment." In a few concise sentences, he explained that the appointee must have diplomatic skills and an appreciation, if not love, for the Philippines and its peoples. He concluded the message by saying that the press, officials, and the public indicated that there were only two acceptable replacements for Gilmore: "Fischer, Director of Forestry and Governor Early."[1] Davis repeated that the situation in the Philippines was delicate, and he needed a capable assistant.

When Gilmore's impending resignation became widely known, people began speculating and advocating for various individuals to replace him. It was common knowledge that Governor-General Davis's short tenure was coming to an end as his wife remained in the United States and was in failing health. The next vice-governor would assuredly step into his role on at least an interim basis.

Without asking Early's permission, a key figure in the Philippines maneuvered to make sure that Early would receive the appointment. On March 6,

Bishop Mosher wrote a confidential letter to Early. In it, he claimed no one was more qualified to fill Gilmore's position than Early. Based on this conviction, he had sent letters to Mrs. Leonard Wood, Secretary Stimson, Governor Forbes, and General Dorey to garner their support for Early's appointment. Mosher possessed considerable influence among decision-makers as many were under his spiritual care during their time in the Philippines. Other officials joined the growing momentum for Early's appointment, including Secretary of the Interior Ray Wilbur, who wrote a personal letter to Hurley about the matter. Ohio Senator Simon Fess wrote in support of Early, as did Dr. Charles A. Prosser, perhaps the most important figure in the US with regard to new theories on education. This latter endorsement was key, as the vice-governor also served as the secretary of public education. Many of these letters included a line from one of Stimson's earlier letters: "Early is the best Provincial Governor in the Philippine Islands today."[2]

Two things kept President Hoover from nominating Early. First, there was the letter that Early wrote before learning of Gilmore's resignation. He had only been back in the Philippines a few weeks and was feeling ill from the long journey across the Pacific. While he was still recovering from surgery and radiation—and with the cancer still growing in his body—he began his trip to the southern Philippines in his new advisory role. During the dark days of pain in Mindanao, he wrote to Stimson, indicating that he was not well. However, after learning about Gilmore's resignation, he changed his tune and wrote to Stimson on March 29 that he was now in much better health. Still, the damage was done. Stimson responded to Early in an April 30 letter: "I had been worried over the remark of your previous letter which indicated that you are not well."[3] On that same day, Stimson responded to Bishop Mosher, "I heartily concur with everything you say with respect to him [Early as vice governor] and your suggestion is one that has already occurred to me."[4] But Early's health was unstable, and surely Candace told her brother about Early's recent letter, which ended with the hope that he might live two more years.

A second problem was that these highly sought appointments were often given as political favors and were not always based on merit. The position was an important stepping stone to greater things. Gilmore, for example, used his position to become the twelfth president of the University of Iowa, where he served until 1940. He also used his time and resources in the Philippines to write a fifteen-volume encyclopedia on modern American law. Both Hurley and Hoover fielded many requests to appoint particular political supporters and relatives of officials. Davis feared this would happen and insisted from the outset that the new vice-governor be admired, known, and respected by the Filipinos. However, his message fell on deaf ears, leading to a major debacle.

Vice-governor Gilmore made his intentions public and said that May 30 would be his last day in office. President Hoover ignored Davis's suggestion that he appoint either Governor Early or Fischer. He had bigger plans. Given the nation's political climate, he believed it was a propitious moment to bolster his party by appointing a Roosevelt who was loyal to the Republican Party. Nicholas Roosevelt (1893–1982), Teddy's first cousin, was Hoover's perfect appointment for vice-governor. From the Oyster Bay branch of the family, Nicholas possessed an impressive resume. A 1914 Harvard graduate, Nicholas was the picture-perfect diplomat: he was highly educated, physically attractive, and a bachelor. He had already served in diplomatic positions in Europe and had traveled extensively throughout Southeast Asia.

But there was a problem. A big one. Following a tour of the Philippines, Roosevelt published a book in 1926 whose title provided a preview of the author's thesis *The Philippines, a Treasure and a Problem*.[5] In it he claimed that "there neither is nor ever has been any desire to 'exploit' the Philippines," and that the US should not provide a timeline for Philippine independence because the Filipinos were two or three generations away from self-government.[6]

Hoover also found opposition to Roosevelt's nomination in the US Senate, and so he appointed Roosevelt as interim vice-governor while the Senate was in summer recess. The growing opposition took Hoover and Roosevelt by surprise. Governor Davis, who had favored Early's nomination and was not consulted on the Roosevelt decision, threatened to resign. The Philippine Legislature unanimously agreed to a resolution against Hoover's choice. Roosevelt's books were burned in Manila's streets and thrown into Manila's bay. Roosevelt was challenged to a duel by a Filipino patriot who was greatly offended by his book.

Hoover would not budge. He insisted that Roosevelt was his man and appointed him as the Philippines' new vice-governor. During his first two months in that role, Roosevelt remained in the US, preparing for his move to the islands. But as each day passed, it became clearer that he would face an insurmountable challenge once he arrived in Manila. On September 24, Roosevelt sent his letter of resignation, opening with: "Unfortunately the Filipino leaders have ignored these views [in my book] and have, instead, broadcast misrepresentations of my writings with an obvious indifference to the correlation between their statements and the facts. In many cases this has been done by persons who apparently have not even read what I have written. . . . This one-sided propaganda has tended to create in the Philippine Islands a state of mind prejudicial to my present usefulness as Vice-Governor."[7]

Hoover reluctantly accepted Roosevelt's resignation and appointed him the US minister to Hungary. Having already decided that the vice-governor must have strong Republican ties, Hoover turned to George Charles Butte, a two-time Republican nominee for governor of Texas. One newspaper article claimed that "Butte is unknown in the islands and the nomination was a surprise. Local leaders said they will give him full cooperation."[8]

Early never mentioned the sting of being passed over for vice-governor. He had many advocates on both sides of the Pacific, but he was not sufficiently politically connected nor a scion of a prominent American family. He was the son of a bankrupt Irish brickmaker. For his name to even come across the US president's desk was monumental.

As the summer rainy season of 1930 gave way to the clear, cooler days of fall in Baguio, Early turned his attention to something that reminded him of his mortality even more than the daily pain of his growing cancer. Bishop Mosher and numerous others had requested that he give the keynote address at a dedication service for Charles Henry Brent and Leonard Wood. The service was to be held at Manila's Cathedral Church of St. Mary and St. John and would include the unveiling of two stained-glass windows honoring Brent and Wood. The service commenced at 10:30 a.m. on Sunday, November 9.

Brent and Wood had graced the covers of *Time* magazine and had profoundly affected the Philippines. Wood died in 1927, Brent in 1929. Wood was certainly a controversial figure, but even Brent was criticized for being either too close or too far from the Roman Catholic Church. Memorializing these men was a tall task to give a man who knew that he himself was close to death. But Early saw this as one of his greatest honors.

The service began with a responsive prayer, a recitation of the Apostles Creed, and a congregational hymn, "For All the Saints." Early then came to the pulpit and delivered an address entitled "Gentleman Adventurers." He began with the remembrance of Wood, emphasizing his accomplished work in the medical field. He scarcely mentioned his role as governor-general, perhaps a tacit acknowledgment that Wood lacked basic diplomatic skills that would have made his tenure more successful. When speaking about Brent, Early lauded the bishop's campaign against opium addiction and businesses that profited from exploiting people. The theme woven throughout the address was how Brent and Wood loved their fellow humans. At a time when little was said about men who love deeply, Early publicly called these men lovers of others. As he drew his address to a close, Early said, "The Author of Justice will gradually draw back the veil and let the names of these great humanitarians shine among these immortal men who gave much because they loved much, who served humanity to the utmost."[9]

As the congregation rose and was dismissed, Early accepted thanks and praise from Bishop Mosher, along with the family and friends of Wood and Brent. No one knows if any participant guessed or anticipated that Early was the next to be eulogized and have a window dedicated in his honor, for he had just one year left to live.

CHAPTER 36

"Please Write Your Story"

Early was in a reflective mood on Saturday, January 3, 1931. The day marked the one-year anniversary of his boarding the SS *Jefferson* for his return trip to the Philippines after he was pronounced cured from cancer. He and Willa were in their house on the beach, and the breezes that flowed through the windows made Manila's humid heat tolerable. The past year included monumental professional and personal changes. For a few months he had been on the precipice of becoming the colony's second-highest official, yet despite numerous advocates for him, he seemed to know that he was not well enough to serve as the vice-governor. He grew weaker and not stronger, the opposite of what a cured patient should experience.

He didn't know it, but this was the last January 3 he would experience. He had exactly one year—365 days—left to live, and it was propitious that he used this day to resurrect a semi-dormant correspondence with an individual who most positively influenced him. He would write him later in 1931: "If I have an interest in geography, an interest in travel, and in people who live on the other side of the world, I owe it to you. . . . If I have made some mark in the Philippines you can claim a generous share of the credit, for without you I perhaps never will have left the boundaries of the United States. All of this I remember—and I am glad to tell you now."[1] The man Early wrote to that Saturday morning was Dr. J. Paul Goode (1862–1932), one of the most influential geographers in America's history.

Goode loved underdogs as he had also overcome long odds to rise above poverty and humble beginnings. He was born on a farm in rural Minnesota near the town of Stewartville, and as a boy he endured the long, harsh Minnesota winters while working to keep the farm afloat. All the while he harbored a burning desire to develop his mind, and he later reminisced about how hard he worked to pay for his schooling. An overview of his post–high school academic career included a bachelor of science degree from the University of Minnesota in 1889 and graduate stints at Harvard and the University of Chicago, culminating in a 1903 PhD in economics from the University of Pennsylvania. He subsequently enjoyed a long and distinguished career as a professor in the Department of Geography at the University of Chicago. Among other things, he is famous for his invention of the homolosine projection of the planet in a spatial form that more accurately demonstrated the planet's ocean and land mass areas. His 1923 Rand McNally Goode's School Atlas became the standard in classrooms with at least twenty-two editions. Goode was also an extremely gifted singer, and while in college he earned money as a performer and continued this passion with musical groups for the rest of his life.

But in 1931, Dr. Paul Goode, like Early, was not doing well. His soft facial features remained the same—he had a cleft chin with thin lips that gave off a sense that he was born to be an academician and not a farmer. But he had a broken heart, figuratively and literally. On December 11, 1927, he suffered a massive heart attack and was ordered to refrain from any exercise and stress. His strain leading up to his heart attack was attributed to caring for his beloved wife Katherine. She was also from Minnesota, and together they made history. She began teaching elementary school when she was fourteen, and they were inseparable—once riding bicycles from St. Paul to New York. An effective advocate for women's rights, Katherine was serving her second term as an Illinois state representative when she suffered a heart attack in the fall of 1927. Following his heart attack, he was not allowed to see or care for his wife per the doctor's orders, and she died on January 13, 1928. He never fully recovered from this loss and referred to the emotional hurt of not seeing his wife during her last four weeks as "the limit in wicked tragedy."[2]

Goode slowly recovered from his heart attack but was warned that he was living on borrowed time. He had to slow down and rest more. He found this impossible as he raced against time to complete his magnum opus—the revised and enlarged edition of his school atlas.

In Goode's full and extraordinary life, where did John Early fit in? How is it that Early received a November 29, 1930, letter from this esteemed scholar with a very personal request? The two men's lives had intertwined when Early was in his early twenties.

In 1885, the Minnesota Legislature passed a law that established a normal school in Morehead, Minnesota. The school opened three years later with twenty-nine enrolled students and four faculty members, plus the president. Goode, who was completing his bachelor's degree, was the only male faculty member. In 1895, Early was looking to become more than a laborer. When he stepped onto the 6-acre Morehead campus, there were still fewer than 150 students. Goode probably saw himself in Early—a common laborer who wanted to expand his mind and experiences. The two men became close and intermittently corresponded with each other for the remainder of their lives. It also happened that Goode visited Mountain Province for several months during the summer of 1911, just after Early had been fired from his post as lieutenant governor. It must have shamed Early for his mentor to witness his professional humiliation. But Goode's confidence in and support for Early never wavered, and Early's vindication brought his mentor great joy.

Thus, when Early set aside his morning to write, it was in response to his mentor and hero. He began the letter apologizing for not corresponding since his return to the Philippines. He explained that he had been promoted to the position of adviser to the governor-general, with a portfolio that now included not only Mountain Province but "also the special provinces in Mindanao and Sulu." Following this little bit of boasting, he noted that his new responsibilities were beyond his abilities due to his failing health. His half-dozen 1931 inspection trips, which took most of the year, were only possible because he remained in bed on the days he was not working.

The bulk of Early's letter responded to something Goode had requested. Goode had closely followed Early's career, and he believed that Early should write an autobiography. It must have taken Early aback that the man he most admired had just one request of him: please tell your story. Early acquiesced to the repeated requests but noted that his health would need to improve. He ended the letter with a vague reference to his health and a more optimistic view of the upcoming year: "My physical condition is improving somewhat, and although I get little encouragement from surgeons and others who claim to know something of my ailment, I have hope to render quite a bit of service to the people in the Special Provinces before the curtain drops."[3]

Goode's January 25 response was overwhelmingly positive. He suggested Early's memoir might take the form of reminiscences, and he was excited to collaborate on the project. It took Early more than a month to respond, but on March 4 he sent the first of the twenty-four chapters he would write in 1931. He explained that his desire in writing a memoir was to highlight the unknown people rather than familiar personalities. His reminiscences did not name drop, and he focused on the Igorots who shaped his life.

Early began his story in 1906 as an aspiring journalist for the *Southern Idaho Review*, and he was unapologetic about bypassing the first thirty-two years of his life. In the first chapter he is critical of both the US government's failure to provide the promised irrigation water to the hundreds of homestead families in Eastern Idaho, and the Western arrogance he witnessed in Shanghai while making his way to the Philippines. Only one chapter accompanied Early's letter to Goode as he wanted to see if his work had the requisite quality and content. But he could not wait for a response. The exercise of recalling his experiences among the Igorots so energized him that three days after sending the first chapter, he sent the next two, and five days later he sent six more. Almost apologetically, Early explained that his explosive writing and creativity were due, in part, to "more than ordinary leisure this week" due to the governor-general's visits to neighboring countries. At the same time, his insecurity about his work comes through, as he closed his letter with this short paragraph: "If I am sending this material so fast that it takes too much of your time or if you are bored with it, please let me know. It really enables me to set down my remembrances more clearly if I know you are to read them."[4]

But Early could not stop writing his story. On April 1, he sent eight more chapters, and one week later he sent three more, all the time wondering about Goode's impressions, sheepishly writing: "I hope you are not too bored with all this, and I would appreciate it if you tell me frankly whether or not it is up to your expectations."[5] While waiting for a response, Early received two heartfelt letters that illustrated the breadth of his influence. The first came from James W. Chapman.

Chapman arrived in the Philippines in 1916 with impressive credentials: a PhD in economic entomology from Harvard University (1913), as well as experiences as an instructor at Tufts College and as an assistant in the Bureau of Entomology, US Department of Agriculture. He met his wife, Ethel Robinson, while they were undergraduate students at Park College, a Presbyterian-affiliated college in Parkville, Missouri. Chapman was especially interested in studying ants. While they faced a promising future in Boston, they decided to serve as teaching missionaries at Silliman College, the Presbyterian school in Negros Oriental. James taught in the science department while Ethel taught English. They remained at Silliman until 1950, evading Japanese soldiers for three years during World War II and writing about it in their memoir, *Escaped to the Hills*. By the time they retired to the US, Chapman had published papers that identified twelve new species of ants in six subfamilies.

Early and Chapman became close friends due to their work together in Negros Oriental. This deep friendship compelled Chapman to write a lengthy personal letter to Early on the first day of spring 1931. He recalled their time together, as well as the numerous ant projects he was involved with. At the end of the letter, he became more solemn: "I do not know just what to say about the condition of your health as it is now and then reported. I hope it has been over exaggerated. If not you know you both have our deepest sympathy. I do not want to wait until it is too late to tell you how much I have always admired you. . . . I cannot begin to set down what is in my heart to say. But consider it all said and more too and just remember always our friendship, as we remember yours."[6]

Four weeks later, Early received a letter from Dr. Hilary Clapp, the adopted son of the Episcopal missionary Walter Clapp. This letter meant to assure Early of the lasting goodwill he had among the Igorots, noting at the end of his letter, "Please feel that you have so many friends in the Mountain Province who are worshiping you."[7] More letters came flooding in from Igorot officials expressing gratitude and well-wishes to their former governor.

While Early enjoyed these sentiments, the letter he really wanted was not mailed to him until May 22, 1931, and not received until the first weeks of June. Finally, Goode commented on the first twenty chapters of Early's memoir, noting in the first sentence that he was delighted with the manuscript. His enthusiasm and exuberance were such that he believed that the University of Chicago Press would be anxious to serve as a publisher for the completed manuscript. His only suggestion was that Early incorporate more anecdotal stories. As an example, Goode recalled an incident he had heard from a source in which Early taught Igorot boys to be proud of their heritage, dignity, and intrinsic worth. Shortly after some of these lessons, an American lieutenant came to Bontoc while Early was lieutenant governor. He came to Early's house while Early was away and reportedly called out to one of the boys, "Here, you g.d. s. of a b., take these boots and clean the mud off of them, and be quick about it!" The young man reprimanded the lieutenant for his manner of speech, which took the American by surprise. Goode wrote, "You must certainly put that story in, and others like it to show the strong independence of character of the mountain people."[8]

While this affirming letter made its way across the Pacific, Early gave his final public address. The setting was the newly constructed amphitheater in Baguio's US military base, Camp John Hay. Given his health, it is probable he knew this would be his last speech. Fittingly, the occasion was a Memorial Day celebration on Saturday, May 30. His brief talk highlighted three things. First, humans are, without choice, tied to the past. He mentioned the growing purely material view of the universe and said that whether one believed in a spiritual or material universe, humans remained connected to the past. He praised the Igorots, who invited their ancestor spirits to join them in their feasts. Secondly, he remembered the life and work of two lieutenant governors, Jeff Gallman and Norman Conner, who effectively brought peace to Ifugao and Apayao, respectively. Both men rose from obscurity and set their subprovinces aright because they realized life was not about them—they chose a higher calling. Finally, Early addressed the growing cynicism and demythologizing of historical figures. He contended that historical context provided a helpful lens when judging the past: "By using this simple formula of disregarding the time environment and refusing to recognize the fact that every time has its own manners, they picture Washington a drunkard, Jefferson a wastrel, Hamilton a

FIGURE 10. John and Willa Early on their final visit to the US as they disembark from the *President Pierce* in San Francisco, March 1929. Historicimages.com.

stock jobber, Lincoln a foul-mouthed jester, and Grant a political crook."[9] In this last speech, Early anticipated how postcolonial scholars would overlook any good that may have come about from outside rule and benevolent assistance. They were not perfect, Early noted, but many had sacrificed to stop the highlanders from perpetual warfare, advance literacy throughout Mountain Province, and introduce modern medicine that saved the lives of Igorot women and children.

Following his talk, Early's fragile health gave way, and he collapsed. Rushed to the hospital, the doctors did what they could to alleviate his suffering. That entire summer, he teetered on the brink of death, enduring two surgeries. The once-muscled farmer, brickmaker, and first-rate hiker of Luzon's northern mountains became a shell of his former self. It took him three months to respond to Goode's positive comments, and Early was diplomatic but frank about his current situation: "I am on my feet again after a most painful and nearly fatal operation, which was, in essential, the burning out of the core of the cancer with a red-hot iron. You can imagine the effect on the sensitive parts of the body of such operation. The surgeon hopes he has given me a few years' lease of life by it, and his hope is that cancer will be conquered before the respite expires."[10]

Like so many cancer patients, Early held hope that a cure might be found before the disease would take his life. It was a fight against time, and he was running out of it. Unbeknownst to Early, Goode had also suffered a major health setback, and he too had just a few months left to live.

Early tried to continue his memoirs through the fall but found it impossible to concentrate. Writing to Goode on November 15, he indicated that he was in hospice-type care and found it impossible to think straight. In his weakened condition, he found it difficult to even provide a proper dedication for the book. He had earlier decided to dedicate his life story to Goode but could not muster the strength to do even this. He closed this letter by saying, "Today I am not feeling very fit; in fact, not fit enough to frame a dedication I would want for you, and I will send it later when I'm feeling more in a mood to pay you a just tribute."[11] Two weeks later, he wrote Goode, grieving that he would not finish his book, and he acknowledged that his story might be lost to history. But should it ever see the light of day, the dedication should read: "To my instructor, counselor and friend John Paul Goode this book is affectionately dedicated."[12]

But then on December 19, Early wrote that he had rallied and had just completed three new chapters of his memoir with more to follow. This was amazing given that he was just days away from death. It showed his grit and determination to record his view of the American presence in Igorot territory.

The Earlys spent Christmas of 1931 in Baguio, and he hoped to gather more strength in his beloved mountain city, with its pines and cloudy early morning mists. Vice-governor Butte and his staff were also in Baguio for the holidays, working on their annual reports. Early's final report to Butte was dated December 31.

On New Year's Day, the staff met for conversation at Baguio's Country Club with an official dinner scheduled for that evening. Early joined in the dinner, but before it was over, he reportedly gave a smile and asked to be excused, retiring to his room. In the early hours of January 2, the staff, led by Butte, were called to Early's bedside, where he was laboring to breathe. At 5:15 a.m., John Chrysostom Early drew in and then exhaled his last breath, having "prepared the world for the use of man but reserved nothing for himself."[13]

Epilogue

Philippine newspapers printed front-page stories about Early's death, as did papers throughout the world, though they were wrong in much of their details regarding his life. A reputable southern US paper noted in their January 2 issue, "John C. Early, governor of Mountain Province . . . and leading figure in Philippine administration, died at Baguio today. . . . Born at Fargo, N.D. in 1882, Early came to the Philippines in 1906 as a teacher."[1] The article was off by nine years on his birth year and wrong about his place of birth. Upon hearing the news, many prominent American officials along with rank-and-file Igorots sent letters to Willa lauding the life and work of her husband. In one newspaper article, the acting governor-general characterized Early's writings as "masterpieces," and Early was noted as someone who never saw himself as "superior" to any Igorot person he served.[2] Those in Bontoc and Ifugao testified to his protection of their rights and property.

He was buried on January 4, just two days after his death, in the Baguio Municipal Cemetery. It was reported that when Early was confirmed as governor of Mountain Province at the start of Stimson's tenure as governor-general, the Bontoc elders said, "We want Governor Early to be our governor always. But we realize this cannot be. Therefore when Governor Early dies we want him to be buried here so that his bones can rest with our bones and his spirit can always remain with our spirits."[3] Early also wanted to be buried in Mountain Province, and so this was prearranged before he died. His pall-bearers included his old friend W. W. Marquardt; Baguio's mayor, James Halsema; and Kalinga's former lieutenant governor and leader of the Bacarri massacre, Walter Hale.

Three years after his death, a special service at Manila's Episcopal Church led by Bishop Mosher dedicated a stained-glass window and a plaque for Early. Willa attended the ceremony and then left the Philippines, never remarried, and lived off of her husband's pension until her death in 1971.

Just three years after Early's death, the Philippines transitioned into a Commonwealth, but those three years were troubling for the Igorots. After Early's death, Dosser returned as governor, but was falsely accused of using his influence to profit from the mining industry. Some Igorot leaders wrote to the vice-governor that "they worshiped Governor Early but did not trust Governor Dosser."[4]

Similar statements of the Igorots' affection and trust for Early after his death are found in scores of documents. They mention his protection of the cargadores, Igorot property rights, human rights, and his care for the environment. But almost a century has passed since his death, and he is mostly forgotten in America and in the Philippines. Even the grave of the once-governor of Mountain Province and protector of its inhabitants can no longer be found. But neither can the burial sites of the Igorots who were slaughtered during the Bacarri massacre or the bones of Lissuag, who was beheaded by rival neighbors. Reading through Early's speeches, letters, and memoirs, it is evident he would have been the first to say that he was not worthier of remembrance than the rank-and-file highlanders, who rose in the morning and walked to their fields to usher in the harvesting season.

Notes

Introduction

1. Stuart Creighton Miller, *Benevolent Assimilation: The American Conquest of the Philippines, 1899-1903* (New Haven, Connecticut: Yale University Press, 1984), 134.

2. For the maternal use of language in colonialism, see Funnie Hsu, "Colonial Articulations: English Instruction and the 'Benevolence' of U.S. Overseas Expansion in the Philippines, 1898–1916" (PhD diss., University of California, Berkeley, 2013).

3. Henry Stimson to Willa Early, January 24, 1932, John C. Early Papers, Bentley Historical Library, University of Michigan, Ann Arbor (hereafter Early Papers).

4. Vincent H. Gowen, *Philippine Kaleidoscope: An Illustrated Story of the Church's Mission* (New York: National Council, Protestant Episcopal Church, 1939), 35–38.

5. Kenton J. Clymer, "Humanitarian Imperialism: David Prescott Barrows and the White Man's Burden in the Philippines," *Pacific Historical Review* 45, no. 4 (November 1976): 498.

6. Daniel Immerwahr, *How to Hide an Empire: A History of the Greater United States* (New York: Farrar, Straus and Giroux, 2019).

7. Andrew Priest, review of *How to Hide an Empire: A History of the Greater United States*, by Daniel Immerwahr, *Diplomacy & Statecraft* 31, no. 1 (2020): 204.

8. Priest, review of *How to Hide*, 204.

9. Julius W. Pratt, *Expansionists of 1898: The Acquisition of Hawaii and the Spanish Islands* (Baltimore: Johns Hopkins Press, 1936); Julius W. Pratt, *America's Colonial Experiment: How the United States Gained, Governed, and in Part Gave Away a Colonial Empire* (New York: Prentice-Hall, 1950).

10. William Thaddeus Sexton, *Soldiers in the Sun: An Adventure in Imperialism* (Harrisburg, PA: The Military Services Publishing Co., 1939); Leon Wolff, *Little Brown Brother: How the United States Purchased and Pacified the Philippines* (Garden City, NJ: Doubleday, 1960).

11. Theodore Friend, *Between Two Empires: The Ordeal of the Philippines, 1929–1946* (New Haven: Yale University Press, 1965); Bonifacio S. Salamanca, *The Filipino Reaction to American Rule, 1901–1913* (Hamden, CT: Shoestring Press, 1968); Peter W. Stanley, *A Nation in the Making: The Philippines and the United States, 1899–1921* (Cambridge, MA: Harvard University Press, 1974); Glenn A. May, *Social Engineering in the Philippines: The Aims and Impact of American Colonial Policy, 1900–1913* (Westport, CT: Greenwood Press, 1980).

12. Michael Hawkins, review of *The Blood of Government: Race, Empire, the United States, & the Philippines*, by Paul A. Kramer, *Crossroads: An Interdisciplinary Journal of Southeast Asian Studies* 19, no. 2 (2008): 189.

13. Vicente L. Rafael, *White Love: And Other Events in Filipino History* (Durham: Duke University Press, 2000). One critic notes that "the book falls short of establishing a firm epistemological foundation upon which to ground many of its conclusions." Cecilia A. Samonte, review of *White Love and Other Events in Filipino History*, by Vicente L. Rafael, *Journal of Asian Studies* 61, no. 3 (2002): 1128.

14. René Alexander D. Orquiza Jr., *Taste of Control: Food and the Filipino Colonial Mentality* (New Brunswick, NJ: Rutgers University Press, 2020).

15. Christopher Capozzola, *Bound by War: How the United States and the Philippines Built America's Pacific Century* (New York: Basic Books, 2020). Guy Emerson Mount, in his review of the book, concludes that "While one could argue that Capozzola stretches his evidence to make the Philippines appear more central to the US than it might have been, the explanatory case on the Philippine side is compelling." *H-Diplo, H-Net Reviews* (January 2021), https://www.h-net.org/reviews/showrev.php?id=55577.

16. See, for example, Kenton J. Clymer, *Protestant Missionaries in the Philippines, 1898–1916: An Inquiry into the American Colonial Mentality* (Urbana: University of Illinois Press, 1986); Susan K. Harris, *God's Arbiters: Americans and the Philippines, 1898–1902* (New York: Oxford University Press, 2011); Sarah Steinbock-Pratt, *Educating the Empire: American Teachers and Contested Colonization in the Philippines* (New York: Cambridge University Press, 2019); Rodney J. Sullivan, *Exemplar of Americanism: The Philippine Career of Dean C. Worcester* (Ann Arbor: University of Michigan, Center for South and Southeast Asian Studies, 1991).

17. Stanley Karnow, *In Our Image: America's Empire in the Philippines* (New York: Random House, 1989); H. W. Brands, *Bound to Empire: The United States and the Philippines* (New York: Oxford University Press, 1992).

18. The Muslim Moros in the southern Philippines have received some significant attention. See, for example, Peter Gowing's pioneering work, *Mandate in Moroland: The American Government of Muslim Filipinos, 1899–1929* (Quezon City, Philippines: New Day, 1983); Michael Hawkins's two books, *Making Moros: Imperial Historicism and American Military Rule in the Muslim Philippines' Muslim South* (DeKalb: Northern Illinois University Press, 2013) and *Semi-Civilized: The Moro Village at the Louisiana Purchase Exposition* (Ithaca: Northern Illinois Press, 2020); Oliver Charbonneau, *Civilizational Imperatives: Americans, Moros, and the Colonial World* (Ithaca, NY: Cornell University Press, 2020); and Ronald K. Edgerton's two books, *People of the Middle Ground: A Century of Conflict and Accommodation in Central Mindanao, 1880s–1980s* (Quezon City, Philippines: Ateneo de Manila University Press, 2008) and *American Datu: John J. Pershing and Counterinsurgency Warfare in the Muslim Philippines, 1899–1913* (Lexington: University Press of Kentucky, 2020).

19. Barbara Crossette explains the unique role of hill stations in Asia, and Robert Reed's volume focuses exclusively on Baguio. These studies concentrate more on the imperialists than the peoples they displaced. Barbara Crossette, *The Great Hill Stations of Asia, Culture, Values & Religion* (Boulder, CO: Westview Press, 1998); Robert Ronald Reed, *City of Pines: The Origins of Baguio as a Colonial Hill Station and Regional Capital*, 2nd ed. (Baguio City, Philippines: A-Seven Pub, 1999).

20. William Henry Scott, *The Discovery of the Igorots: Spanish Contacts with the Pagans of Northern Luzon* (Quezon City, Philippines: New Day, 1974).

21. Frank L. Jenista, *The White Apos: American Governors on the Cordillera Central*, 2nd ed. (Quezon City, Philippines: New Day, 1989); Edward P. Dozier, *The Kalinga of*

Northern Luzon, Philippines, Case Studies in Cultural Anthropology (New York: Holt, Rinehart and Winston, 1967).

22. Howard T. Fry, *A History of the Mountain Province* (Quezon City, Philippines: New Day, 1989). As Bruce Cruikshank writes in his review of the book, "This book is exhaustively researched, and promises to be the definitive book of its sort henceforth." Bruce Cruikshank, review of *A History of the Mountain Province*, by Howard T. Fry, *The Journal of Asian Studies* 44, no. 3 (May 1985): 668.

23. Alfred W. McCoy, *Policing America's Empire: The United States, the Philippines, and the Rise of the Surveillance State* (Madison: University of Wisconsin Press, 2009).

24. Roy Franklin Barton, *The Half-Way Sun: Life among the Headhunters of the Philippines* (New York: AMS Press, 1978); Claire Prentice, *The Lost Tribe of Coney Island: Headhunters, Luna Park, and the Man Who Pulled Off the Spectacle of the Century* (Boston: Houghton Mifflin Harcourt, 2014).

25. Stanley, *A Nation in the Making*, 202.

26. See Kenton Clymer, "Humanitarian Imperialism: David Prescott Barrows and the White Man's Burden in the Philippines," *Pacific Historical Review* 45, no. 4 (1976): 495–517; and Sullivan, *Exemplar of Americanism*.

27. Joseph Ralston Hayden, *The Philippines: A Study in National Development, World Affairs: National and International Viewpoints* (1942, repr., New York: Arno Press, 1972).

1. The Making of a Governor

1. Typescript of "Reminiscences of John C. Early" by John C. Early, 1931, Early Papers.

2. Washington Agricultural College Yearbook, *1902 Chinook: Volume II* (Pullman, WA: Published by the Junior Class, 1903), 294.

3. Washington Agricultural College Yearbook, *1904 Chinook: Volume III* (Pullman, WA: Published by the Junior Class, 1905), 114.

4. Enoch A. Bryan to John Early, March 12, 1905, box 35, President: Enoch A. Bryan Records 1888–1952, Washington State University Libraries, Pullman (hereafter Bryan Records).

5. "First Heyburn Schoolteacher Had All Kinds of Jobs in Order to Raise Money to Pay for His Homestead," in *The Minidoka County News Golden Anniversary Edition, 1905–1955* (Minidoka, ID: Minidoka County House, 1955), 18.

6. Early, "Reminiscences of John C. Early," 1.

7. Early, "Reminiscences of John C. Early," 3.

8. Early, "Reminiscences of John C. Early," 4.

2. Eight Million Souls for Twenty Million Dollars

1. León Ma Guerrero, *The First Filipino. A Biography of José Rizal* (Manila: Publications of the National Heroes Commission, 1963), xiii.

2. George Washington to Gilbert du Motier, Marquis de Lafayette, August 15, 1786, *Founders Online*, National Archives, https://founders.archives.gov/documents/Washington/04-04-02-0200.

3. John Leddy Phelan, *The Millennial Kingdom of the Franciscans in the New World*, 2nd ed. (Berkeley: University of California Press, 1970), 11.

4. General James Rusling, "Interview with President William McKinley," *The Christian Advocate*, January 22, 1903, 17. Reprinted in Daniel Schirmer and Stephen Rosskamm Shalom, eds., *The Philippines Reader* (Boston: South End Press, 1987), 22–23.

3. War and Colonial Policies

1. Henry R. Pattengill, ed., "Report of the Philippine Commission," *Timely Topics* 4, no. 5 (October 6, 1899): 151.
2. Helen Herron Taft, *Recollections of Full Years* (New York: Dodd, Mead & Company, 1914), 32.
3. Taft, *Recollections of Full Years*, 87.
4. David Barrows, "The Prospects for Education in the Philippines," *The Philippine Teacher* 1, no. 1 (December 1904): 7.
5. May, *Social Engineering in the Philippines*, 105.
6. Early, "Reminiscences of John C. Early," 6.

4. The Discovery of the Igorots

1. Scott, *The Discovery of the Igorots*, 7.
2. John Leddy Phelan, *The Hispanization of the Philippines: Spanish Aims and Filipino Responses* (Madison: University of Wisconsin Press, 1959), 13.
3. Scott, *The Discovery of the Igorots*, 292.
4. Sullivan, *Exemplar of Americanism*, 98.
5. Dean Conant Worcester, *The Philippines Past and Present* (New York: Macmillan Company, 1930), 377–79.
6. Typescript of David P. Barrows's memoirs, 1873–1954, David P. Barrows Papers, The Bancroft Library, University of California, Berkeley, 78 (hereafter Barrows Papers).
7. David P. Barrows's memoirs, 79.
8. David P. Barrows's memoirs, 97.
9. David P. Barrows's memoirs, 99.
10. Early, "Reminiscences of John C. Early," 15.

5. The Philippine Constabulary

1. McCoy, *Policing America's Empire*, 82.
2. *Annual Reports of the War Department for the Fiscal Year Ended June 30, 1904, Volume XI, Report of the Philippine Commission, Part One* (Washington, DC: Government Printing Press Office, 1905), 575.
3. Jenista, *The White Apos*, 43–45.
4. Jenista, *The White Apos*, 60.
5. Jenista, *The White Apos*, 66–67.

6. John Early in the Cordillera

1. Early, "Reminiscences of John C. Early," 5.
2. Early, "Reminiscences of John C. Early," 7.
3. Early, "Reminiscences of John C. Early," 7.

4. Early, "Reminiscences of John C. Early," 10.

5. Early, "Reminiscences of John C. Early," 12.

6. Early, "Reminiscences of John C. Early," 13.

7. *Seventh Annual Report of the Philippine Commission, 1906, Part 2* (Washington, DC: Government Printing Office, 1907), 284.

8. Early, "Reminiscences of John C. Early," 18.

9. Early, "Reminiscences of John C. Early," 21.

10. Early, "Reminiscences of John C. Early," 23–24.

11. Early, "Reminiscences of John C. Early," 27.

12. Bontoc Provincial Commander to Adjutant Philippine Constabulary, August 19, 1918, Record Group 350, Records of the Bureau of Insular Affairs, National Archives, Washington, DC (hereafter, Record Group 350, Records of the Bureau of Insular Affairs will be referred to as BIA Group 350).

13. Early, "Reminiscences of John C. Early," 28.

14. Assistant of the Chief of Bureau of Insular Affairs to Maria Mekota, June 14, 1926, BIA Group 350, National Archives, Washington, DC.

7. Dean Worcester and the Making of Mountain Province

1. Lewis E. Gleeck, *American Institutions in the Philippines, 1898–1941* (Manila: Historical Conservation Society, 1976), 190.

2. Karnow, *In Our Image*, 174.

3. Dean C. Worcester, *The Philippine Islands and Their People* (New York: The Macmillan Company, 1898), 377.

4. Sullivan, *Exemplar of Americanism*, 28.

5. Pattengill, "Report of the Philippine Commission," 151.

6. G. A. Painton, "United States Non-Christian Policy" (master's thesis, James Cook University of North Queensland, 1981).

8. Early's Move to Bontoc

1. Early, "Reminiscences of John C. Early," 40.

2. Early "Reminiscences of John C. Early," 51.

3. Samuel Kane, *Life or Death in Luzon: Thirty Years of Adventure with the Philippine Headhunters* (Indianapolis, IN: Bobbs-Merrill Company, 1933), 282. Published in the same year as *Thirty Years with the Philippine Headhunters* (New York: Grosset & Dunlap, 1933).

4. Early, "Reminiscences of John C. Early," 52.

5. Early, "Reminiscences of John C. Early," 56.

6. Early, "Reminiscences of John C. Early," 53.

7. Early, "Reminiscences of John C. Early," 66.

9. Lieutenant Governor of Amburayan

1. Early, "Reminiscences of John C. Early," 66.

2. "Annual Report of the Provincial-Governor of the Mountain Province, Fiscal Year Ending June 30, 1910," in *Report of the Philippine Commission to the Secretary of War, 1911* (Washington, DC: Government Printing Office, 1911), 14.

3. Early, "Reminiscences of John C. Early," 67.

4. Early, "Reminiscences of John C. Early," 67.

5. Early, "Reminiscences of John C. Early," 68–69.

6. Early, "Reminiscences of John C. Early," 68.

7. J. M. Dickinson, *Special Report of J. M. Dickinson to the President on the Philippines* (Washington, DC: Government Printing Office, 1911), 20.

8. Camillus Gott, "William Cameron Forbes and the Philippines, 1904–1946" (PhD diss., Indiana University, 1974), 41.

9. Gott, "William Cameron Forbes and the Philippines," 62.

10. Lieutenant Governor of Bontoc

1. S. L. Williams, "The Governor of Paragua," *Munsey's Magazine*, May 1905, 136.

2. "Wanted: A New King for Palawan," *The San Francisco Sunday Call*, October 2, 1910, 11.

3. *Seventh Annual Report of the Secretary of the Interior to the Philippine Commission: For the Fiscal Year Ended, June 30, 1908* (Manila: Bureau of Printing, 1908, repr., London: Forgotten Books, 2019), 66.

4. "Wanted: A New King for Palawan," 11.

5. Early, "Reminiscences of John C. Early," 80.

6. Early, "Reminiscences of John C. Early," 80.

7. *War Department, U.S.A. Annual Reports, 1907: Volume VII, The Philippine Commission* (Washington, DC: Government Printing Office, 1908), 282.

8. "Annual Report of the Provincial-Governor of the Mountain Province, Fiscal Year Ending June 30, 1909," in *The Philippine Commission Report for the Year 1909* (Washington, DC: Government Printing Office, 1910), 17.

9. Harry H. Woodring to Senator Morris Sheppard, March 6, 1939, BIA Group 350, William Pack file.

10. Worcester, *The Philippines Past and Present*, 506.

11. Laurence L. Wilson, "Sapao: Walter Franklin Hale," *Journal of East Asiatic Studies* 5, no. 2 (1956): 15.

12. Brian McAllister Linn, "The Thirty-Third Infantry, United States Volunteers: An American Regiment in the Philippine Insurrection, 1899–1901" (PhD diss., Ohio State University, 1981), 24.

13. Linn, "The Thirty-Third Infantry," 26.

14. Linn, "The Thirty-Third Infantry," 36.

15. Matthew Westfall, *The Devil's Causeway: The True Story of America's First Prisoners of War in the Philippines, and the Heroic Expedition Sent to Their Rescue* (Guilford, CT: Lyons Press, 2012).

16. Linn "The Thirty-Third Infantry," 102.

17. Kane, *Life or Death in Luzon*, 49. Frank Jenista notes that "Kane's book was heavily romanticized to encourage sales in the United States and must be treated with some caution by the serious scholar." Jenista, *The White Apos*, 275.

18. Kane, *Life or Death in Luzon*, 105.

19. Kane, *Life or Death in Luzon*, 214.

20. Kane, *Life or Death in Luzon*, 250–51.

11. Alcohol, Labor, and Land

1. Kane, *Life or Death in Luzon*, 281.

2. Fry, *A History of the Mountain Province*, 10.

3. Early, "Reminiscences of John C. Early," 83.

4. Charles W. Olson to Charles C. Batchelder, November 9, 1915 (Olson Papers in the possession of Professor Frank Jenista, Emeritus of Cedarville University; hereafter Olson Papers).

5. Early, "Reminiscences of John C. Early," 89.

6. Early, "Reminiscences of John C. Early," 82.

7. Worcester, *The Philippines Past and Present*, 41.

8. Worcester, *The Philippines Past and Present*, 46.

9. Worcester, *The Philippines Past and Present*, 46.

10. Jose Mencio Molintas, "The Philippine Indigenous Peoples' Struggle for Land and Life: Challenging Legal Texts," *Arizona Journal of International & Comparative Law* 21, no. 1 (2004): 275.

11. Hayden, *The Philippines*, ix.

12. Charles W. Olson diary entry, June 8, 1911, digital reproduction of original manuscript (Olson Papers), 67.

13. Fry, *A History of the Mountain Province*, 120.

14. Early, "Reminiscences of John C. Early," 94–95.

12. The Problem of Kalinga and the Hale Solution

1. Mr. Simms to Mr. Dorsey, August 12, 1906, quoted in Fry, *A History of the Mountain Province*, 29.

2. Cornelis DeWitt Willcox, *Head Hunters of Northern Luzon: From Ifugao to Kalinga, a Ride through the Mountains of Northern Luzon* (London: Forgotten Books, 2016), 223.

3. Kane, *Life or Death in Luzon*, 286.

4. Wilson, "Sapao: Walter Franklin Hale," 8.

5. Fry, *A History of the Mountain Province*, 46.

6. Edward P. Dozier, *Mountain Arbiters: The Changing Life of a Philippine Hill People* (Tucson: University of Arizona Press, 1966), 39.

7. Wilson, "Sapao: Walter Franklin Hale," 5.

8. Wilson, "Sapao: Walter Franklin Hale," 8.

9. Wilson, "Sapao: Walter Franklin Hale," 2.

10. Dozier, *Mountain Arbiters*, 39.

11. Wilson, "Sapao: Walter Franklin Hale," 29.

12. Wilson, "Sapao: Walter Franklin Hale," 22.

13. Dozier, *Mountain Arbiters*, 40.

14. Wilson, "Sapao: Walter Franklin Hale," 32.

15. Wilson, "Sapao: Walter Franklin Hale," 16.

16. Wilson, "Sapao: Walter Franklin Hale," 31.

17. Winfred Denison to Edward Bowditch Jr., July 17, 1914, box 1, Dean C. Worcester Papers: 1887–1925, Bentley Historical Library, University of Michigan, Ann Arbor (hereafter Worcester Papers).

13. The Bacarri Problem

1. Walter Hale, "Final and Formal Report on the Guinabal Expedition," January 30, 1911, *Guinabal Expedition Report*, Worcester Papers, box 1, 1.

2. McCoy, *Policing America's Empire*, 223.

3. Hale, "Final and Formal Report," 2.

4. Governor William F. Pack to Wallace Cadet Taylor, telegram, January 4, 1911, Guinabal Expedition Report, October 6, 1911, Worcester Papers, box 1, 17.

5. Wallace Cadet Taylor to Governor William F. Pack, telegram, January 5, 1911, *Guinabal Expedition Report*, October 6, 1911, Worcester Papers, box 1, 17.

6. Governor-General Forbes to Governor Pack, January 27, 1911, *Guinabal Expedition Report*, October 6, 1911, Worcester Papers, box 1, 16.

7. Charles Penningroth, *Then 'Til Now* (Cedar Rapids, IA: n.p., 1967), 4–5.

8. Penningroth, *Then 'Til Now*, 26.

9. Penningroth, *Then 'Til Now*, 19–20.

10. Penningroth, *Then 'Til Now*, 30.

11. Governor William F. Pack to J. C. Early, January 7, 1911, *Guinabal Expedition Report*, October 6, 1911, Worcester Papers, box 1, 23.

12. Early, "Reminiscences of John C. Early," 90.

13. Early, "Reminiscences of John C. Early," 92–93.

14. The Bacarri Massacre

1. Walter Penningroth, "Report on the Guinabal Expedition," January 23, 1911, *Guinabal Expedition Report*, October 6, 1911, Worcester Papers, box 1, 28.

2. Penningroth, "Report on the Guinabal Expedition," 28.

3. Hale, "Final and Formal Report," 62.

4. Early, "Reminiscences of John C. Early," 92.

5. Lieutenant Harris, "Report on the Guinabal Expedition," January 27, 1911, *Guinabal Expedition Report*, October 6, 1911, Worcester Papers, box 1, 39.

6. Harris, "Report on the Guinabal Expedition," 40.

7. Penningroth, "Report on the Guinabal Expedition," 29.

8. Hale, "Final and Formal Report," 67.

9. Harris, "Report on the Guinabal Expedition," 42.

15. The Report

1. Charles Penningroth, "Final and Formal Report on the Guinabal Expedition," January 30, 1911, *Guinabal Expedition Report*, Dean C. Worcester Papers: 1887–1925, box 1, Bentley Historical Library, University of Michigan, 30.

2. William E. Moore to Harry H. Bandholtz, January 29, 1911, *Guinabal Expedition Report*, Worcester Papers, box 1, 44.

3. Wallace Cadet Taylor to Harry H. Bandholtz, January 31, 1911, *Guinabal Expedition Report*, Worcester Papers, box 1, 26.

4. Harry H. Bandholtz to Charles Elliott, February 3, 1911, *Guinabal Expedition Report*, Worcester Papers, box 1, 26.

5. Charles Elliott to Cameron Forbes, February 7, 1911, *Guinabal Expedition Report*, Worcester Papers, box 1, 27.

6. William F. Pack, "Report to Governor-General Forbes," March 27, 1911, *Guinabal Expedition Report*, Worcester Papers, box 1, 46.

7. William F. Pack, "Report to Governor-General Forbes," 48.

8. "Stenographer's Report of Interview between Lieutenant Governor Hale, Dean C. Worcester, and people of the Guinabal district at Lubuagan," n.d., *Guinabal Expedition Report*, Worcester Papers, box 1, 87.

9. "Stenographer's Report of Interview," 89.

10. "Stenographer's Report of Interview," 90.

11. "Stenographer's Report of Interview," 91.

12. Dean Worcester to Cameron Forbes, October 6, 1911, *Guinabal Expedition Report*, Worcester Papers, box 1, 3.

13. Worcester to Forbes, 11.

14. Cameron Forbes to Dean Worcester, January 5, 1912, *Guinabal Expedition Report*, Worcester Papers, box 1, 94.

15. Forbes to Worcester, 94.

16. Forbes to Worcester, 95.

17. Wallace Cadet Taylor to Executive Inspector, Bureau of Constabulary, January 17, 1911, *Guinabal Expedition Report*, Worcester Papers, box 1, 97.

18. Dean Worcester to Charles Elliott, February 7, 1912, *Guinabal Expedition Report*, Worcester Papers, box 1, 97.

19. Penningroth, *Then 'Til Now*, 31.

16. Igorots on Display

1. Early, "Reminiscences of John C. Early," 93.

2. Richard Schneidewind to Cameron Forbes, February 3, 1911, *Schneidewind and Baber Report*, March 20, 1911, BIA Group 350, 1. This fourteen-page report was from Richard Schneidewind and Captain Baber to Calvin Brown of Paris's Magic City. It contains copies of official communications between February 3, 1911, and March 18, 1911, and it is one of the documents in the larger report on the Igorot Fair in Ghent, Belgium.

3. Rudyard Kipling, "The White Man's Burden," *Modern History Sourcebook*, Fordham University, https://sourcebooks.fordham.edu/mod/kipling.asp.

4. Philippine Exposition Board, *Report of the Philippine Exposition Board in the United States for the Louisiana Purchase Exposition* (Washington, DC: Bureau of Insular Affairs, 1905), 30.

5. Philippine Exposition Board, *Report of the Philippine Exposition Board*, 27.

6. Sharra L. Vostral, "Imperialism on Display: The Philippine Exhibition at the 1904 World's Fair," *Gateway Heritage* 13, no. 4 (Spring 1993): 18–31.

7. Vostral, "Imperialism on Display," 19.

8. Quoted in Claire Prentice, *The Lost Tribe of Coney Island: Headhunters, Luna Park, and the Man Who Pulled Off the Spectacle of the Century* (Boston: Houghton Mifflin Harcourt, 2014), 179.

9. Prentice, *The Lost Tribe of Coney Island*, 180.

10. Deana L. Weibel, "A Savage at the Wedding and the Skeletons in My Closet: My Great-Grandfather, 'Igorotte Villages,' and the Ethnological Expositions of the 1900s," in *Mutuality: Anthropology's Changing Terms of Engagement*, ed. Roger Sanjek (Philadelphia: University of Pennsylvania Press, 2015), 101.

11. "Honeymoon to Be Spent with Band of Filipino Savages," *Detroit Free Press*, October 5, 1906, 5.

17. Schneidewind Meets His Match

1. Richard Schneidewind to Cameron Forbes, February 3, 1911, *Schneidewind and Baber Report*, BIA Group 350, 1.

2. Cameron Forbes to Richard Schneidewind, February 4, 1911, *Schneidewind and Baber Report*, BIA Group 350, 1.

3. A. V. Dalrymple to Richard Schneidewind, telegram, n.d., *Schneidewind and Baber Report*, BIA Group 350, 2.

4. Richard Schneidewind to A. V. Dalrymple, telegram, n.d., *Schneidewind and Baber Report*, BIA Group 350, 2.

5. George Harvey to John Early, n.d., *Schneidewind and Baber Report*, BIA Group 350, 2.

6. The following uncited quotes are from Schneidewind and Baber's reporting of the interactions with those who assisted or hindered Schneidewind's project, from the *Schneidewind and Baber Report*, BIA Group 350, 4.

18. New Players, New Problems

1. Richard Schneidewind to O'Brien and DeWitt, telegram, n.d., *Schneidewind and Baber Report*, BIA Group 350, 4.

2. Clyde DeWitt to Schneidewind, telegram, n.d., *Schneidewind and Baber Report*, BIA Group 350, 4.

3. Cameron Forbes to John Early, telegram, February 23, 1911, *Schneidewind and Baber Report*, BIA Group 350, 5.

4. Prentice, *The Lost Tribe of Coney Island*, 324.

5. Walter Clayton Clapp, *A Vocabulary of the Igorot Language as Spoken by the Bontok Igorots* (London: Forgotten Books, 2018), 6.

6. Richard Schneidewind to Captain Baber, telegram, February 28, 1911, *Schneidewind and Baber Report*, BIA Group 350, 5.

19. Early's Last Stand

1. Clyde DeWitt to Sheldon O'Brien, telegram, March 1, 1911, *Schneidewind and Baber Report*, BIA Group 350, 6.

2. Sheldon O'Brien to Clyde DeWitt, telegram, March 2, 1911, *Schneidewind and Baber Report*, BIA Group 350, 6.

3. Captain Baber to William Pack, telegram, March 2, 1911, *Schneidewind and Baber Report*, BIA Group 350, 6–7.

4. Clyde DeWitt to Thomas Welch, telegram, March 2, 1911, *Schneidewind and Baber Report*, BIA Group 350, 7.

5. Thomas Welch to William Pack, telegram, March 6, 1911, *Schneidewind and Baber Report*, BIA Group 350, 8.

6. William Pack to Thomas Welch, telegram, March 6, 1911, *Schneidewind and Baber Report*, BIA Group 350, 8.

7. The following uncited quotes are Schneidewind and Baber's reporting of their interactions with those involved in assisting or hindering Schneidewind's project, from the *Schneidewind and Baber Report*, March 20, 1911, BIA Group 350.

8. The following uncited quotes are Schneidewind and Baber's reporting of their interactions with those involved in assisting or hindering Schneidewind's project, from the *Schneidewind and Baber Report*, March 20, 1911, BIA Group 350.

20. Tragedy in Europe

1. Albert Johnson to William Jennings Bryant, December 31, 1913, *Schneidewind and Baber Report*, BIA Group 350, 2.

2. Johnson to Bryant, *Schneidewind and Baber Report*, 3.

3. James Amok and Ellis Tongai to President Woodrow Wilson, October 21, 1913, *Schneidewind and Baber Report*, BIA Group 350.

4. Frank McIntyre to Francis Burton Harrison, November 3, 1913, *Schneidewind and Baber Report*, BIA Group 350.

5. William Jennings Bryan to Albert Johnson, December 10, 1913, *Schneidewind and Baber Report*, BIA Group 350, 2.

21. Early's Exile South

1. Samuel Kane memo, Joseph Ralston Hayden papers: 1899–1945, box 27, folder 9, Bentley Historical Library, University of Michigan, Ann Arbor (hereafter Hayden Papers).

2. Early, "Reminiscences of John C. Early," 95.

3. Augusto V. de Viana, "The Philippines' Typhoon Alley: The Historic Bagyos of the Philippines and Their Impact," *Jurnal Kajian Wilayah* 5, no. 2 (2014): 184–216.

4. Early, "Reminiscences of John C. Early," 96.

5. Early, "Reminiscences of John C. Early," 98.

6. Richard Campbell to John Early, January 17, 1912, Early Papers.

7. Melvin Lewis to John Early, November 10, 1922, Early Papers.

8. Campbell to Early, January 17, 1912.

9. Early, "Reminiscences of John C. Early," 101.

10. "For Filipino Uplift: Committee Formed to Aid Bishop Brent in His Labors," *Baltimore Sun*, October 8, 1913, 7.

11. R. T. McCutchen, "The Moro Agricultural School of Jolo, P.I.," *The Spirit of Missions* 83, no. 10 (October 1913): 675.

12. Brent to Early, June 5, 1915, Early Papers, 1.

13. Brent to Early, June 5, 1915, 4.

14. Brent to Early, August 27, 1915, Early Papers.

15. Brent to Early, August 27, 1915.

16. *Report of the Governor General of the Philippine Islands to the Secretary of War, 1919* (Washington, DC: Government Printing Office, 1920), 24.

17. Caridad Aldecoa-Rodríguez, *Negros Oriental from American Rule to the Present: A History* (Tokyo, Japan: Toyota Foundation, 1989), 79–82.

18. Early, "Reminiscences of John C. Early," 113.

19. Aldecoa-Rodrigues, *Negros Oriental*, 132.

20. Aldecoa-Rodrigues, *Negros Oriental*, 133.

21. Willa Early to Walter William Marquardt, March 16, 1920, Early Papers.

22. Willa Early to Walter William Marquardt, March 18, 1920, Early Papers.

23. Walter William Marquardt to Willa Early, March 24, 1920, Early Papers.

22. Changes in Mountain Province

1. Cameron Forbes, *Journals of W. Cameron Forbes*, first series, vol 4., April 14, 1911, W. Cameron Forbes Papers, Houghton Library, Harvard University, Cambridge, Massachusetts, 357 (hereafter Forbes Papers).

2. Karnow, *In Our Image*, 244.

3. Francis Burton Harrison to US Secretary of War, May 8, 1914, BIA Group 350, box 1239, folder 113.

4. Worcester, *The Philippines Past and Present*, 717.

5. Worcester, *The Philippines Past and Present*, 717.

6. William Oliver Stevens, *Mystery of Dreams* (New York: Routledge, 2017), n.p.

7. Charles Clarence Batchelder, "The Grain of Truth in the Bushel of Christian Science Chaff," *Popular Science Monthly* 72 (March 1908): 223.

8. Fry, *A History of the Mountain Province*, 250.

9. *Manila Times*, May 24, 1915. Quoted in Fry, *A History of the Mountain Province*, 105.

10. Wilson, "Sapao: Walter Franklin Hale," 36.

11. Francis Burton Harrison, *The Corner-Stone of Philippine Independence: A Narrative of Seven Years* (New York: Century, 1922), 142.

12. Napoleon Jimenez Casambre, "Francis Burton Harrison: His Administration in the Philippines, 1913–1921" (PhD diss., Stanford University, 1968), 36.

13. Casambre, "Francis Burton Harrison," 29.

14. Charles Batchelder, "Economic Pressure as a Cause of the Revolt of the Asiatic Peoples against Occidental Exploitation," *The Annals of the American Academy of Political and Social Science* 112, no. 1 (March 1, 1924), 266.

15. "A New Philippine Administrator," *The Independent Weekly, New York* 76 (December 18, 1913), 545.

16. "Winfred T. Denison Commits Suicide," *New York Times*, November 6, 1919, 16.

17. Fry, *A History of the Mountain Province*, 105–6.

18. "Former U.S. Official Dies in New York," *The Times Dispatch*, Richmond, Virginia, May 6, 1946, 16.

23. Colonial Policies

1. Karnow, *In Our Image*, 242.

2. Democratic National Committee, *The Democratic Textbook, 1912* (New York: Democratic National Committee, 1912), 30.

3. Roy Watson Curry, "Woodrow Wilson and Philippine Policy," *The Mississippi Historical Review* 41, no. 3 (December 1954): 436.

4. Doris Kearns Goodwin, *The Bully Pulpit: Theodore Roosevelt, William Howard Taft, and the Golden Age of Journalism* (New York: Simon & Schuster, 2013), 260.

5. Barrows, "The Prospects for Education in the Philippines," 105.

6. Karnow, *In Our Image*, 238.

7. Karnow, *In Our Image*, 241.

24. World War I and a Troubled Yet Vibrant Economy

1. Westel Woodbury Willoughby, Charles G. Fenwick, and the United States Department of State, *Types of Restricted Sovereignty and of Colonial Autonomy* (Ann Arbor: Reprint from the collection of the University of Michigan Library, 2012), 163.

2. Frank H. Golay, *Face of Empire: United States-Philippine Relations, 1898–1946* (Madison: University of Wisconsin–Madison, Center for Southeast Asian Studies, 1998), 208. See also Colin D. Moore, *American Imperialism and the State, 1893–1921* (Cambridge, UK: Cambridge University Press, 2017), 101–57.

3. Golay, *Face of Empire*, 205.

4. Golay, *Face of Empire*, 205.

5. Golay, *Face of Empire*, 209.

6. Golay, *Face of Empire*, 212.

7. Golay, *Face of Empire*, 220.

8. "Summary Report of Haskins and Sells, Co., as of May 19, 1921," portions printed in the *Manila Times*, August 19, 1923.

9. Victor G. Heiser, *An American Doctor's Odyssey: Adventures in Forty-Five Countries* (New York: W. W. Norton & Company, 1936), 188–89.

10. *Philippine Independence Hearings: Testimony before the Committee on the Philippines, U.S. Senate, and the Committee on Insular Affairs, House of Representatives*, 66th Cong., 1919, 105 (statement of Francis Burton Harrison, Governor-General of the Philippines).

25. Marriages and Scandals

1. Carlos P. Romulo and Beth Day Romulo, *The Philippine Presidents: Memoirs Of* (Quezon City, Philippines: New Day, 1987), 17.

2. "The Francis Burton Harrisons Parted," *Brooklyn Life*, May 25, 1918, 10.

3. "How Burton Harrison Voted," *San Francisco Daily Times*, February 11, 1911, 15.

4. Golay, *Face of Empire*, 222.

5. "Francis Burton Harrison again Ventures into Matrimony," *The Coronado Strand*, June 7, 1919, 4.

6. Clarence George Wrentmore, resignation letter, in "Memoir," *Faculty History Project*, University of Michigan, http://faculty-history.dc.umich.edu/faculty/clarence-george-wrentmore/memoir.

7. "Romance of Gen. Harrison's Child Bride-to-Be," *The Tennessean*, May 4, 1919, 70.

8. "Harrison's Father-in-Law Given Political Snap in Philippines," *Oakland Tribune*, October 18, 1920, 18.

9. "Harrison in New Love Row," *Oakland Tribune*, July 31, 1934, 9.

10. "Obituary of Clarence G. Wrentmore," *The Detroit Free Press*, March 3, 1934, 5.

11. "Tucson Woman Takes Life at Coronado," *Los Angeles Times*, June 2, 1941, 34.

26. Wilson's Parting Shot and the Republicans Return

1. Woodrow Wilson, "Address at Luncheon, Hotel Portland, Portland, Oreg.," September 15, 1919, *Addresses of President Wilson*, 66th Cong., 1st sess., Library of Congress, Washington, DC, 201–206.

2. Woodrow Wilson, "President's Annual Message," *Congressional Record*, 66th Cong., 3rd sess., December 7, 1920, vol. 60, pt. 1, Senate, 26, https://www.congress.gov/bound-congressional-record/1920/12/07/daily-digest?p=0.

3. Frederick Gilman Hoyt, "The Wood-Forbes Mission to the Philippines, 1921" (PhD diss., Claremont Graduate School, 1979), 7.

4. Francis Burton Harrison to Frank McIntyre, November 14, 1920, Burton Norvell Harrison Family Papers, box 26, Manuscript Division, Library of Congress, Washington, DC (hereafter Harrison Papers).

27. The Wood-Forbes Mission

1. Manuel Quezon to Jaime de Veyra, cablegram, March 17, 1921, BIA Group 350, Wood-Forbes Mission file, 56.

2. Cameron Forbes, *Journals of W. Cameron Forbes*, first series, vol. 2, W. Cameron Forbes Papers, Houghton Library, Harvard University, Cambridge, Massachusetts, 45–46 (hereafter Forbes Papers).

3. Yeater to Weeks, cablegram, September 11, 1921, BIA Group 350, Wood-Forbes Mission file.

4. Leonard Wood and Cameron Forbes to John Wingate Weeks, cablegram, June 10, 1921, BIA Group 350, Wood-Forbes Mission file.

5. Leonard Wood to Charles Bishop, June 9, 1921, Wood Papers, box 155.

6. E. J. Westerhouse to Francis Burton Harrison, June 3, 1921, Harrison Papers, box 43.

7. Manuel Quezon to Francis Burton Harrison, Manila July 11, 1921, Harrison Papers, box 44.

8. Leonard Wood to John Wingate Weeks, cablegram, July 25, 1921, BIA Group 350, Wood-Forbes Mission file.

9. Leonard Wood, *Diaries, 1875–1927*, June 7, 1921, Leonard Wood Papers, 1825–1942, Library of Congress, Washington, DC, box 14.

10. Copy of correspondence from William Howard Taft to Leonard Wood, April 5, 1921, *Journals of W. Cameron Forbes*, second series, vol. 4, Forbes Papers, 335.

11. Wood, *Diaries, 1875–1925*, June 4, 1921.

12. Forbes, *Journals of W. Cameron Forbes*, second series, vol. 4, 77–78.

13. Manuel Quezon to Francis Burton Harrison, March 4, 1921, Harrison Papers, box 44.

14. Francis Burton Harrison, *Origins of the Philippine Republic: Extracts from the Diaries and Records of Francis Burton Harrison*, ed. Michael Paul Onorato (Ithaca, NY: Cornell Department of Asian Studies, 1974), 34.

28. Governor-General Wood

1. Golay, *Face of Empire*, 231.
2. Golay, *Face of Empire*, 237.
3. *Congressional Record*, 67th Cong., 2nd sess., January 20, 1922, vol. 62, pt. 2, H., 1483–86.
4. Golay, *Face of Empire*, 243.
5. Golay, *Face of Empire*, 246.
6. Harrison, *Origins of the Philippine Republic*, 76.
7. Golay, *Face of Empire*, 247.

29. Vindication

1. *An Act to Declare the Purpose of the People of the United States as to the Future Political Status of the People of the Philippine Islands, and to Provide a More Autonomous Government for Those Islands*, Pub. L. No. 64–240, 39 Stat. 545 (1916).
2. Francis Burton Harrison, *The Corner-Stone of Philippine Independence*, 141.
3. Fry, *A History of the Mountain Province*, 110.
4. Fry, *A History of the Mountain Province*, 111.
5. Igorot Elders to Wood-Forbes Mission, Kabayan, Benguet, March 24, 1921, BIA Group 350, Wood-Forbes Mission file.
6. "Mountain Province Letters," March 17, 1923, Joseph Ralston Hayden Papers: 1854–1975, box 29, Bentley Historical Library, University of Michigan, Ann Arbor, Michigan, 13 (hereafter Hayden Papers).
7. "Filipinos Divided," *Los Angeles Times*, June 1, 1921, 1.
8. "Filipinos Not All Agreed on Independence," *San Francisco Chronicle*, June 1, 1921, 4.
9. "Filipinos Are Friendly with the United States," *The Selma Times-Journal*, September 2, 1921, 1.
10. William Cameron Forbes, *The Philippine Islands, Volume 2* (New York: Houghton Mifflin, 1928), 249.
11. Harrison, *The Corner-Stone of Philippine Independence*, 142.
12. Dean Worcester to Leonard Wood and Cameron Forbes, Manila, August 4, 1921, BIA Group 350, Wood-Forbes Mission file.
13. Fry, *A History of the Mountain Province*, 119.
14. Early, "Reminiscences of John C. Early," 116.
15. Leonard Wood to John Early, July 7, 1922, Early Papers.
16. Leonard Wood to Chief Engineer US Reclamation Service, July 13, 1922, Early Papers.
17. Limericks for May 19, 1923, Dinner at Baguio Teachers Camp, Early Papers.
18. *Annual Report of the Governor General, Philippine Islands, 1923* (Washington, DC: Washington Government Printing Office, 1924), 15.
19. *Annual Report of the Governor General, Philippine Islands, 1924* (Washington, DC: Washington Government Printing Office, 1925), 10.

30. Political Deadlock

1. Early, "Reminiscences of John C. Early," 132.

2. Leonard Wood to John Early, December 26, 1926, Early Papers.

3. "Gen. Wood Badly Shaken When His Auto Ditched," *The Brooklyn Daily Eagle,* May 7, 1927.

4. Hermann Hagedorn, *Leonard Wood: A Biography* (repr., New York: Kraus, 1969), 2: 477.

5. "Wood Gives Report to President," *Los Angeles Times,* June 24, 1927, 2.

6. "Wood Gives Report to President," 2.

7. Jack McCallum, "Leonard Wood: Rough Rider, Surgeon, Architect of American Imperialism," Filmed December 27, 2005, in Fort Worth, TX, C-Span video, 47:32, https://www.c-span.org/video/?190324-1/leonard-wood-rough-rider-surgeon-architect-american-imperialism (37.30).

8. "Address of Governor J. C. Early at the Necrological Services in Commemoration of the Death of Governor-General Leonard Wood," Baguio Auditorium, August 13, 1927, Early Papers.

31. "We Felt It Was Our Duty to Confirm Him"

1. *Appointment of Governors of the Non-Christian Provinces in the Philippine Islands, Hearing before the Committee on Territories and Insular Possessions, United States Senate, Seventieth Congress, First Session on S. 2787,* sess. 2 (February 1, 1928).

2. *Appointment of Governors of the Non-Christian Provinces,* 3.

3. *Appointment of Governors of the Non-Christian Provinces,* 15.

4. *Appointment of Governors of the Non-Christian Provinces,* 15.

5. *Appointment of Governors of the Non-Christian Provinces,* 16.

6. Gouverneur Frank Mosher to John Early, September 12, 1927, Early Papers.

7. John Early to Charles Olson, November 2, 1927, Olson Papers.

8. Early to Olson, November 2, 1927.

9. Early to Olson, November 2, 1927.

10. Hillary Clapp to John Early, April 14, 1931, Early Papers.

32. Henry Stimson

1. Godfrey Hodgson, *The Colonel: The Life and Wars of Henry Stimson, 1867–1950* (New York: Knopf, 1990), 18–19.

2. Henry Stimson, "Future Philippine Policy under the Jones Act," *Foreign Affairs,* April 1927; "First-Hand Impressions of the Philippine Problem," *Saturday Evening Post,* March 19, 1927, 6–7.

3. Hodgson, *The Colonel,* 134.

4. Hodgson, *The Colonel,* 134.

5. Hodgson, *The Colonel,* 139.

6. Lewis E. Gleeck, *The American Governors-General and High Commissioners,* 233.

7. Henry L. Stimson and McGeorge Bundy, *On Active Service in Peace and War* (New York: Harper, 1948), 138–39.

8. Hodgson, *The Colonel*, 71.

9. Walter Robb, "Brief Tribute to John C. Early," *The American Chamber of Commerce Journal* 12 (January 1932): 9.

10. Henry Stimson, *Diaries 1909–1945*, August 12, 1926, Henry Lewis Stimson Papers, 1846–1966, Yale University Library, New Haven, Connecticut (hereafter Stimson Papers).

11. Henry Stimson, "Trip to Bontoc: Observations in Ifugao Agriculture," April 22, 1928, volume 8, Stimson Papers, 69.

12. Stimson, Diaries 1900-1945, October 12, 1928.

13. Early, "Reminiscences of John C. Early," 72–73.

14. Stimson, *Diaries 1909–1945*, October 12, 1928.

15. James Fugate to John Early, March 10, 1929, Early Papers.

33. Dark Days

1. Robert H. Ferrell, *American Diplomacy in the Great Depression: Hoover-Stimson Foreign Policy, 1929–1933* (New Haven, CT: Yale University Press, 1957), 195.

2. "Surprises Await Political World in Hoover Cabinet," *The Austin American*, January 14, 1929, 2.

3. "Stimson Asked by Hoover to Return to U.S.," *The Brooklyn Daily Eagle*, February 6, 1929, 1.

4. "Personalities in the News of the Week," *New York Times, Mid-Week Pictorial*, April 6, 1929.

5. "Stimson Is Opposed to Tax on Philippines Sugar," *Oakland Tribune*, March 21, 1929, 3.

6. Peter C. English, *Shock, Physiological Surgery, and George Washington Crile: Medical Innovation in Progressive Era* (Westport, CT: Greenwood Press, 1980), 51.

7. Thomas E. Jones, "The Technique of Abdominoperineal Resection for Carcinoma of the Rectum," *Cleveland Clinical Journal of Medicine* 2, no. 2 (April 1935): 7.

8. Jones, "The Technique of Abdominoperineal Resection," 15.

9. Henry Stimson to F. Le J. Parker, April 10, 1929, Early Papers.

10. Bureau of Insular Affairs to John Early, May 7, 1929, Early Papers.

11. Siddhartha Mukherjee, *The Emperor of All Maladies: A Biography of Cancer* (New York: Scribner, 2010), 78.

12. Mabel Stimson to Willa Early, May 25, 1929, Early Papers.

13. Frank Mosher to John Early, June 15, 1929, Early Papers.

14. A. Faculo to Willa Early, July 29, 1929, Early Papers.

15. Henry Stimson to John Early, July 22, 1929, Early Papers.

16. John Early to Bureau of Insular Affairs Purchasing Agent, July 26, 1929, Early Papers.

17. "Former Butte Man Visitor from Islands," *Great Falls Tribune*, August 15, 1929, 8.

18. Henry Stimson to John Early, September 20, 1929, Early Papers.

19. Dwight Davis to Henry Stimson, November 1, 1929, Stimson Papers.

20. Henry Stimson to Dwight Davis, cablegram, November 2, 1929, Stimson Papers.

21. Henry Stimson to Dwight Davis, November 12, 1929, Stimson Papers.

22. Keller, Chief of the Surgical Service, Walter Reed General Hospital, to Whom It May Concern, December 13, 1929, Early Papers.

34. Advisor to the Governor-General

1. Francis Kester, "The Dog Watch," *Oakland Tribune*, January 2, 1930, 47.
2. Lewis E. Gleeck, *The American Governors-General and High Commissioners*, 236.
3. Gleeck, *The American Governors-General and High Commissioners*, 238.
4. Gleeck, *The American Governors-General and High Commissioners*, 254.
5. Gleeck, *The American Governors-General and High Commissioners*, 251.
6. William Pack to Francis Parker, December 4, 1929, BIA Group 350, Pack file.
7. Francis Parker to William Pack, January 10, 1930, BIA Group 350, Pack file.
8. William Pack to Francis Parker, January 14, 1930, BIA Group 350, Pack file.
9. John Early to Dwight Davis, January 31, 1930, Early Papers.
10. Dwight Davis to John Early, January 31, 1930, Early Papers.
11. John Early, "Memorandum for the Governor-General: Provincial Government—Davao," September 8, 1930, Hayden Papers, 5.
12. John Early, "Memorandum for the Governor-General: Japanese and Filipino Pioneer in Davao," August 28, 1930, Hayden Papers, 12.
13. John Early to Candace Stimson, June 5, 1930, Early Papers.

35. Vice-Governor

1. Cablegram no. 141 from Dwight Davis to President Hoover and Secretary of War Hurley, March 8, 1930, BIA Group 350, Dwight Davis file.
2. Stimson to Parker, April 10, 1929, Early Papers.
3. Henry Stimson to John Early, April 30, 1930, Early Papers.
4. Henry Stimson to Frank Mosher, April 30, 1930, Hayden Papers.
5. Charles Roosevelt, *The Philippines: A Treasure and a Problem* (New York: J. H. Sears, 1926).
6. Roosevelt, *The Philippines*, 281.
7. Resignation letter from Nicholas Roosevelt to Herbert Hoover, September 24, 1930, *The American Presidency Project*, University of California, Santa Barbara, https://www.presidency.ucsb.edu/node/211786.
8. "Manila Favors Butte Choice," *Honolulu Star-Bulletin*, December 5, 1930, 21.
9. John Early, "Gentleman Adventurers," November 9, 1930, Early Papers.

36. "Please Write Your Story"

1. John Early to Paul Goode, November 2, 1931, Early Papers.
2. William H. Haas and Harold B. Ward, "J. Paul Goode," *Annals of the Association of American Geographers* 23, no. 4 (December, 1933): 245.
3. John Early to Paul Goode, January 3, 1931, Early Papers.
4. John Early to Paul Goode, March 12, 1931, Early Papers.
5. John Early to Paul Goode, April 1, 1931, Early Papers.
6. James Chapman to John Early, March 21, 1931, Early Papers.
7. Hillary Clapp to John Early, April 14, 1931, Early Papers.
8. Paul Goode to John Early, May 22, 1931, Early Papers.
9. John Early, "Memorial Day Address," Camp John Hay Amphitheater, Mary 30, 1931, Early Papers.

10. John Early to Paul Goode, September 13, 1931, Early Papers.

11. John Early to Paul Goode, November 16, 1931, Early Papers.

12. John Early to Paul Goode, December 2, 1931, Early Papers.

13. Quote from the plaque in Manila's Episcopal Church dedicating the Transfiguration Window to John C. Early, September 1, 1935, Early Papers.

Epilogue

1. "John C. Early," *The Atlanta Constitution*, January 2, 1932, 3.

2. "A Man of the Mountains," *Philippine Press*, January 9, 1932, 8.

3. "A Man of the Mountains," 8.

4. "Memorandum to His Excellency, the Governor General: Fragmentary Comments on the Fairchild and Other Mine Cases in the Mountain Province," May 9, 1935, Hayden Papers, 2.

BIBLIOGRAPHY

Manuscript Collections

Burton Norvell Harrison Family Papers. Manuscript Division, Library of Congress, Washington, DC.

David P. Barrows Papers, 1890–1954. The Bancroft Library, University of California, Berkeley, CA.

Dean C. Worcester Papers: 1887–1925. Bentley Historical Library, University of Michigan, Ann Arbor, MI.

Henry Lewis Stimson Papers, 1846–1966. Yale University Library, New Haven, CT.

John C. Early Papers: 1911–1942. Bentley Historical Library, University of Michigan, Ann Arbor, MI.

Joseph Ralston Hayden Papers: 1854–1975. Bentley Historical Library, University of Michigan, Ann Arbor, MI.

Leonard Wood Papers, 1825–1942. Library of Congress, Washington, DC.

Olson Papers. In the possession of Professor Frank Jenista, Emeritus of Cedarville University.

President: Enoch A. Bryan Papers, 1843–1989. Manuscripts, Archives, and Special Collections, Washington State University Libraries, Pullman, WA.

Record Group 350—Records of the Bureau of Insular Affairs. National Archives, Washington, DC. (BIA Group 350)

W. Cameron Forbes Papers. Houghton Library, Harvard University, Cambridge, MA.

Government Documents

An Act to Declare the Purpose of the People of the United States as to the Future Political Status of the People of the Philippine Islands, and to Provide a More Autonomous Government for Those Islands. Pub. L. No. 64–240, 39 Stat. 545 (1916).

Annual Report of Governor General Philippine Islands, 1923. Washington, DC: Washington Government Printing Office, 1924.

Annual Report of Governor General, Philippine Islands, 1924. Washington, DC: Washington Government Printing Office, 1925.

"Annual Report of the Provincial-Governor of the Mountain Province, Fiscal Year Ending June 30, 1909." In *The Philippine Commission Report for the 1909.* Washington, DC: Government Printing Office, 1910.

"Annual Report of the Provincial-Governor of the Mountain Province, Fiscal Year Ending June 30, 1910." In *Report of the Philippine Commission to the Secretary of War, 1911.* Washington, DC: Government Printing Office, 1911.

Annual Reports of the War Department for the Fiscal Year Ended June 30, 1904, Volume XI, Report of the Philippine Commission, Part One. Washington, DC: Government Printing Press Office, 1905.

Appointment of Governors of the Non-Christian Provinces in the Philippine Islands, Hearing before the Committee on Territories and Insular Possessions, United States Senate, 70th Congress, 1st Session on S. 2787. (February 1, 1928): 2.

Congressional Record. 66th Congress, 3rd session, December 7, 1920. Volume 60, part 1. Senate, 26.

Congressional Record. 67th Congress, 2nd session, January 20, 1922. Volume 62, part 2. House of Representatives, 1483–86.

Dickinson, J. M. *Special Report of J. M. Dickinson to the President on the Philippines.* Washington, DC: Government Printing Office, 1910.

Philippine Exposition Board. *Report of the Philippine Exposition Board in the United States for the Louisiana Purchase Exposition.* Washington, DC: Bureau of Insular Affairs, 1905.

Philippine Independence Hearings: Testimony before the Committee on the Philippines, U.S. Senate, and the Committee on Insular Affairs, House of Representatives. 66th Congress, 1919. (Statement of Francis Burton Harrison, Governor-General of the Philippines.)

Report of the Governor General of the Philippine Islands to the Secretary of War, 1919. Washington, DC: Government Printing Office, 1920.

Schneidewind, Richard, and A. M. Baber. *Schneidewind and Baber Report, March 20, 1911.* BIA Group 350. National Archives, Washington, DC.

Seventh Annual Report of the Philippine Commission, 1906, Part 2. 3 volumes. Washington, DC: Government Printing Office, 1907.

Seventh Annual Report of the Secretary of the Interior to the Philippine Commission: For the Fiscal Year Ended, June 30, 1908. Manila, Philippines: Bureau of Printing, 1908. Reprint, London: Forgotten Books, 2019.

War Department, U.S.A. Annual Reports, 1907: Volume VII, The Philippine Commission. 10 volumes. Washington, DC: Government Printing Office, 1908.

Wilson, Woodrow. "Address at Luncheon, Hotel Portland, Portland, Oreg." September 15, 1919. *Addresses of President Wilson.* 66th Congress, 1st session. Library of Congress, Washington, DC, 201–206.

Wilson, Woodrow. "President's Annual Message." *Congressional Record,* 66th Congress, 3rd session, December 7, 1920, volume 60, part 1, Senate, 26. https://www.congress.gov/bound-congressional-record/1920/12/07/daily-digest?p=0.

Other Primary and Secondary Sources

Aldecoa-Rodriguez, Caridad. *Negros Oriental from American Rule to the Present: A History.* Tokyo, Japan: Toyota Foundation, 1989.

Barrows, David. "The Prospects for Education in the Philippines," *The Philippine Teacher* 1, no. 1 (December 1904): 7.

Barton, Roy Franklin. *The Half-Way Sun: Life among the Headhunters of the Philippines.* New York: AMS Press, 1978.

Batchelder, Charles. "Economic Pressure as a Cause of the Revolt of the Asiatic Peoples against Occidental Exploitation." *The Annals of the American Academy of Political and Social Science* 112, no. 1 (March 1, 1924): 258–68.

Batchelder, Charles Clarence. "The Grain of Truth in the Bushel of Christian Science Chaff." *Popular Science Monthly* 72 (March 1908): 211–23.

Brands, H. W. *Bound to Empire: The United States and the Philippines*. New York: Oxford University Press, 1992.

Bryan, Enoch A. Enoch A. Bryan to John Early, March 12, 1905. box 35. President: Enoch A. Bryan Papers. Manuscripts, Archives, and Special Collections, Washington State University Libraries, Pullman, Washington.

Capozzola, Christopher. *Bound by War: How the United States and the Philippines Built America's Pacific Century*. New York: Basic Books, 2020.

Casambre, Napoleon Jimenez. "Francis Burton Harrison: His Administration in the Philippines, 1913–1921." PhD diss., Stanford University, 1968.

Charbonneau, Oliver. *Civilizational Imperatives: Americans, Moros, and the Colonial World*. Ithaca, NY: Cornell University Press, 2020.

Clapp, Walter Clayton. *A Vocabulary of the Igorot Language as Spoken by the Bontok Igorots*. London: Forgotten Books, 2018.

Clymer, Kenton J. "Humanitarian Imperialism: David Prescott Barrows and the White Man's Burden in the Philippines." *Pacific Historical Review* 45, no. 4 (November, 1976): 495–517.

Clymer, Kenton J. *Protestant Missionaries in the Philippines, 1898–1916: An Inquiry into the American Colonial Mentality*. Urbana: University of Illinois Press, 1986.

Crossette, Barbara. *The Great Hill Stations of Asia*. Boulder, CO: Westview Press, 1998.

Cruikshank, Bruce. Review of *A History of the Mountain Province*, by Howard T. Fry. *The Journal of Asian Studies* 44, no. 3 (May, 1985): 668.

Curry, Roy Watson. "Woodrow Wilson and Philippine Policy." *The Mississippi Historical Review* 41, no. 3 (December 1954): 435–52.

Democratic National Committee. *The Democratic Textbook, 1912*. New York: Democratic National Committee, 1912.

de Viana, Augusto V. "The Philippines' Typhoon Alley: The Historic Bagyos of the Philippines and Their Impact." *Jurnal Kajian Wilayah* 5, no. 2 (2014): 184–216.

Dozier, Edward P. *Mountain Arbiters: The Changing Life of a Philippine Hill People*. Tucson: University of Arizona Press, 1966.

Dozier, Edward P. *The Kalinga of Northern Luzon, Philippines*. Case Studies in Cultural Anthropology. New York: Holt, Rinehart and Winston, 1967.

Edgerton, Ronald K. *American Datu: John J. Pershing and Counterinsurgency Warfare in the Muslim Philippines, 1899–1913*. Lexington: University Press of Kentucky, 2020.

Edgerton, Ronald K. *People of the Middle Ground: A Century of Conflict and Accommodation in Central Mindanao, 1880s–1980s*. Quezon City, Philippines: Ateneo de Manila Press, 2008.

English, Peter C. *Shock, Physiological Surgery, and George Washington Crile: Medical Innovation in Progressive Era*. New York: Greenwood Press, 1980.

Ferrell, Robert H. *American Diplomacy in the Great Depression: Hoover-Stimson Foreign Policy, 1929–1933*. New Haven, CT: Yale University Press, 1957.

Forbes, William Cameron. *The Philippine Islands, Volume 2*. New York: Houghton Mifflin, 1928.

Friend, Theodore. *Between Two Empires: The Ordeal of the Philippines, 1929–1946*. New Haven, CT: Yale University Press, 1965.

Fry, Howard T. *A History of the Mountain Province*. Quezon City, Philippines: New Day, 1989.

Gleeck, Lewis E. *The American Governors-General and High Commissioners in the Philippines: Proconsuls, Nation-Builders and Politicians*. Quezon City, Philippines: New Day, 1986.

Gleeck, Lewis E. *American Institutions in the Philippines, 1898–1941*. Manila, Philippines: Historical Conservation Society, 1976.

Golay, Frank H. *Face of Empire: United States-Philippine Relations, 1898–1946*. Madison: University of Wisconsin–Madison, Center for Southeast Asian Studies, 1998.

Goodwin, Doris Kearns. *The Bully Pulpit: Theodore Roosevelt, William Howard Taft, and the Golden Age of Journalism*. New York: Simon & Schuster, 2013.

Gott, Camillus. "William Cameron Forbes and the Philippines, 1904–1946." PhD diss., Indiana University, 1974.

Gowen, Vincent H. *Philippine Kaleidoscope: An Illustrated Story of the Church's Mission*. New York: National Council, Protestant Episcopal Church, 1939.

Gowing, Peter. *Mandate in Moroland: The American Government of Muslim Filipinos, 1899–1929*. Quezon City, Philippines: New Day, 1983.

Guerrero, León Ma. *The First Filipino: A Biography of José Rizal*. Manila: Publications of the National Heroes Commission, 1963.

Haas, William H., and Harold B. Ward. "J. Paul Goode." *Annals of the Association of American Geographers* 23, no. 4 (December 1933): 241–46.

Hagedorn, Hermann. *Leonard Wood: A Biography*. Reprint, New York: Krause, 1969.

Harris, Susan K. *God's Arbiters: Americans and the Philippines, 1898–1902*. New York: Oxford University Press, 2011.

Harrison, Francis Burton. *The Corner-Stone of Philippine Independence: A Narrative of Seven Years*. New York: Century, 1922.

Harrison, Francis Burton. *Origins of the Philippine Republic: Extracts from the Diaries and Records of Francis Burton Harrison*. Edited by Michael Paul Onorato. Ithaca, NY: Cornell Department of Asian Studies, 1974.

Hawkins, Michael. *Making Moros: Imperial Historicism and American Military Rule in the Muslim Philippines' Muslim South*. DeKalb: Northern Illinois University Press, 2013.

Hawkins, Michael. Review of *The Blood of Government: Race, Empire, the United States, & the Philippines*, by Paul A. Kramer. *Crossroads: An Interdisciplinary Journal of Southeast Asian Studies* 19, no. 2 (2008): 186–89.

Hawkins, Michael. *Semi-Civilized: The Moro Village at the Louisiana Purchase Exposition*. DeKalb: Northern Illinois University Press, 2020.

Hayden, Joseph Ralston. *The Philippines: A Study in National Development*. World Affairs: National and International Viewpoints. New York: Arno Press, 1972.

Heiser, Victor G. *An American Doctor's Odyssey: Adventures in Forty-Five Countries*. New York: W. W. Norton & Company, 1936.

Hodgson, Godfrey. *The Colonel: The Life and Wars of Henry Stimson, 1867–1950*. New York: Knopf, 1990.

Hoyt, Frederick Gilman. "The Wood-Forbes Mission to the Philippines, 1921." PhD diss., Claremont Graduate School, 1979.

Hsu, Funnie. "Colonial Articulations: English Instruction and the 'Benevolence' of U.S. Overseas Expansion in the Philippines, 1898–1916," PhD diss., University of California, Berkeley, 2013.

Immerwahr, Daniel. *How to Hide an Empire: A History of the Greater United States*. New York: Farrar, Straus and Giroux, 2019.

Jenista, Frank L. *The White Apos: American Governors on the Cordillera Central*. 2nd ed. Quezon City, Philippines: New Day, 1989.

Jones, Thomas E. "The Technique of Abdominoperineal Resection for Carcinoma of the Rectum." *Cleveland Clinical Journal of Medicine* 2, no. 2 (April 1935): 7–15.

Kane, Samuel. *Life or Death in Luzon: Thirty Years with the Philippine Headhunters*. Indianapolis, IN: Bobbs-Merrill Company, 1933.

Kane, Samuel. *Thirty Years with the Philippine Headhunters*. New York: Grosset & Dunlap, 1933.

Karnow, Stanley. *In Our Image: America's Empire in the Philippines*. New York: Random House, 1989.

Kipling, Rudyard. "The White Man's Burden." *Modern History Sourcebook*, Fordham University. https://sourcebooks.fordham.edu/mod/kipling.asp.

Linn, Brian McAllister. "The Thirty-Third Infantry, United States Volunteers: An American Regiment in the Philippine Insurrection, 1899–1901." PhD diss., Ohio State University, 1981.

May, Glenn Anthony. *Social Engineering in the Philippines: The Aims, Execution, and Impact of American Colonial Policy, 1900–1913*. Westport, CT: Greenwood Press, 1980.

McCallum, Jack. "Leonard Wood: Rough Rider, Surgeon, Architect of American Imperialism." Filmed December 27, 2005, in Fort Worth, TX. C-Span video, 47:32. https://www.c-span.org/video/?190324-1/leonard-wood-rough-rider-surgeon-architect-american-imperialism.

McCoy, Alfred W. *Policing America's Empire: The United States, the Philippines, and the Rise of the Surveillance State*. Madison: University of Wisconsin Press, 2009.

McCutchen, R. T. "The Moro Agricultural School of Jolo, P.I." *The Spirit of Missions* 83, no. 10 (October 1913): 675–78.

Molintas, Jose Mencio. "The Philippine Indigenous Peoples Struggle for Land and Life: Challenging Legal Texts." *Arizona Journal of International & Comparative Law* 21, no. 1 (2004): 269–306.

Moore, Colin D. *American Imperialism and the State, 1893–1921*. Cambridge, United Kingdom: Cambridge University Press, 2017.

Mount, Guy Emerson. Review of *Bound by War: How the United States and the Philippines Built America's Pacific Century*, by Christopher Capozzola. H-Diplo, H-Net Reviews (January 2021). https://www.h-net.org/reviews/showrev.php?id=55577.

Mukherjee, Siddhartha. *The Emperor of All Maladies: A Biography of Cancer*. New York: Scribner, 2010.

Orquiza, René Alexander D., Jr. *Taste of Control: Food and the Filipino Colonial Mentality*. New Brunswick, NJ: Rutgers University Press, 2020.

Painton, G. A. "United States Non-Christian Policy." Master's thesis, James Cook University of North Queensland, 1981.

Pattengill, Henry R., ed. "Report of the Philippine Commission." *Timely Topics* 4, no. 5 (October 6, 1899): 151.

Penningroth, Charles. *Then 'Til Now*. Cedar Rapids, IA: n.p., 1967.

Phelan, John Leddy. *The Hispanization of the Philippines: Spanish Aims and Filipino Responses*. Madison: University of Wisconsin Press, 1959.

Phelan, John Leddy. *The Millennial Kingdom of the Franciscans in the New World*. 2nd ed. Berkeley: University of California Press, 1970.

Pratt, Julius W. *America's Colonial Experiment: How the United States Gained, Governed, and in Part Gave Away a Colonial Empire*. New York: Prentice-Hall, 1950.

Pratt, Julius W. *Expansionists of 1898: The Acquisition of Hawaii and the Spanish Islands*. Baltimore: Johns Hopkins Press, 1936.

Prentice, Claire. *The Lost Tribe of Coney Island: Headhunters, Luna Park, and the Man Who Pulled Off the Spectacle of the Century*. Boston: Houghton Mifflin Harcourt, 2014.

Priest, Andrew. Review of *How to Hide an Empire: A History of the Greater United States*, by Daniel Immerwahr. *Diplomacy & Statecraft* 31, no. 1 (2020): 203–205.

Rafael, Vicente L. *White Love: And Other Events in Filipino History*. Durham, NC: Duke University Press, 2000.

Reed, Robert Ronald. *City of Pines: The Origins of Baguio as a Colonial Hill Station and Regional Capital*. 2nd ed. Baguio City, Philippines: A-Seven Pub, 1999.

Robb, Walter. "Brief Tribute to John C. Early." *The American Chamber of Commerce Journal* 12 (January 1932): 9.

Romulo, Carlos P., and Beth Day Romulo. *The Philippine Presidents: Memoirs Of.* Quezon City, Philippines: New Day, 1987.

Roosevelt, Charles. *The Philippines: A Treasure and a Problem*. New York: J. H. Sears, 1926.

Roosevelt, Nicholas. Resignation letter from Nicholas Roosevelt to Herbert Hoover, September 24, 1930. *The American Presidency Project*, University of California, Santa Barbara. https://www.presidency.ucsb.edu/node/211786.

Salamanca, Bonifacio S. *The Filipino Reaction to American Rule, 1901–1913*. Hamden, CT: Shoestring Press, 1968.

Samonte, Cecilia A. Review of *White Love and Other Events in Filipino History*, by Vicente L. Rafael. *Journal of Asian Studies* 61, no. 3 (2002): 1126–28.

Schirmer, Daniel, and Stephen Rosskamm Shalom, eds. *The Philippines Reader*. Boston: South End Press, 1987.

Scott, William Henry. *The Discovery of the Igorots: Spanish Contacts with the Pagans of Northern Luzon*. Quezon City, Philippines: New Day, 1974.

Sexton, William Thaddeus. *Soldiers in the Sun: An Adventure in Imperialism*. Harrisburg, PA: The Military Services Publishing Co., 1939.

Stanley, Peter W. *A Nation in the Making: The Philippines and the United States, 1899–1921*. Cambridge, MA: Harvard University Press, 1974.

Steinbock-Pratt, Sarah. *Educating the Empire: American Teachers and Contested Colonization in the Philippines*. New York: Cambridge University Press, 2019.

Stevens, William Oliver. *Mystery of Dreams*. New York: Routledge, 2017.

Stimson, Henry L., and McGeorge Bundy. *On Active Service in Peace and War*. New York: Harper, 1948.

Sullivan, Rodney J. *Exemplar of Americanism: The Philippine Career of Dean C. Worcester*. Ann Arbor: The University of Michigan Center for South and Southeast Asian Studies, 1991.

Taft, Helen Herron. *Recollections of Full Years*. New York: Dodd, Mead & Company, 1914.

Vostral, Sharra L. "Imperialism on Display: The Philippine Exhibition at the 1904 World's Fair." *Gateway Heritage* 13, no. 4 (Spring 1993): 18–31.

Washington, George. Correspondence from George Washington to Gilbert du Motier Marquis de Lafayette, August 15, 1786. *Founders Online*, National Archives, https://founders.archives.gov/documents/Washington/04-04-02-0200.

Washington Agricultural College. *1902 Chinook: Volume III* (yearbook). Pullman, WA: Published by the Junior Class, 1903.

Weibel, Deana L. "A Savage at the Wedding and the Skeletons in My Closet: My Great-Grandfather, 'Igorotte Villages,' and the Ethnological Expositions of the 1900s." In *Mutuality: Anthropology's Changing Terms of Engagement*, edited by Roger Sanjek, 99–117. Philadelphia: University of Pennsylvania Press, 2015.

Westfall, Matthew. *The Devil's Causeway: The True Story of America's First Prisoners of War in the Philippines, and the Heroic Expedition Sent to Their Rescue*. Guilford, CT: Lyons Press, 2012.

Willcox, Cornelis DeWitt. *Head Hunters of Northern Luzon: From Ifugao to Kalinga, a Ride through the Mountains of Northern Luzon*. London: Forgotten Books, 2016.

Williams, S. L. "The Governor of Paragua." *Munsey's Magazine* (May 1905): 136.

Willoughby, Westel Woodbury, Charles G. Fenwick, and United States Department of State. *Types of Restricted Sovereignty and of Colonial Autonomy*. Ann Arbor, MI: Reprints from the Collection of the University of Michigan Library, 2012.

Wilson, Laurence L. "Sapao: Walter Franklin Hale." *Journal of East Asiatic Studies* 5, no. 2, (1956): 1–38.

Wolff, Leon. *Little Brown Brother: How the United States Purchased and Pacified the Philippines*. Garden City, NJ: Doubleday, 1960.

Worcester, Dean C. *The Philippine Islands and Their People*. New York: The Macmillan Company, 1898.

Worcester, Dean Conant. *The Philippines Past and Present*. New York: Macmillan Company, 1930.

Wrentmore, Clarence George. Resignation letter. In "Memoir," *Faculty History Project*, University of Michigan. http://faculty-history.dc.umich.edu/faculty/clarence-george-wrentmore/memoir.

INDEX

Page numbers in italic indicate figures.

Printed in the USA
CPSIA information can be obtained
at www.ICGtesting.com
LVHW040012210324
775082LV00032B/611